National Grange

The Glory of Cooking

To Linda Kercheval
from

Sacramento Grange #12 - G.W.A.
(Grange Women's Activities)

Library of Congress Cataloging in Publication Data on Page 303.

Dear Members and Friends:

The publication of "The Glory of Cooking" by the National Grange is dedicated to the Bicentennial Celebration of the United States Constitution. The signing of the Constitution took place on September 17, 1787 and it became the supreme law of the nation on March 4, 1789.

The National Grange, state and local Granges across the country will be celebrating the Bicentennial with special programs and events, the first of which is the publication of "The Glory of Cooking." We feel that being the country's first farm organization, this cookbook is an especially appropriate project for the Grange.

This is the third cookbook published by the National Grange in which we promote the use of American agriculture products. All of the recipes call for real ingredients. In this book we offer both classic American and Old World recipes. Many were brought over from the "Old Country" and handed down from one generation to the next. And in keeping with the times, there is a section with microwave recipes, too.

As an added surprise, there are a number of recipes throughout the book from special friends such as the President and Vice President and all 12 Governors whose state representatives were the original signers of the Constitution, and some others as well.

Our sincerest thanks to the thousands of Grange members and friends who took the time to send us their favorite recipes. We wish we could have used them all. And, as always, we are much appreciative of the guidance and counsel of our publisher, Favorite Recipes Press.

Sincerely,

Mary R. Buffington
Director of Women's Activities

BOARD OF ADVISORS
COOKBOOK COMMITTEE

Coordinator

Judy Taylor Massabny
Director of Information and Public Relations

Consultants

Darlene Andersen
Wife, National Master

Mary R. Buffington
Director of Women's Activities

Georgia M. Taylor
Resales Director

Mary Jane Blount
Favorite Recipes Press

Cover design: Barbara Covington-Jones
Graphics Coordinator-National Grange

Contents

Appetizers and Beverages

An array of tempting appetizers, whether a table full of hors d'oeuvres or a single dip surrounded by garden-fresh vegetables and crisp crackers, is a welcome preamble to dinners everywhere. Coming to us from the Russian *Zambrouska*, the Swedish *Smörgåsbord,* and the Italian *Antipasto*, these now thoroughly American treats are served anywhere people gather for good food, from the kitchen to the banquet hall. Like their old world predecessors, the appetizers in *The Glory of Cooking* are unusual and delicious. And to suit the way we live today, many are portable, easily increased to serve a group, and nutritious as well.

We are also universally united by our love of something to sip together — beverages both hot and cold that wake us, accompany family meals, and spark friendly get-togethers. The beverages in this section include such old favorites as *Switchel* from Holland, as well as milk drinks which supplement daily nutrition, punches for a crowd, and cups that cheer any time.

BEAN DIP

Yields: 16 servings	Pan Size: two 9 x 13 inch	Preheat: 350°

3 lb. ground beef	4 avocados, mashed
3 pkg. taco seasoning mix	3 c. sour cream
2 lg. cans refried beans	2 tomatoes, chopped
3 cans chopped green chilies	Pinch of garlic salt
1 bottle of taco sauce	Dash of Tabasco sauce
1 lb. Monterey Jack cheese,	Dash of Worcestershire sauce
shredded	1 can chopped black olives

Brown ground beef in skillet, stirring until crumbly; drain. Add taco seasoning mix using package directions. Cook using package directions. Stir in refried beans. Spread in baking dishes. Sprinkle chilies over ground beef mixture. Drizzle taco sauce over chilies. Sprinkle with cheese. Bake for 20 to 30 minutes or until heated through. Mash avocados with 2 tablespoons sour cream. Add tomatoes and seasonings. Spread remaining sour cream over hot baked layers. Spoon avocado mixture over top. Sprinkle with olives. Serve hot with taco chips.

Janet Gwin, Cedar Grange, Washington

BEEF DIP IN PUMPERNICKEL

Yields: 6 to 8 servings

1 round loaf pumpernickel	3 to 4 oz. dried beef, chopped
bread	2 tbsp. minced onion
1½ c. mayonnaise	2 tbsp. parsley flakes
¼ c. sour cream	2 tsp. dillweed

Scoop out center of loaf to form shell; cut center into chunks for dipping. Combine remaining ingredients in bowl; mix well. Spoon into bread shell. Place on serving plate. Serve with reserved bread.

Bette Kirby, Hamilton Grange, New Jersey

HOT CHIPPED BEEF DIP

Yields: 12 servings	Pan Size: 3 cup	Preheat: 350°

8 oz. cream cheese, softened	¾ c. chopped dried beef
1 tbsp. milk	1 tbsp. minced onion
½ c. sour cream	2 tbsp. chopped green pepper
¼ tsp. pepper	¼ c. chopped nuts

Blend cream cheese and milk in bowl. Add sour cream and pepper; mix well. Stir in dried beef, onion and green pepper. Spoon into ungreased casserole. Bake for 15 minutes or until bubbly. Sprinkle with nuts. Place in warming server. Serve with vegetables or crackers.

Lela Patterson, Lake Grange, Ohio

GOVERNMENT HOUSE CRAB DIP

Yields: 16 servings

1½ tbsp. flour	½ tbsp. lemon juice
1½ tbsp. unsalted butter, melted	Salt and white pepper to taste
½ c. milk	1 tsp. Worcestershire sauce
2 tbsp. grated Swiss cheese	½ c. heavy cream
4 shallots, minced	1½ tsp. Sherry
¼ c. unsalted butter	1½ tsp. Cognac
1 lb. crab meat	

Blend flour with melted butter in saucepan. Stir in milk gradually. Cook until thickened, stirring constantly. Stir in cheese; blend well. Sauté shallots in ¼ cup butter in saucepan over medium heat. Add crab meat, lemon juice, salt and pepper. Cook until warmed through. Stir in cheese sauce, Worcestershire sauce and cream. Add Sherry and Cognac 10 minutes before serving time. Adjust seasonings; do not oversalt. Spoon into chafing dish. Serve with hard crackers.

Harry Hughes
Governor of Maryland

SHRIMP DIP

Yields: 15 servings

8 oz. cream cheese, softened	1 tsp. mustard
3 tbsp. mayonnaise	½ tsp. seasoned salt
1 clove of garlic, pressed	1 can small shrimp,
1 tbsp. soy sauce	drained, crumbled

Beat cream cheese and mayonnaise in mixer bowl until smooth. Add garlic, soy sauce, mustard, seasoned salt and shrimp; mix well. Spoon into serving bowl. Serve with deep-fried flour tortilla wedges.

Clare L. Berryhill
Director, California Department of Food and Agriculture

DIP OLÉ

Yields: 6 to 10 servings   Pan Size: Crock•Pot

1 lb. ground beef	½ c. picante sauce
2½ tbsp. chili powder	1 can refried beans
1 lb. Velveeta cheese, cubed	½ can chopped green chilies

Brown ground beef and chili powder in skillet, stirring until crumbly; drain. Melt cheese with picante sauce in saucepan; mix well. Combine ground beef, cheese mixture, beans and chilies in Crock•Pot; mix well. Heat on Low. Serve with nacho or tortilla chips.

Connie Nickerson, Corry Grange, Pennsylvania

CURRY DIP FOR RAW VEGETABLES

Yields: 12 servings

2 c. mayonnaise	1 tbsp. curry powder
3 tbsp. chili sauce	½ tsp. garlic salt
1 tbsp. Worcestershire sauce	½ tsp. salt
1 tsp. instant onion	Pepper to taste

Combine all ingredients in bowl; mix well. Spoon into serving bowl in center of serving plate. Arrange fresh vegetables around dip.

Dick and Ginny Thornburgh
Governor of Pennsylvania

GINGER-ALMOND DIP

Yields: 8 servings

8 oz. cream cheese, softened	½ c. minced candied ginger
½ c. sour cream	½ c. slivered blanched almonds

Blend cream cheese and sour cream in bowl. Add ginger and almonds; mix well. Chill overnight to blend flavors. Spoon into serving dish.

Clarence Heinrich, Walterville Grange, Oregon

YUMMY DIP FOR APPLES

Yields: 8 servings

8 oz. cream cheese, softened	¾ c. packed brown sugar
¼ c. sugar	1 tsp. vanilla extract

Combine cream cheese, sugar, brown sugar and vanilla in mixer bowl; beat until smooth. Chill in refrigerator. Spoon into serving bowl. Serve with sliced apples.

Mrs. John Rorabaugh, Sugar Grove Grange, Iowa

HOT ARTICHOKE SPREAD

Yields: 3 cups   Pan Size: 1 quart   Preheat: 350°

1 14-oz. can artichoke hearts	1 c. Parmesan cheese
1 4-oz. can chopped green chilies	Dash each of garlic powder and salt
1 c. mayonnaise	

Drain artichoke hearts and chilies; chop artichoke hearts. Combine with remaining ingredients in casserole. Bake for 20 minutes or until bubbly.

Catherine Coleman, Pierstown Grange, New York

GARLIC-SEED SPREAD

Yields: 12 to 16 servings   Pan Size: baking sheet   Preheat: 400°

½ c. margarine, softened
¼ c. sesame seed
¼ c. caraway seed
¼ c. poppy seed

8 oz. Tillamook cheese, grated
1 tbsp. garlic powder
1 loaf French bread

Combine margarine, sesame seed, caraway seed, poppy seed, cheese and garlic powder in bowl; mix well. Split French bread lengthwise. Spread halves with garlic spread. Place on baking sheet. Bake, covered with foil, for 10 minutes. Cut into serving pieces.
Note: May substitute Cheddar cheese for Tillamook.

Audrey D. Edmonds, Silverdale Grange, Washington

CHEESE BALL

Yields: 15 servings

16 oz. cream cheese, softened
2 c. shredded Cheddar cheese
1 tsp. chopped onion
1 tsp. chopped green pepper

1 tsp. chopped pimento
2 tsp. Worcestershire sauce
1 tsp. lemon juice
Finely chopped pecans

Combine cream cheese, Cheddar cheese, onion, green pepper, pimento, Worcestershire sauce and lemon juice in bowl; mix well. Shape into ball. Roll in pecans. Chill for several hours. Place on serving plate. Serve with crackers.

Susie Culler, Glade Valley Grange, Maryland

CLAM-CHEESE LOG

Yields: 20 servings

1 lb. sharp Cheddar cheese,
    grated
6 oz. cream cheese, softened
¼ c. butter, softened
3 tbsp. chopped parsley
1 tsp. grated onion

2 tsp. Worcestershire sauce
¾ tsp. Tabasco sauce
2   7-oz. cans minced clams,
    drained
3 tbsp. chopped parsley
½ c. finely chopped nuts

Combine Cheddar cheese, cream cheese, butter, 3 tablespoons parsley, onion, Worcestershire sauce, Tabasco sauce and clams in mixer bowl; mix well. Chill until mixture can be easily handled. Shape into log. Roll in mixture of remaining parsley and nuts. Chill until serving time.

Marian Levasseur, East Barnard Grange, Vermont

COLD SALMON APPETIZER

Yields: 8 servings

2 c. cooked fresh salmon	1 tbsp. olive oil
8 oz. cream cheese, softened	Freshly ground pepper
2 green onions, minced	½ red onion, finely chopped
¼ tsp. garlic powder	¼ c. capers
1 lg. dill pickle, finely chopped	1 lg. tomato, chopped
Juice of ½ lemon	

Combine salmon, cream cheese, green onions, garlic powder, pickle, lemon juice and olive oil in bowl; mix well. Spread in shallow serving dish. Sprinkle with pepper, onion, capers and tomato. Garnish with parsley and lemon slices. Serve with crackers. *Note:* If canned salmon is substituted for fresh salmon, omit olive oil.

Mrs. George M. Ray, Sauvies Island Grange, Oregon

SALMON PARTY LOG

Yields: 15 servings

1 16-oz. can salmon	¼ tsp. liquid smoke
8 oz. cream cheese, softened	¼ tsp. salt
2 tsp. grated onion	½ c. chopped pecans
1 tbsp. lemon juice	3 tbsp. chopped parsley

Drain and flake salmon. Combine with cream cheese, onion, lemon juice, liquid smoke and salt in bowl; mix well. Chill for several hours. Shape into 2x8-inch log. Roll in mixture of pecans and parsley. Chill in refrigerator. Place on serving plate. Serve with assorted crackers.

Darlene Andersen
First Lady of the National Grange

SHRIMP MOLD

Yields: 12 servings   Pan Size: 4 cup

1 env. unflavored gelatin	½ c. finely chopped celery
½ c. tomato soup	¼ c. finely chopped onion
3 oz. cream cheese, softened	2 cans sm. shrimp, drained
¾ c. mayonnaise	

Soften gelatin in *1 tablespoon cold water*. Bring soup to a simmer in saucepan. Add gelatin; stir until gelatin dissolves. Blend in cream cheese and mayonnaise. Add celery and onion; mix well. Stir in shrimp. Pour into mold. Chill for 2 hours to overnight. Unmold onto serving plate. Serve with crackers.

Helen E. Verge, Fidelity Grange, New Hampshire

BACON AND WATER CHESTNUTS

Yields: 30 servings	Pan Size: baking sheet	Preheat: 350°

2 lb. bacon
2 cans whole water chestnuts
1 8-oz. can tomato sauce
¼ c. molasses

¼ c. A-1 sauce
¼ c. packed brown sugar
2 tbsp. soy sauce

Cut bacon strips and water chestnuts into halves. Wrap water chestnuts with bacon; secure with toothpick. Place on baking sheet. Bake for 45 minutes. Drain on paper towel. Combine remaining ingredients in saucepan. Simmer for 10 minutes, stirring frequently. Add water chestnuts. Simmer for 10 minutes. Serve hot or cold.

Lois Pifer, Henderson Grange, Pennsylvania

FRENCH-FRIED CHEESE BITES

Yields: 4 servings	Pan Size: 2 quart	Preheat: 325°

8 oz. Fontina cheese
1 egg

½ c. dried bread crumbs
Oil for deep frying

Cut cheese into bite-sized cubes. Beat egg and *2 tablespoons water* with fork. Dip cheese cubes 1 at a time into egg mixture and roll in bread crumbs to coat; repeat process. Place coated cheese cubes on waxed paper-lined plate. Refrigerate until ready to fry. Heat 1-inch oil in saucepan to 325 degrees. Deep-fry cheese cubes several at a time for 1 minute or until golden brown. Drain on paper towels. Serve hot with mustard sauce for dipping.

Ann Wehr, Valley Grange, Pennsylvania

MEATBALL HORS D'OEUVRES

Yields: 12 to 16 servings

2 lb. lean ground beef
1 med. onion, finely chopped
1 egg
1 tsp. salt
Bread crumbs

1 c. grape jelly
¼ c. packed brown sugar
12 oz. chili sauce
1 tbsp. lemon juice

Combine ground beef, onion, egg and salt in bowl; mix well. Add enough bread crumbs to bind mixture. Shape into small balls. Brown in skillet; remove to chafing dish. Combine remaining ingredients in saucepan. Heat until bubbly; mix well. Pour over meatballs. Serve with wooden picks.

Ellen McClelland, Williamsport Grange, Ohio

PARTY TUNA ROLLS

Yields: 6 to 12 servings	Pan Size: baking sheet	Preheat: 350°

1 7-oz. can tuna, flaked	½ can condensed consommé
1 c. dry bread crumbs	¼ c. mayonnaise
¼ c. minced onion	1 tbsp. mustard
1 egg, beaten	1 tsp. poultry seasoning
2 tbsp. chopped parsley	Cornflake crumbs

Combine tuna, bread crumbs, onion, egg, parsley, consommé, mayonnaise, mustard and poultry seasoning in bowl; mix well. Shape into small balls. Roll in cornflake crumbs, coating well. Place on greased baking sheet. Bake for 8 to 10 minutes or until heated through. Arrange on serving plate.

Edith M. Prescott, Bellbrook Grange, Ohio

OPEN-FACED CRAB AND MUSHROOM SANDWICHES

Yields: 6 servings	Pan Size: baking sheet	Preheat: 400°

3 slices bacon	½ c. mayonnaise
¼ c. chopped onion	Butter, softened
4 oz. mushrooms, sliced	6 English muffins, split
1 c. crab meat	Paprika to taste
1 c. grated Swiss cheese	Pepper to taste
⅓ c. Parmesan cheese	

Fry bacon in skillet until crisp. Drain on paper towel; crumble. Sauté onion and mushrooms in bacon drippings. Add crumbled bacon. Cool. Combine crab meat, cheeses and mayonnaise in bowl. Add bacon mixture; mix well. Chill until serving time. Spread evenly on buttered English muffins. Sprinkle with paprika and pepper. Place on baking sheet. Bake for 15 minutes. Serve hot.

Judy A. Boring, Lookout Mountain Grange, Oregon

FIRESIDE SANDWICHES

Yields: 8 servings	Pan Size: baking sheet	Preheat: 350°

2 c. finely chopped ham	2 tsp. mustard
1 c. shredded sharp cheese	2 tbsp. mayonnaise
2 tsp. grated onion	8 sandwich buns, split
½ tsp. horseradish	

Combine ham, cheese, onion, horseradish, mustard and mayonnaise in bowl; mix well. Fill buns; wrap individually in foil. Bake for 10 minutes. Serve hot with sliced tomatoes, potato chips and pickles.

Grace C. Hopkins, Henlopen Grange, Delaware

BANANA GRANOLA

Yields: 6 cups	Pan Size: baking sheet	Preheat: 300°

3 c. oats	½ c. chunky peanut butter
½ c. wheat germ	2 tbsp. oil
2 med. bananas, mashed	1 tsp. cinnamon
⅓ c. packed brown sugar	1 c. raisins

Mix oats and wheat germ in bowl. Add mixture of bananas, brown sugar, peanut butter, oil and cinnamon; mix well. Spread in pan. Bake for 45 to 50 minutes, stirring occasionally. Cool. Stir in raisins. Store in airtight container.

Mary E. Herron, Fairview Grange, West Virginia

TOASTY NUT GRANOLA

Yields: 9 cups	Pan Size: two 9 x 13 inch	Preheat: 350°

6 c. quick-cooking oats	1 c. chopped nuts
½ c. packed brown sugar	½ c. (or more) oil
¾ c. wheat germ	¼ c. honey
½ c. flaked coconut	1½ tsp. vanilla extract
¼ c. sesame seed	

Spread oats in ungreased baking pan. Bake for 10 minutes. Combine with brown sugar, wheat germ, coconut, sesame seed and nuts in bowl. Add oil, honey and vanilla; toss to mix well. Spread in baking pans. Bake for 20 to 26 minutes or until golden brown, stirring occasionally. Cool. Store in airtight container.

Martha A. Cullen, Round Butte Grange, Montana

NUTS AND BOLTS

Yields: 5 quarts	Pan Size: roaster	Preheat: 225°

1½ c. butter, melted	1 med. package Wheat Chex
1 tsp. each garlic salt, onion salt	1 med. package Cheerios
	4 oz. pretzels
1 tbsp. Worcestershire sauce	4 oz. each cashews, peanuts
1 med. package Rice Chex	and pecans

Mix butter, garlic salt, onion salt and Worcestershire sauce. Pour over mixture of cereals, pretzels and nuts in baking pan; mix well. Bake for 4 hours, stirring every 30 minutes. Cool on paper towels. Store in airtight container.

Lillie Jane Casler, Litchfield Grange, New York

EGG COFFEE (SCANDINAVIA)

Yields: 20 servings

1 egg	**½ c. plus 2 tbsp.**
Pinch of salt	**ground coffee beans**

Bring *19 cups water* to a boil in enamel pan. Combine egg and salt with *2 tablespoons cold water* in bowl; mix with fork. Add coffee; moisten well. Stir into boiling water. Bring to a boil; reduce heat. Simmer for 3 minutes; remove from heat. Pour *1 cup cold water* over coffee to settle grounds. Let stand for several minutes. Pour carefully into serving pot.

Leona Ball, Rogue River Valley Grange, Oregon

GOGOZZA (SWITZERLAND) Lemonade

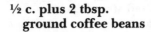

Yields: 10 quarts

2 lb. sugar	**2 tsp. (heaping) cream of**
4 lemons, sliced	**tartar**

Bring *2 quarts water* to a boil in saucepan. Add sugar; mix well. Boil for 5 minutes. Add lemons. Boil for 15 minutes. Dissolve cream of tartar in a small amount of water. Stir into lemon mixture. Strain into *8 quarts cold water* in 3-gallon container; mix well. Pour into bottles; seal for storage.

Rita F. Bradley, Sierra Valley Grange, California

HOT APPLE CIDER NOG

Yields: 6 servings

1 c. apple cider	**¼ tsp. salt**
2 eggs, beaten	**3 c. milk**
½ c. sugar	**½ c. whipping**
¼ tsp. cinnamon	**cream,**
⅛ tsp. nutmeg	**whipped**

Combine cider, eggs, sugar, spices and salt in bowl; beat until smooth. Bring milk to a boil in saucepan. Stir a small amount of hot milk into egg mixture; stir egg mixture into milk. Cook until thickened, stirring constantly. Pour into mugs. Top with stiffly whipped cream.

MILK PUNCH

Yields: 50 servings

6 c. mashed strawberries
3 c. sugar
Pinch of salt
4 qt. cold milk

2 qt. strawberry ice cream,
softened
1 qt. mint ice cream,
softened

Combine strawberries, sugar and salt in large bowl. Stir in milk. Fold in ice cream. Pour into punch bowl. Garnish with whole strawberries. Ladle into punch cups.

Dorothy Stewart, Victory Grange, Ohio

DAIRY ORANGE PICK-ME-UP

Yields: 5 servings   Pan Size: blender

½ c. frozen orange juice
concentrate, thawed
2 tbsp. honey

1 egg
4 c. cold milk
2 scoops vanilla ice cream

Combine orange juice, honey, egg and milk in blender container. Add ice cream. Process until smooth. Serve immediately.
Note: May substitute other ice cream flavors or several ice cubes for vanilla ice cream.

Michelle Stewart, Marion Grange, Pennsylvania

SWITCHEL (HOLLAND)

Yields: 8 cups

¼ c. sugar
¼ c. vinegar

1 tbsp. ginger

Combine sugar, vinegar and ginger with *2 quarts water* in pitcher; mix well. Chill in refrigerator. Serve cold.

Frances Casler, Litchfield Grange, New York

WEDDING PUNCH

Yields: 100 servings

6 tea bags
6 c. sugar
1 lg. can grapefruit juice
2 lg. cans pineapple juice
1 lg. can frozen lemonade
concentrate

2 lg. cans frozen orange juice
concentrate
1½ c. finely chopped
maraschino cherries
5 qt. ginger ale

Pour *3 quarts boiling water* over tea bags in large container. Steep for several minutes; remove tea bags. Bring sugar and *6 cups water* to a boil in saucepan; stir until sugar dissolves. Add to tea mixture. Add juices and cherries; mix well. Chill in refrigerator. Stir in ginger ale gently at serving time. Pour into punch bowl. Ladle into punch cups.

Mildred P. Lockcuff, Bottle Run Grange, Pennsylvania

SHERBET PUNCH

Yields: 40 servings   Pan Size: punch bowl

2   46-oz. cans pineapple juice
1 qt. orange juice
½ c. lemon juice

2 qt. ginger ale
¼ gal. pineapple sherbet, softened

Chill juices and ginger ale. Combine juices in punch bowl. Add ginger ale and sherbet just before serving; mix gently. Ladle into punch cups.

Lelah M. Fiori, Rinn Valley Grange, Colorado

FRUIT SLUSH

Yields: 20 servings

6 oz. frozen orange juice concentrate
6 oz. frozen pink lemonade concentrate
1   16-oz. can crushed pineapple

16 oz. 7-Up
1 c. sugar
2 lg. bananas, mashed
2   10-oz. packages frozen raspberries

Thaw frozen ingredients. Combine all ingredients in bowl; mix well. Freeze until firm. Thaw for 30 minutes. Stir until slushy. Spoon into glasses.

Lona Adkins, Victor Grange, Iowa

PINK RHUBARB REFRESHER

Yields: 24 servings

2 lb. tender pink rhubarb, chopped
2 c. sugar

2½ to 3 c. grapefruit juice
¼ c. lemon juice
1 qt. ginger ale

Combine rhubarb with sugar and *5 cups boiling water* in saucepan. Cook until mushy. Strain through cheesecloth. Measure syrup. Combine ½ cup grapefruit juice for each cup rhubarb syrup in punch bowl. Add lemon juice; mix well. Add ginger ale just before serving; mix gently. Garnish with mint springs. Ladle into punch cups.
Serving suggestion: Freeze pink lemonade in ring mold to float in punch bowl.

Alta B. Arlen, Holland Grange, New York

ICED TEA

Yields: 16 servings

5 tea bags
1 bunch fresh mint

1¾ c. sugar
⅓ c. lemon juice concentrate

Pour *4 cups boiling water* over tea bags and mint. Steep for 15 minutes; remove tea bags and mint. Add mixture of sugar, lemon juice and *4 cups cold water*; mix until sugar dissolves. Combine with *4 cups ice water* in gallon container. Chill until serving time. Serve over ice.

Miriam E. Robenold, Washington Grange, Pennsylvania

THREE-FRUIT PUNCH

Yields: 42 6-ounce servings

12 oz. frozen lemonade
 concentrate, thawed
12 oz. frozen orange juice
 concentrate, thawed

46 oz. pineapple juice
1 c. sugar
1 qt. ginger ale

Combine lemonade concentrate, orange juice concentrate and pineapple juice in large container. Dissolve sugar in *½ cup water*. Add sugar and *11 cups water* to juices; mix well. Add ginger ale just before serving time; mix gently. Pour over ice in punch bowl. Ladle into punch cups.

Thelma Meyer, Millville Grange, California

TOMATO JUICE COCKTAIL

Yields: 16 servings

48 oz. tomato juice
1 tbsp. grated onion
2 tbsp. grated celery
1½ tsp. Worcestershire sauce

¼ c. lemon juice
1 tbsp. sugar
1 tsp. salt

Place tomato juice in large pitcher. Rinse tomato juice can with *½ cup water*; add to juice. Add remaining ingredients and *2 cups water*; mix well. Chill for several hours. Strain into glasses.

Home Economics Committee, Williamsport Grange, Ohio

Accompaniments

Homemade relishes, pickles, preserves, sauces, jam, jelly and marmalade are perfect accompaniments to family and company meals, adding zest and variety to any menu. Preserving food is an old art, growing out of the need to conserve nature's bounty for times of less abundance and our American taste for "sweet and sour" dates back to Colonial kitchens. Colorful jars of foods put up with love and care are a feast for the eye and palate as well as a tasty link with our past.

The collection of accompaniments in *The Glory of Cooking* includes recipes—old and new—which are not only economical and free from commercial additives, but which also add the spice of imagination to naturally delicious ingredients: green beans pickled with cayenne, garlic, and dill; crab apples spiced with cinnamon, ginger, cloves, and nutmeg; mustard blended with white wine and honey; delectable fruit combinations preserved in jam, jelly and marmalade. Packaged in eye-catching containers—Brandy snifters, sherbet glasses, earthenware crocks, or graceful bottles and jars—these treasures are welcomed gifts or additions to any table.

NEW ENGLAND BEET RELISH

Yields: 2 quarts

1 qt. finely chopped fresh cabbage	**2 c. sugar**
1 qt. finely chopped cooked beets	**1 tbsp. salt**
½ c. grated horseradish	**1 tsp. pepper**
	¼ tsp. red pepper
	Cider vinegar

Combine cabbage, beets, horseradish, sugar and seasonings in bowl; mix well. Spoon into jars. Add enough vinegar to cover. Store, covered, in refrigerator.

Susan M. Lynch, San Marcos Grange, California

FRESH CRANBERRY SAUCE

Yields: 4 cups   Pan Size: 2 quart

4 c. fresh cranberries	**2 c. sugar**

Combine cranberries, sugar and *2 cups water* in saucepan. Cook over medium heat until sugar dissolves, stirring constantly. Boil for 5 minutes or until cranberries pop. Serve warm or cold.

Photograph for this recipe on page 135.

HOT DOG RELISH

Yields: 10 to 12 pints   Pan Size: stockpot

20 green tomatoes	**12 c. sugar**
4 c. chopped cabbage	**8 c. vinegar**
8 c. chopped onions	**3 tbsp. mustard seed**
24 green peppers, chopped	**3 tbsp. celery seed**
12 red peppers, chopped	**1 tbsp. turmeric**
1 c. salt	**3 tbsp. dry mustard**

Grind tomatoes, cabbage, onions and peppers. Mix with salt in crock. Let stand overnight. Drain. Combine ground vegetables with sugar, vinegar, mustard seed, celery seed, turmeric, dry mustard and *4 cups water* in stockpot. Bring to a boil. Cook for 3 minutes. Spoon into hot sterilized jars, leaving ½-inch headspace; seal with 2-piece lids. Process in boiling water bath for 10 minutes.

Hazel Weaver, Smith Grange, Ohio

DILLY BEAN PICKLES

Yields: 8 pints	Pan Size: 3 quart

2 lb. whole green beans, trimmed	8 heads of dill
4 tsp. cayenne pepper	2½ c. vinegar
8 cloves of garlic	¼ c. salt

Cook green beans in water to cover in saucepan until tender-crisp. Drain and cool. Pack lengthwise into sterilized jars. Add ½ teaspoon cayenne pepper, 1 clove of garlic and 1 head of dill to each jar. Bring vinegar, salt and *2½ cups water* to a boil in saucepan. Pour over beans, leaving ½-inch headspace; seal with 2-piece lids. Process in boiling water bath for 10 minutes. Let stand for 2 weeks before serving.

Bethel Croghan, Rockwall Grange, Oregon

GALLON-JUG DILL PICKLES

Yields: 1 gallon	Pan Size: 3 quart

2 cloves of garlic	2 c. vinegar
1 gal. small cucumbers	¼ c. salt
4 tsp. dillseed	1 tsp. pickling spice

Place garlic in wide-mouth 1-gallon container. Add cucumbers. Sprinkle with dillseed. Bring vinegar, salt, pickling spice and *4 cups water* to a boil in saucepan. Pour over cucumbers. Let stand, tightly covered, for 24 hours. Chill in refrigerator for 3 days before serving. Store in refrigerator.

Esther Hopewell, Bottle Run Grange, Pennsylvania

KOSHER-STYLE DILL PICKLES

Yields: 6 to 8 quarts	Pan Size: 5 quart

20 to 25 4-inch cucumbers	1 qt. cider vinegar
6 to 8 cloves of garlic	½ tbsp. powdered alum
4 to 5 tbsp. dillseed	1 c. salt

Wash cucumbers. Combine with cold water to cover in crock. Let stand overnight. Drain. Pack cucumbers into hot sterilized quart jars. Add 1 clove of garlic and 2 teaspoons dillseed to each jar. Combine vinegar, alum, salt and *3 quarts water* in saucepan. Bring to a boil. Pour over cucumbers, leaving ½-inch headspace; seal with 2-piece lids. Process in boiling water bath for 20 minutes.

Gloria E. Lessard, Stonyford Grange, California

GRANDMOTHER'S SPICED CRAB APPLE PICKLES

Yields: 1 to 2 pints   Pan Size: 3 quart

2 lb. crab apples	**1 tsp. cinnamon**
2 lb. sugar	**½ tsp. each ginger, cloves**
½ c. vinegar	** and nutmeg**

Combine quartered crab apples, sugar, vinegar, spices and *1 cup water* in saucepan. Cook, covered, over low heat for 30 minutes. Cook, uncovered, until of desired consistency, stirring frequently. Spoon into sterilized jars, leaving ½-inch headspace; seal with 2-piece lids. Process in boiling water bath for 20 minutes.

Doris Getchell, Houlton Grange, Maine

CUCUMBER CINNAMON RINGS

Yields: 8 pints

2 gal. large cucumbers	**10 c. sugar**
2 c. lime	**2 c. vinegar**
2 c. vinegar	**8 sticks cinnamon**
1 tbsp. powdered alum	**8 oz. red hot candies**

Peel, slice and core cucumbers. Place in large crock. Add lime and *2 gallons water*. Let stand for 24 hours, stirring frequently. Drain. Rinse and drain. Place in crock. Add cold water to cover. Let stand for 1 hour. Drain. Combine with 2 cups vinegar, alum, *1 ounce red food coloring* and water to cover in stockpot. Simmer for 2 hours. Drain. Return cucumbers to crock. Mix sugar, 2 cups vinegar, cinnamon, candies and *2 cups water* in saucepan. Bring to a boil, stirring to dissolve sugar and candies. Pour over cucumbers. Let stand for 24 hours. Drain, reserving syrup. Bring syrup to a boil. Pour over cucumbers. Let stand for 24 hours. Repeat process 2 times. Pack cucumbers into hot sterilized jars. Pour boiling syrup into jars, leaving ½-inch headspace; seal with 2-piece lids. Process in boiling water bath for 15 minutes.

Shirley Wasko, Fairview Grange, Idaho

BREAD AND BUTTER PICKLES

Yields: 5 to 6 pints   Pan Size: 5 quart

4 qt. sliced cucumbers	**3 c. 4% white vinegar**
1 qt. sliced onions	**5 c. sugar**
1 pt. sweet red pepper strips	**2 tbsp. mustard seed**
⅓ c. salt	**½ tsp. each celery seed, turmeric**

Layer vegetables, salt and ice cubes in crock. Let stand overnight. Drain. Bring remaining ingredients to a boil in large saucepan. Add vegetables. Bring to a boil. Cook for 1 minute, stirring frequently. Spoon into hot sterilized jars, leaving ½-inch headspace; seal with 2-piece lids. Process in boiling water bath for 10 minutes.

Hilda Wolbaugh, Smithville Grange, Ohio

FROZEN PICKLES

Yields: 4 pints   Pan Size: 2 quart

2 qt. sliced unpeeled cucumbers   **1½ c. sugar**
1 (or more) onion, chopped   **½ c. vinegar**
2 tbsp. salt

Mix cucumbers, onion and salt in large bowl. Let stand for 2 hours. Combine sugar and vinegar in saucepan. Bring to a boil, stirring until sugar dissolves; syrup will be thick. Cool. Drain cucumbers, pressing out as much liquid as possible. Pack cucumbers into freezer containers. Pour syrup over cucumbers. Store in freezer. Store opened pickles in refrigerator.

Ruth Schilliger, Ashley Grange, Ohio

PICKLED CAULIFLOWER

Yields: 4 quarts   Pan Size: 8 quart

2 heads cauliflower   **½ c. dried onion flakes**
4 tsp. salt   **2 tbsp. mustard seed**
4 c. sliced carrots   **2 tsp. turmeric**
1 qt. white vinegar   **4 peppercorns**
1 c. sugar

Cut cauliflower into large flowerets; slice. Place in large bowl; sprinkle with 2 teaspoons salt. Sprinkle 2 teaspoons salt over carrots in bowl. Let stand, covered, for 2 hours. Rinse under running water; drain well. Combine vinegar and remaining ingredients in saucepan. Bring to a boil; add carrots. Simmer, covered, for 5 minutes. Add cauliflower. Simmer, covered, for 6 minutes or until tender-crisp. Pack vegetables into hot sterilized jars. Add boiling liquid, leaving ½-inch headspace; seal with 2-piece lids. Process in boiling water bath for 10 minutes.

SPICY BARBECUE SAUCE

Yields: 2½ cups   Pan Size: 10 inch

1 med. onion, chopped
⅓ c. corn oil
½ c. dark corn syrup
½ c. catsup
⅓ c. vinegar

2 tbsp. mustard
2 tbsp. Worcestershire sauce
2 tsp. salt
½ tsp. pepper

Sauté onion in oil in skillet. Add remaining ingredients and *½ cup water*; mix well. Simmer for 15 minutes, stirring occasionally.

Gladys Tarpley, Statesville Grange, Tennessee

BARBECUE SAUCE

Yields: 2½ cups   Pan Size: 1 quart

1 c. tomato sauce
1 med. onion, chopped
¼ c. oil
1 tbsp. sugar
1 tbsp. mustard

¼ c. vinegar
½ tsp. chili powder
½ tsp. salt
¼ tsp. pepper

Combine all ingredients and *¼ cup water* in saucepan; mix well. Bring to a boil; reduce heat. Simmer for 10 minutes, stirring frequently. Cool. Store in covered container in refrigerator. Use with beef, pork, chicken and fish.

Connie Mills, Quilcene Grange, Washington

CHILI SAUCE

Yields: 8 quarts   Pan Size: stockpot

60 ripe tomatoes, chopped
6 lg. onions, chopped
6 red peppers, chopped
6 green peppers, chopped
2 jalapeño peppers,
** chopped**

10 c. sugar
5 c. vinegar
1 tbsp. each ginger, cloves
5 tbsp. salt
1 tbsp. pepper

Combine vegetables in stockpot. Cook for 1 hour, stirring frequently. Add remaining ingredients; mix well. Cook until of desired consistency, stirring frequently. Spoon into sterilized jars, leaving ½-inch headspace; seal with 2-piece lids. Process in boiling water bath for 15 minutes.

Jeanne Gee, Lickly Corners Grange, Michigan

SALSA

Yields: 4 pints	Pan Size: 2 quart

8 lg. tomatoes, peeled, chopped	1 8-oz. can tomato sauce
2 lg. onions	2 tbsp. vinegar
4 jalapeño peppers, chopped	1 tsp. sugar
2 cloves of garlic, chopped	2 tsp. salt

Combine tomatoes, onions, peppers and garlic in saucepan. Add tomato sauce, vinegar, sugar and salt; mix well. Simmer for 30 minutes or to desired consistency. Spoon into sterilized jars, leaving ½-inch headspace; seal with 2-piece lids. Process in boiling water bath for 35 minutes. Serve with pinto beans, nachos and other Mexican dishes or mix with sour cream for spicy dips.

Delores Clocker, Barberton Grange, Washington

MOTHER'S CATSUP

Yields: 10 quarts	Pan Size: stockpot

1 bu. ripe tomatoes	1 oz. mace
1 oz. ground red pepper	Mustard seed to taste
2 oz. black pepper	Salt to taste
2 oz. allspice	Vinegar to taste

Chop tomatoes. Simmer in stockpot until tender. Press through coarse sieve to remove skin and seed. Combine with remaining ingredients in stockpot. Simmer for 6 hours, stirring frequently. Pour into sterilized bottles, leaving 1-inch headspace; seal. Process in boiling water bath for 10 minutes.
Note: Original recipe calls for 10 cents worth of mustard seed.

Emeline Frace, San Marcos Grange, California

HOT SWEET MUSTARD

Yields: 4 cups	Pan Size: double boiler

1 4-oz. can dry mustard	2 eggs
½ c. vinegar	½ c. honey
¾ c. white wine	2 c. mayonnaise

Combine dry mustard, vinegar and wine in bowl; mix well. Let stand, covered, overnight. Mix eggs and honey in double boiler. Cook until thickened, stirring constantly. Cool slightly. Add mustard mixture and mayonnaise; mix well. Store in covered jar in refrigerator.

Wilma V. Corbin, Pleasant Valley Grange, Washington

TANGY MUSTARD SAUCE

Yields: 2 cups	Pan Size: 1 quart

1 2-oz. can dry mustard	**¼ c. sugar**
½ c. vinegar	**Dash of salt**
1 egg, beaten	**1 c. mayonnaise**

Blend dry mustard and vinegar in small bowl. Let stand, covered, for 24 to 36 hours. Mix egg, sugar, salt and mustard mixture in saucepan. Cook until mixture coats spoon, stirring constantly. Cool. Stir in mayonnaise. Store in covered container in refrigerator.

Myrta D. Forbes, Hamer Grange, New York

ZAPPLESAUCE

Yields: 1 pint	Pan Size: 1½ quart/blender

5 c. chopped seeded peeled zucchini	**½ c. sugar**
½ c. pineapple juice	**¼ c. lemon juice**

Combine zucchini, pineapple juice, sugar and lemon juice in saucepan. Cook until zucchini is tender. Cool. Process in blender until puréed. Store in refrigerator. Use as substitute for applesauce with meals or in recipes.
Note: Larger quantities may be preserved. Reheat purée to the boiling point. Spoon into hot sterilized jars, leaving ½-inch headspace; seal with 2-piece lids. Process in boiling water bath for 15 minutes.

Cathy Higman, Lakevista Grange, Colorado

CORN COB JELLY

Yields: 2 to 3 pints	Pan Size: 2 quart

12 corn cobs	**Several drops of yellow food coloring**
1 pkg. pectin	
4 c. sugar	

Combine corn cobs with *4 cups water* in saucepan. Boil for 10 minutes. Strain liquid; measure 3 cups. Cool. Combine 3 cups liquid and pectin in saucepan. Bring to a boil. Add sugar. Simmer until sugar and pectin dissolve. Skim off foam. Stir in food coloring. Pour into hot sterilized jars, leaving ½-inch headspace; seal with 2-piece lids. Process in boiling water bath for 4 minutes.
Note: This jelly tastes like honey.

Marie Byers, Salmon River Grange, Oregon

PEPPER JELLY

Yields: 6 cups　　　　　　　Pan Size: 2 quart

¾ c. ground green peppers
¼ c. ground hot red peppers
6 c. sugar

1½ c. white vinegar
1 6-oz. package Certo

Bring peppers, sugar and vinegar to a boil in saucepan. Boil for 1 minute, stirring constantly. Remove from heat. Stir in Certo. Let stand for 5 minutes. Skim off foam. Pour into hot sterilized jars, leaving ¼-inch headspace; seal with 2-piece lids. Process in boiling water bath for 5 minutes. Let stand until partially cooled. Invert jars. Cool completely. Serve on crackers with cream cheese.

Margaret S. Maple, Lawrenceville Grange, New Jersey

BLUE PLUM-RASPBERRY JAM

Yields: 4 pints　　　　　　　Pan Size: 3 quart

6 to 8 lb. blue prune plums
1 10-oz. package frozen
　raspberries

1 pkg. Sure-Jel
6½ c. sugar

Put plums through food grinder. Measure 6 cups. Combine with raspberries in saucepan. Bring to a boil over low heat. Cook for 1 minute, stirring constantly. Stir in Sure-Jel and sugar. Cook for 1 minute, stirring constantly. Pour into hot sterilized jars, leaving ½-inch headspace; seal with 2-piece lids. Process in boiling water bath for 5 minutes.

Mary Wirich, Friend of Cherryvale Grange, Kansas

LUCKY LEAF JELLY

Yields: 2 to 4 pints　　　　　Pan Size: stockpot

1 gal. red clover blossoms
Juice of 1 lemon
1 pkg. pectin

4 c. sugar
3 to 4 drops of red food
　coloring

Bring clover blossoms and water to cover to a boil in stockpot. Simmer for 8 to 10 minutes, stirring occasionally. Let stand for several minutes. Strain liquid through 3 thicknesses of cheesecloth. Measure 2 cups liquid. Combine with lemon juice and pectin in saucepan. Bring to a boil. Add sugar and food coloring. Boil for 1 minute. Pour into sterilized jars, leaving ½-inch headspace; seal with 2-piece lids. Process in boiling water bath for 5 minutes.

Helen Metcalf, Saxtons River Grange, New Hampshire

ORANGE MARMALADE WITH GALLIANO

Yields: 6 pints   Pan Size: 3 quart

6 med. oranges, thinly
   sliced
¾ cup lemon juice
9 c. sugar

¼ tsp. margarine
¾ c. Galliano
1 pkg. pectin

Combine orange slices, lemon juice and *6 cups water* in saucepan. Bring to a boil over high heat; reduce heat. Simmer for 1 hour or until orange rind is tender. Measure 7 cups. Combine with sugar in saucepan. Bring to a rolling boil. Stir in margarine. Boil for 4 minutes; remove from heat. Skim off foam. Stir in Galliano and pectin. Pour into sterilized jars, leaving ½-inch headspace; seal with 2-piece lids. Process in boiling water bath for 5 minutes.

Jackie Criswell, Friend of Brush College Grange, Oregon

PEAR AND PINEAPPLE MARMALADE

Yields: 5 pints   Pan Size: 5 quart

7 c. chopped peeled pears
3 oranges, seeded

2 c. crushed pineapple
7 c. sugar

Grind pears and oranges. Combine pears, oranges, pineapple and sugar in saucepan. Cook for 20 minutes or until very thick. Pour into hot sterilized jars, leaving ½-inch headspace; seal with 2-piece lids. Process in boiling water bath for 5 minutes.
Note: May add 1 package Sure-Jel using package directions.

Virginia Shannon, St. Johns Grange, Ohio

RHUBARB AND ORANGE MARMALADE

Yields: 15 pints   Pan Size: 3 quart

6 lb. rhubarb, finely
   chopped
2 c. sugar

6 sweet oranges
Sugar

Combine rhubarb and 2 cups sugar in large bowl. Let stand, covered, overnight. Slice unpeeled oranges. Combine with water to cover in saucepan. Simmer for 1 hour or until orange rind is tender. Let stand, covered, overnight. Measure rhubarb and oranges. Combine with 1 cup sugar for each cup rhubarb and oranges in saucepan. Bring to a boil over low heat. Simmer for 1 hour or until thick. Test for desired consistency by cooling a small amount on cold saucer. Spoon into jars, leaving ¼-inch headspace; seal with 2-piece lids. Process in boiling water bath for 5 minutes.

Roselyn Teelin, South Trenton Grange, New York

Soups

Everyone loves soup. A potful simmering on the stove recalls memories of fragrant kitchens from our past, and no food is more satisfying or comforting. Somehow, a hot soup on a winter night is heartier and more warming while a chilled soup on a summer day is more refreshing than the same ingredients served separately. Soups are important in every ethnic cuisine, and those traditional old-world recipes are savory ties to the past. And today, as in the past, preparing soup offers the cook unlimited opportunity to be creative with the ingredients on hand and favorite herbs and spices.

The soups in *The Glory of Cooking* rise to any occasion, from brunch to dinner. A substantial protein-rich soup is an informal one-dish supper. Lighter soups are gracious first courses or tasty lunches. A cold soup transported in a thermos is perfect for a picnic. And fruit soups make an unusual brunch dish or dessert. Serve several soups with homemade bread and a rich dessert for a memorable party. Anytime, ladle soups from handsome tureens, stockpots, or casseroles; pour from pitchers into mugs or pretty stemmed glasses; top with toasted nuts, croutons, grated cheese, or sour cream. Steaming or frosty, simple or elegant, soups are versatile and delicious.

ALMA CEBERE (HUNGARY) Apple Soup

Yields: 4 servings	Pan Size: 2 quart

6 med. apples, peeled, chopped	**5 tbsp. cornstarch**
1 c. sour cream	**Salt, pepper and sugar to taste**

Combine apples and *1½ cups water* in saucepan. Cook until tender. Blend sour cream and cornstarch in bowl. Stir a small amount of hot liquid into sour cream. Stir sour cream into hot mixture. Simmer for several minutes. Season to taste.

Elizabeth Mecera, North Elyria Grange, Ohio

FRUIT SOUP (NORWAY)

Yields: 8 to 10 servings	Pan Size: 4 quart

2 c. dried prunes	**1½ c. sugar**
2 c. raisins	**½ lemon, thinly sliced**
2 sticks cinnamon	**1 tbsp. vinegar**
⅓ c. Minute tapioca	

Soak prunes and raisins in *8 cups water* in saucepan overnight. Bring to a boil. Add cinnamon. Boil for 15 minutes. Add tapioca. Cook for 10 minutes. Add sugar. Cook for 10 minutes. Add lemon. Cook for 10 minutes. Remove cinnamon sticks. Stir in vinegar. Serve hot or cold. May garnish cold soup with sweetened whipped cream.

Alma Irey, Rogue River Valley Grange, Oregon

STRAWBERRY SOUP

Yields: 4 servings	Pan Size: blender

3 c. fresh strawberries	**2 tbsp. sugar**
1 c. sour cream	**1 c. sliced strawberries**
1 c. heavy cream	

Purée 3 cups strawberries in blender container. Press through sieve to remove seed. Combine with sour cream in bowl; mix well. Stir in cream and sugar gradually. Chill, covered, until serving time. Serve in chilled bowls. Garnish with sliced strawberries.

Mrs. George Boyer, Smithville Grange, Ohio

BONGO BONGO SOUP

Yields: 4 servings   Pan Size: 1 quart

9 fresh oysters	**1 tsp. Worcestershire sauce**
¼ c. spinach	**Dash of salt and pepper**
½ c. cream	**1½ c. milk**
2 tbsp. butter	**1 tbsp. cornstarch**
Dash of garlic salt	**Whipped cream**

Combine first 8 ingredients in blender container. Process until blended. Blend a small amount of milk with cornstarch. Heat remaining milk in saucepan. Add oyster purée and cornstarch mixture. Cook until thickened, stirring constantly. Spoon into ovenproof tureen. Top with whipped cream. Brown under broiler.

Irene M. Gormley, East Wenatchee Grange, Washington

ALL-AMERICAN CLAM CHOWDER

Yields: 4 servings   Pan Size: 3 quart

3 slices bacon	**1 c. chopped potatoes**
½ c. minced onion	**1 can cream of celery soup**
1 7½-oz. can minced clams	**1½ c. milk**
	Dash of pepper

Cook bacon in saucepan until crisp; drain on paper towel. Break bacon into 1-inch pieces. Sauté onion in bacon drippings. Drain clams, reserving liquid. Add clam liquid and potatoes to saucepan. Cook, covered, over low heat for 15 minutes or until potatoes are tender. Add bacon, clams, soup, milk and pepper; mix well. Heat to serving temperature; do not boil. Ladle into soup bowls. Garnish with bacon.

George and Barbara Bush
Vice President of the United States

CLAM CHOWDER

Yields: 10 servings   Pan Size: 3 quart

1 to 1½ qt. clams	**1 lb. potatoes, chopped**
Bit of salt pork	**1 qt. milk**
1¼ lb. Spanish onions, chopped	**3 tbsp. butter**

Cook clams in boiling water to cover in saucepan for 5 to 10 minutes or until shells open. Discard unopened clams. Remove clams from shells and chop. Strain cooking liquid, reserving 2 cups. Render salt pork in saucepan. Add onions. Sauté until transparent. Add potatoes and reserved liquid. Cook until potatoes are tender. Stir in clams, milk and butter. Heat to serving temperature, stirring constantly.

John H. Sununu
Governor of New Hampshire

NEW ENGLAND FISH AND VEGETABLE CHOWDER

Yields: 6 servings   Pan Size: 4 quart

¼ lb. bacon, chopped	2 lb. haddock, cut into chunks
2 med. onions, sliced	2 med. potatoes, peeled, chopped
1 leek, sliced	2 tbsp. chopped parsley
¼ c. chopped green pepper	⅜ tsp. thyme
1 stalk celery, chopped	¼ tsp. each basil, salt, pepper
1 clove of garlic, crushed	3 c. milk

Cook bacon in saucepan until crisp; remove bacon. Sauté onions, leek, green pepper, celery and garlic in bacon drippings. Add *4 cups water*, haddock, potatoes and seasonings. Simmer for 15 minutes or until potatoes are tender. Stir in milk and bacon. Heat to serving temperature.

Photograph for this recipe on page 67.

BEEF-BARLEY SOUP

Yields: 12 servings   Pan Size: Dutch oven

2 lb. boneless beef chuck, cubed	1 c. chopped onion
2 tbsp. oil	3 stalks celery, chopped
½ to ¾ c. medium barley	1 16-oz. can tomatoes, chopped
3 carrots, chopped	Salt and pepper to taste

Brown beef in oil in Dutch oven. Add *10 cups water*. Bring to a boil; skim off foam. Simmer, covered, for 1 hour. Add remaining ingredients. Simmer, uncovered, for 1 hour or until beef and barley are tender.

Patricia Hardisty, Monterey Grange, Massachusetts

LEEK SOUP (WALES)

Yields: 4 servings   Pan Size: 2 to 3 quart

1 bunch leeks, chopped	½ c. flour
4 med. potatoes, peeled, chopped	6 slices crisp-fried bacon,
3 c. milk	crumbled
Salt and pepper to taste	½ c. grated Cheddar cheese
¼ c. melted butter	¼ c. chopped parsley

Blanch leeks in boiling water in saucepan; drain. Add potatoes, milk, salt and pepper. Cook until vegetables are tender. Drain, reserving liquid. Blend butter and flour in saucepan. Add reserved liquid gradually, stirring constantly. Cook until thickened, stirring constantly. Add leeks and potatoes. Ladle into soup bowls. Top with bacon, cheese and parsley.

Patricia Hillman, Antelope Grange, California

BEAN SOUP (PORTUGAL)

Yields: 6 servings   Pan Size: 3 quart

1 Portuguese or Polish sausage, sliced	**2 cans red kidney beans**
2 carrots, chopped	**2 cans tomato sauce**
2 potatoes, chopped	**Salt to taste**
2 onions, chopped	**½ head cabbage, chopped**
	1 c. macaroni, cooked

Combine sausage, carrots, potatoes, onions, beans with liquid, tomato sauce and salt in saucepan. Simmer, covered, until sausage is cooked through. Add cabbage and macaroni. Bring to a boil. Simmer for 20 minutes or until vegetables are tender, adding water if necessary to make of desired consistency. Chill for 24 hours or longer. Reheat to serving temperature. Ladle into soup bowls. Serve with garlic bread.

Jack K. Suwa
Chairman, Hawaii Board of Agriculture

NINE-BEAN SOUP

Yields: 4 recipes soup   Pan Size: 4 quart

1 lb. Great Northern beans	**1 lb. split green peas**
1 lb. garbanzo beans	**1 lb. black-eyed peas**
1 lb. kidney beans	**1 lb. pearl barley**
1 lb. pinto beans	**1 med. onion, chopped**
1 lb. baby lima beans	**1 ham bone**
1 lb. black beans	**1 c. grated carrots**

Combine dried beans, peas and barley in bowl; mix well. Divide into 4-cup portions. Store in covered containers. Place 4 cups bean mixture in saucepan. Add *8 cups water*. Bring to a boil; turn off heat. Let stand for 2 hours. Add onion and ham bone. Cook until beans and ham are tender. Add carrots. Cook for 15 minutes longer.

Mr. and Mrs. Ronald Fier, Hope Chapel Grange, Ohio

GRUN BOHNE SUPPE (GERMANY) Green Bean Soup

Yields: 4 to 6 servings   Pan Size: 3 quart

5 c. cut green beans	**3 c. chopped potatoes**
3 tbsp. minced onion	**3 c. rich milk**
2 tsp. salt	**1 c. half and half**
⅛ tsp. pepper	**½ c. butter**

Combine beans, onion, salt, pepper and *6 cups water* in kettle. Cook until beans are almost tender. Add potatoes. Cook until vegetables are tender. Add milk and half and half. Bring just to the boiling point. Add butter. Stir until butter melts.

Mary Fendel, Roy Grange, Washington

CORN CHOWDER

Yields: 10 servings   Pan Size: 3 quart

¾ c. sliced onion
2 20-oz. cans cream-style corn
2 tsp. salt
⅛ tsp. pepper

½ tsp. celery salt
2 c. evaporated milk
2 hard-boiled eggs,
  sliced

Combine onion, corn, seasonings, *3 cups water* and evaporated milk in saucepan. Simmer for 1 hour, stirring frequently. Add eggs just before serving.

Ann Ehrig, Ripon Grange, California

COLD CUCUMBER SOUP

Yields: 5 servings   Pan Size: 2½ quart

3 med. cucumbers
1 med. onion, chopped
2 bay leaves
3 c. chicken broth
1 tbsp. flour

1 tsp. salt
1 c. light cream
⅓ c. sour cream
2 tbsp. lemon juice
Dash of dillweed

Peel cucumbers; remove seed. Chop 2 cucumbers. Combine chopped cucumbers, onion and bay leaves in saucepan. Stir in mixture of broth, flour and salt. Simmer, covered, for 25 to 30 minutes or until cucumbers are very tender. Cut remaining cucumber into thirds. Process cooked mixture and cucumber ⅓ at a time in blender container until smooth. Chill in refrigerator. Blend in mixture of light cream, sour cream, lemon juice and dillweed. Chill for 24 hours.

Shirley Connor, Friend of Pittsfield Grange, Massachusetts

VEGETABLE CHOWDER

Yields: 6 servings   Pan Size: stockpot

1 c. chopped celery
1 c. chopped onion
1 clove of garlic, minced
¼ c. Mazola margarine
4 c. beef bouillon
3 c. chopped potatoes

1 17-oz. can whole kernel corn
1 16-oz. can tomatoes
2 c. sliced carrots
½ tsp. celery seed
½ tsp. each thyme, salt
2 tbsp. cornstarch

Sauté celery, onion and garlic in margarine in stockpot. Add next 8 ingredients. Simmer, covered, for 30 minutes or until vegetables are tender. Stir in mixture of cornstarch and *¼ cup water*. Bring to a boil over medium heat, stirring constantly. Cook for 1 minute longer.

Photograph for this recipe on page 33.

HAMBURGER-VEGETABLE-LENTIL SOUP

Yields: 12 to 15 servings   Pan Size: 6 quart

1 lb. ground beef
5¾ c. tomato juice
1 c. lentils
1 c. each chopped carrots, cabbage and celery

½ c. chopped onion
1 tsp. salt
½ tsp. pepper
½ green pepper, chopped
1 bay leaf

Brown ground beef in saucepan, stirring until crumbly; drain. Add tomato juice and *4 cups water*. Bring to a boil. Add remaining ingredients. Simmer for 1½ hours.

Doris McPherson, McIntosh Grange, Washington

BROCCOLI-CHEESE SOUP

Yields: 6 to 8 servings   Pan Size: 2 quart

1   10-oz. package frozen broccoli
2 tbsp. chopped onion
1 c. chicken broth
3 tbsp. melted butter

3 tbsp. flour
2 c. milk
½ tsp. salt
¼ tsp. pepper
1 c. grated American cheese

Cook broccoli with onion in broth in small saucepan until tender. Do not drain. Blend butter and flour in saucepan. Stir in milk. Cook until thickened, stirring constantly. Season with salt and pepper. Add cheese. Heat until cheese melts. Add vegetable mixture and broth. Simmer for 10 to 15 minutes.

Evelyn Rahn, Rock Creek Grange, Illinois

CABBAGE SOUP (CZECHOSLOVAKIA)

Yields: 10 to 12 servings   Pan Size: large kettle

2 lb. beef bones
1 c. chopped onion
3 carrots, coarsely chopped
2 cloves of garlic, chopped
1 bay leaf
2 lb. beef short ribs
1 tsp. thyme
½ tsp. paprika

8 c. coarsely shredded cabbage
2   16-oz. cans tomatoes
2 tsp. salt
½ to ¾ tsp. Tabasco sauce
¼ c. chopped parsley
3 tbsp. lemon juice
3 tbsp. sugar
1 lb. sauerkraut

Layer beef bones, onion, carrots, garlic and bay leaf in roasting pan. Add ribs, thyme and paprika. Roast, uncovered, at 450 degrees for 20 minutes or until brown. Place in kettle. Add *8 cups water*, cabbage, tomatoes, salt and Tabasco sauce. Simmer, covered, for 1½ hours. Skim. Add parsley, lemon juice, sugar and sauerkraut. Simmer, uncovered, for 1 hour. Cut meat from bones; return meat to kettle. Simmer for 5 minutes longer. Discard bay leaf. Ladle into soup bowls. Garnish with sour cream.

Photograph for this recipe on page 34.

OLD-FASHIONED MICHIGAN MUSHROOM SOUP

Yields: 8 servings   Pan Size: 4 quart/blender

1 lb. fresh Michigan mushrooms	2 cans condensed beef broth
2 c. finely chopped carrots	3 tbsp. tomato paste
2 c. finely chopped celery	¼ tsp. salt
1 c. finely chopped onion	¹⁄₁₆ tsp. ground black pepper
1 clove of garlic, finely minced	2 tbsp. butter
¼ c. butter	3 tbsp. dry Michigan Sherry

Chop half the mushrooms; slice remaining mushrooms. Sauté chopped vegetables and garlic in ¼ cup butter in saucepan for 5 minutes. Stir in beef broth, *3 broth cans water*, tomato paste, salt and pepper. Bring to a boil; reduce heat. Simmer, covered, for 1 hour. Purée soup in blender; return to saucepan. Sauté sliced mushrooms in 2 tablespoons butter in skillet for 5 minutes. Add sautéed mushrooms and Sherry to soup. Heat to serving temperature. Ladle into soup bowls. Serve with sour cream.

Paul Kindinger
Director, Michigan Department of Agriculture

CREOLE-STYLE PEANUT SOUP

Yields: 6 servings   Pan Size: 2 quart

1 c. chopped peanuts	½ c. butter
1 c. chopped carrots	¼ c. flour
½ c. chopped celery	2 14-oz. cans chicken broth
¼ c. chopped green onions	1 c. milk
1 clove of garlic, crushed	

Sauté first 5 ingredients in butter in saucepan over medium heat until tender. Add flour; mix well. Stir in broth gradually. Cook until thickened, stirring constantly. Simmer for 15 minutes. Stir in milk. Heat to serving temperature.

FRENCH ONION SOUP WITH CHEESE TOAST

Yields: 4 servings	Pan Size: 3 quart

2 lg. yellow onions, sliced	⅛ tsp. pepper
2 tbsp. butter	4 slices French bread,
1 tsp. flour	¾ in. thick
4 c. beef broth	1 tbsp. butter
¼ tsp. salt	4 thin slices Swiss cheese

Sauté onions in butter in saucepan over medium-low heat for 10 minutes, stirring occasionally. Stir in flour. Cook for 1 minute. Add broth, salt and pepper. Simmer, covered, for 10 minutes. Spread bread with remaining 1 tablespoon butter. Top with cheese. Place on baking sheet. Broil just until cheese melts. Place 1 slice in each soup bowl. Fill with hot soup.

Yvonne Martz, Henlopen Grange, Delaware

ONION-WINE SOUP

Yields: 6 to 8 servings	Pan Size: 3 quart

5 lg. onions, chopped	1 tbsp. vinegar
¼ c. butter	2 tsp. sugar
5 c. beef broth	1 c. light cream
½ c. celery leaves	1 tbsp. minced parsley
1 lg. potato, sliced	Salt and pepper to taste
1 c. dry white wine	

Sauté onions lightly in butter in saucepan. Add beef broth, celery leaves and potato. Bring to a boil. Simmer, covered, for 30 minutes. Purée soup in blender; return to saucepan. Blend in wine, vinegar and sugar. Bring to a boil. Simmer for 5 minutes. Stir in cream, parsley and seasonings. Heat to serving temperature; do not boil. Ladle into soup bowls.

Nancy Reagan
The White House

ARTSOPPPA (SWEDEN) Pea Soup

Yields: 6 to 8 servings	Pan Size: 4 quart

1 lb. dried whole yellow peas	1½ lb. side pork
1 med. onion, chopped	2 med. carrots, finely chopped

Wash, rinse and drain peas. Soak in *9 cups water* in saucepan overnight. Bring to a boil; skim off shells. Add onion and pork. Simmer for 1 hour. Add carrots. Cook for 30 minutes longer. Remove pork. Cut into small portions. Serve soup with sliced pork, mustard and dark rye bread.

Ruth S. Carlson, Mountain Grange, Pennsylvania

POTATO SOUP

Yields: 6 to 8 servings	Pan Size: 4 quart

8 med. potatoes, peeled, cubed	4 chicken bouillon cubes
1 med. onion, chopped	1 stick margarine
2 carrots, chopped	1 13-oz. can evaporated milk
3 or 4 stalks celery, chopped	Pepper to taste
1 tsp. salt	

Combine vegetables, salt and *6 cups water* in saucepan. Bring to a boil. Add bouillon cubes. Simmer until vegetables are tender. Add margarine and evaporated milk. Bring to a boil. Season with pepper.

Mrs. Frank Stevenson, Newark Grange, Ohio

SQUASH SOUP

Yields: 2 servings	Pan Size: 1½ quart

2 med. yellow squash, sliced	½ tsp. salt
1 sm. potato, chopped	1 c. milk
½ sm. onion, chopped	1 slice cheese
½ carrot, grated	1 tsp. butter
Leaves of 1 stalk celery	

Combine first 6 ingredients and a small amount of water in saucepan. Bring to a boil. Cook for 12 minutes. Add milk, cheese and butter. Bring to the simmering point. Turn off heat. Let stand, covered, for several minutes.

Helen Johnson, Temple Grange, Maryland

TOMATO SOUP

Yields: 8 servings	Pan Size: 3 quart

2 c. thinly sliced onion	2½ lb. fresh tomatoes, cored
2 sprigs of fresh thyme	3 tbsp. tomato paste
4 basil leaves	¼ c. flour
Salt and pepper to taste	3¾ c. chicken broth
1 stick butter	1 tsp. sugar
2 tbsp. olive oil	1 c. cream

Sauté onion, thyme and basil with salt and pepper in mixture of butter and olive oil in saucepan until onion is tender. Add tomatoes and tomato paste. Simmer for 10 minutes or until tomatoes are soft. Blend flour and 5 tablespoons broth in small bowl. Stir into tomato mixture. Add remaining broth. Simmer for 30 minutes, stirring frequently. Put mixture through sieve or food mill. Return to heat. Add sugar and cream. Heat to serving temperature.

Helen S. Bungay, Fruitland Grange, Delaware

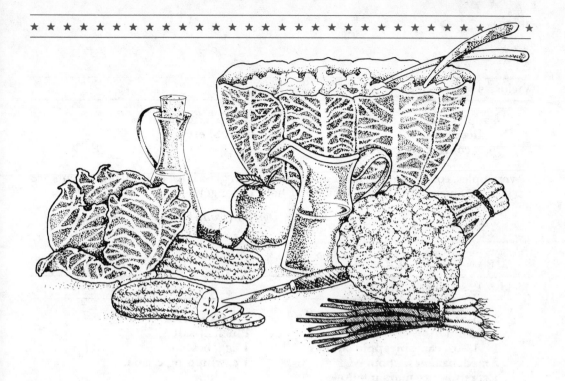

Salads

The first salads were edible herbs or plants dressed with the universal preservative, salt; in fact, the word *salad* comes from the Latin word for salt, *sal*. From this simple beginning, our idea of salads has expanded to include every ingredient imaginable, served cold or hot, simply tossed or elaborately molded. *The Glory of Cooking* contains recipes for all kinds of salads—all delicious.

Perhaps more than any type of food, salads can be served as any course on the menu. Tart, marinated vegetables or spicy aspic make an interesting first course. Salads filled with seafood, poultry, meat, eggs, or cheese are filling main dishes. Rice, bulgur, or pasta salads may be served as a side dish. And fruit salads, rich with cream, are delectable desserts. Serve a sampling of several for a salad supper. Simple or elaborate, salads call for imaginative preparation. Include a variety of greens—light with dark, mild with tangy. Vary dressing ingredients with flavored vinegar, citrus juices, or pungent herbs. Add nuts, cooked vegetables, raisins, tangy red apple or grapefruit sections for texture, color, and flavor. Pile abundantly onto platters lined with frilly greens; layer prettily in glass dishes; unmold on a handsome tray; garnish to suggest the flavor—and serve with confidence and pride on any occasion.

APPLE SALAD

Yields: 4 to 6 servings

6 apples, peeled, thinly sliced	¼ tsp. cinnamon
¼ c. confectioners' sugar	½ c. Sherry

Layer apples, confectioners' sugar and cinnamon in glass bowl until all ingredients are used. Pour Sherry over layers. Chill for 1 hour or longer.

Dorothy Heinrich, Walterville Grange, Oregon

COMPANY SALAD BOWL

Yields: 12 servings

2 3-oz. packages lemon gelatin	1½ tbsp. flour
1 13-oz. can pineapple chunks	Pinch of salt
2 med. bananas, chopped	1 egg, beaten
1 c. miniature marshmallows	1 c. whipping cream, whipped
½ c. sugar	Toasted slivered almonds

Dissolve gelatin in *2 cups boiling water* in bowl. Stir in *2 cups cold water*. Chill until partially set. Drain pineapple, reserving 1 cup juice. Fold pineapple, bananas and marshmallows into gelatin mixture. Pour into 2-quart glass bowl. Chill until almost set. Blend reserved juice into mixture of sugar, flour and salt in saucepan. Cook over medium heat until thickened, stirring constantly. Stir a small amount of hot mixture into beaten egg; stir egg into hot mixture. Cook for 1 minute, stirring constantly. Cool. Fold in stiffly whipped cream. Spread over gelatin. Top with almonds. Chill until serving time.

Rose E. Simmons, Victor Grange, New York

CRANAPPLE SALAD

Yields: 20 servings   Pan Size: 12 cup

2 oranges	2 3-oz. packages red gelatin
3 c. cranberries	3 c. sweet cider
3 med. unpeeled tart apples	1 c. sugar
1 c. nuts	

Put oranges, cranberries, apples and nuts through food grinder. Dissolve gelatin in 2 cups boiling cider in bowl. Add 1 cup cold cider and 1 cup sugar; stir until sugar dissolves. Stir in ground fruit and nuts; mix well. Spoon into mold. Chill until set. Unmold onto serving plate.

Viola K. Lees, Henrietta Grange, Ohio

WILLIAMSPORT GRANGE'S CRANBERRY SALAD

Yields: 25 servings   Pan Size: two   8 cup

1 lb. cranberries, ground	3 3-oz. packages cherry
6 c. ground apples	gelatin
3 c. sugar	1 20-oz. can crushed pineapple

Combine cranberries, apples and sugar in bowl; mix well. Let stand overnight. Dissolve gelatin in *2 cups boiling water* in bowl. Chill until partially set. Stir in cranberry mixture and pineapple. Spoon into molds. Chill until set. Unmold onto serving plates.

Home Economics Committee, Williamsport Grange, Ohio

FRUIT TOSS WITH ORANGE-PECAN DRESSING

Yields: 10 servings

1 med. honeydew melon	¼ c. orange juice
2 c. blueberries	¼ c. confectioners' sugar
2 c. strawberries	½ c. finely chopped toasted
1 c. sour cream	pecans

Peel and seed melon; cut into 1-inch pieces. Combine with blueberries and strawberries in salad bowl; mix gently. Chill until serving time. Combine sour cream, orange juice and confectioners' sugar in small bowl; mix well. Stir in pecans. Chill until serving time. Serve dressing with salad.

Jean D. Bolaski, Bartonsville Grange, Vermont

ORANGE CUSTARD SALAD

Yields: 12 servings

½ to ¾ c. sugar	Grated rind of 1 orange
2 tbsp. flour	4 c. Royal Anne cherries
Dash of salt	2 c. pineapple chunks
¾ c. orange juice	2 c. mandarin oranges
2 tbsp. lemon juice	2 c. miniature marshmallows
2 eggs, separated	½ c. blanched almonds
1 tbsp. butter	1 c. whipping cream, whipped

Blend sugar, flour, salt, orange juice and lemon juice in double boiler. Cook until thickened, stirring constantly. Stir a small amount of hot mixture into mixture of beaten egg yolks, butter and orange rind; stir egg yolks into hot mixture. Cook until thickened, stirring constantly. Cool. Combine drained cherries, pineapple and oranges with marshmallows and almonds in large salad bowl; mix gently. Fold stiffly beaten egg whites and stiffly whipped cream into cooled custard. Fold gently into fruit mixture.

Nancy Wheeler, Sauvies Island Grange, Oregon

COLD CHICKEN-RICE SUMMER SALAD

Yields: 6 servings

1 c. chicken broth	1 bunch scallions, chopped
1 c. rice	½ c. oil
2 chicken breasts, baked	3 tbsp. tarragon wine vinegar
1 green pepper, finely chopped	1 tbsp. Dijon mustard
1 jar chopped pimento	1 tbsp. sugar
½ c. finely chopped parsley	Salt and pepper to taste

Bring broth and *1 cup water* to a boil in saucepan. Add rice. Cook for 20 minutes or until tender. Combine with chopped chicken, green pepper, pimento, parsley and scallions in salad bowl. Blend remaining ingredients in small bowl. Add to salad; mix lightly. Chill for several hours to overnight.

Mrs. Michael Phillips, Skaneateles Grange, New York

LUAU PINEAPPLE-CHICKEN SALAD

Yields: 5 to 6 servings

2½ lb. chicken breasts	¾ tsp. seasoned salt
2 tsp. salt	¾ c. mayonnaise
½ tsp. curry powder	1 30-oz. can pineapple
2 stalks celery, chopped	chunks, drained
1 onion, cut into quarters	1 c. sliced celery
4 tsp. chopped chutney	1 tbsp. each chopped green onion,
4 tsp. tarragon vinegar	green pepper, and pimento

Bring chicken breasts, *1½ quarts water*, salt, curry powder, 2 stalks chopped celery and onion to a boil in saucepan; reduce heat. Simmer, covered, for 20 to 25 minutes or until chicken is tender. Cool in broth. Drain, bone and chop chicken. Combine chutney, vinegar, seasoned salt and mayonnaise in small bowl; mix well. Chill, covered, for 1 hour or longer. Combine chicken, pineapple, 1 cup celery, green onion, green pepper and pimento in bowl. Add chutney-mayonnaise dressing; mix well. Spoon into lettuce-lined salad bowl. Garnish with raisins, coconut and nuts.

Virginia Seitz, Boerne Grange, Texas

HAM, ASPARAGUS AND PEAS WITH PASTA SHELLS

Yields: 8 servings

1 lb. pasta shells, cooked	8 oz. ricotta cheese, mashed
1½ c. cooked peas	1½ c. chopped cooked ham
1½ c. cooked cut asparagus	Salt and pepper to taste

Chill pasta, peas and asparagus. Combine all ingredients in salad bowl; toss lightly.

Susie A. Pfaff, Windfall Grange, Pennsylvania

FRUIT AND CURRY PORK SALAD

Yields: 4 to 5 servings

2½ to 3 c. thinly sliced
   cooked pork strips
1 lg. apple, chopped
1 banana, sliced
⅓ c. flaked coconut

¼ c. raisins
⅓ c. mayonnaise
3 tbsp. chopped chutney
½ tsp. curry powder

Combine pork with apple, banana, coconut and raisins in bowl; mix well. Mix remaining ingredients in small bowl. Pour over pork mixture; toss lightly.

Mary Beth Heberer
Director of Junior Grange Activities, National Grange

BROWN RICE SALAD

Yields: 6 to 8 servings

¾ c. grape jelly
½ c. fresh lemon juice
¼ c. olive oil
2 tbsp. dried mint leaves
½ tsp. salt

1 c. brown rice, cooked
1 c. chopped parsley
2 cucumbers, peeled, chopped
1 c. chopped radishes
½ c. chopped green onions

Process first 5 ingredients in blender container until smooth. Layer rice, parsley and half the cucumbers in glass salad bowl. Pour dressing over top. Chill for several hours to overnight. Add remaining vegetables; toss to mix. Serve on lettuce-lined salad plates or roll in large lettuce leaves and eat as for sandwich.

TABOULI (LEBANON) Salad Supreme

Yields: 4 to 8 servings

¾ c. bulgur	1 or 2 lg. tomatoes, chopped
2 lg. bunches parsley, finely chopped	⅛ tsp. cinnamon
1 c. chopped fresh mint	2 to 3 tsp. salt
1 bunch green onions with tops, finely chopped	Pepper to taste
	½ to ⅔ c. lemon juice
	½ c. olive oil

Rinse bulgur; drain, pressing out as much liquid as possible. Layer bulgur, parsley, mint, green onions and tomatoes in salad bowl. Add cinnamon, salt, pepper and lemon juice; toss to mix well. Add olive oil just before serving; toss to mix well.

Charles F. Thomas, Yellow Creek Grange, Ohio

TABOULI (SAUDI ARABIA) Bulgur Salad

Yields: 4 to 8 servings

1 c. bulgur	1 c. finely chopped fresh mint
4 tomatoes, finely chopped	Salt to taste
4 cucumbers, peeled, chopped	Cayenne pepper to taste
4 green onions with tops, finely chopped	Juice of 2 (or more) lemons
2 c. chopped fresh parsley	½ c. (or more) olive oil

Soak bulgur in cold water to cover in bowl for 10 minutes. Drain and squeeze dry. Combine with tomatoes, cucumbers, green onions, parsley and mint in deep salad bowl; mix gently. Let stand for 30 minutes. Add salt and cayenne pepper; mix well. Add lemon juice and olive oil just before serving; toss to mix well.
Note: May be eaten with fork, but is traditionally rolled in small lettuce or vine leaves.

Eileen Rhyner, Corral de Tierra Grange, California

ALL GREEN SALAD

Yields: 10 servings

½ head lettuce, chopped	1 sm. zucchini, chopped
2 spears broccoli, chopped	1 med. green pepper, chopped
4 green onions, sliced	⅓ c. broken cashews
2 stalks celery, sliced	½ tsp. seasoned salt
1 cucumber, chopped	¼ tsp. garlic powder

Combine vegetables in salad bowl. Add remaining ingredients; mix well. Chill until serving time. Spoon onto salad plates. Serve with ranch-style or Italian dressing. Garnish with alfalfa sprouts and croutons.

Estella McCahill, Rogue River Valley Grange, Oregon

ASPARAGUS MOLD

Yields: 6 to 8 servings   Pan Size: 1½ quart

2 tbsp. unflavored gelatin	½ c. chopped stuffed green
½ c. vinegar	olives
¾ c. sugar	½ c. chopped pecans
1 20-oz. can asparagus,	Juice of ½ lemon
drained, chopped	½ tsp. salt
1 c. chopped celery	½ c. mayonnaise
2 tsp. grated onion	½ c. sour cream
2 pimentos, chopped	

Soften gelatin in *½ cup cold water* for 5 minutes. Bring vinegar, sugar and *1 cup water* to a boil in saucepan. Cook for 2 minutes. Add gelatin; stir until gelatin dissolves. Add next 8 ingredients; mix well. Pour into mold. Chill for 3 to 4 hours or until set. Unmold onto serving plate. Serve with mixture of mayonnaise and sour cream.

Dee Haynes Goldner, Wallingford Grange, Connecticut

BROCCOLI-CAULIFLOWER SALAD

Yields: 6 to 8 servings

Flowerets of 1 bunch broccoli	2 tbsp. vinegar
Flowerets of ½ head cauliflower	⅓ c. sugar
1 c. raisins	4 slices crisp-fried bacon,
1 med. onion, chopped	crumbled
1 c. mayonnaise	

Combine broccoli and cauliflower in salad bowl. Add raisins and onion; mix well. Mix mayonnaise, vinegar and sugar in small bowl. Add to salad; mix well. Chill for 1 hour or longer. Sprinkle with bacon at serving time.

Grace Rauch, Pleasant Grange, Ohio

PACIFIC CARROT MOLD

Yields: 15 to 20 servings   Pan Size: two 6 cup

1 6-oz. package orange	4 c. grated carrots
gelatin	2 c. small curd cottage
¼ c. pineapple juice	cheese
1 c. drained crushed	1 c. mayonnaise
pineapple	½ c. chopped walnuts

Dissolve gelatin in *2 cups boiling water* in bowl. Add pineapple juice. Chill until partially set. Beat until frothy. Fold in remaining ingredients. Spoon into molds. Chill until set. Unmold onto serving plates.

Eleanor Rogers, Hamilton Grange, New Jersey

GARDEN SALAD WITH TOMATO-CREAM CHEESE DRESSING

Yields: 8 servings

3 oz. cream cheese, softened	½ c. sliced radishes
½ c. undiluted tomato soup	Rings of 3 slices onion
¾ c. mayonnaise	2 tomatoes, cut into wedges
2 tsp. lemon juice	1 sm. cucumber, sliced
½ tsp. salt	1 c. chopped celery
Flowerets of 1 sm. head	Lettuce leaf cups
cauliflower	Hard-boiled eggs, sliced
1 c. chopped carrots, cooked	1 green pepper, cut into rings

Combine first 5 ingredients in blender container. Process until smooth. Spoon dressing into serving bowl. Chill until serving time. Cook cauliflower in a small amount of salted water in saucepan for 5 to 8 minutes or until tender-crisp; drain. Chill in refrigerator. Mix cauliflower with next 6 vegetables in bowl. Spoon into lettuce cups. Top with egg slices and green pepper rings. Serve with dressing.

Charlotte Mallet-Prevost, Carroll Manor Grange, Maryland

WILTED LETTUCE SALAD

Yields: 6 servings

6 slices bacon	½ tsp. salt
½ c. sliced green onions	8 c. torn leaf lettuce
¼ c. vinegar	6 radishes, thinly sliced
4 tsp. sugar	1 hard-boiled egg, chopped

Fry bacon in skillet until crisp. Remove bacon and crumble. Sauté green onions in bacon drippings. Add vinegar, sugar, salt, bacon and *¼ cup water*. Bring to a boil, stirring constantly. Pour over lettuce in salad bowl; toss to coat well. Top with radishes and egg. Serve immediately.

Donna Cross, Hawks Mountain Grange, Vermont

ZIPPY MUSHROOMS

Yields: 6 to 8 servings

⅔ c. tarragon vinegar	Dash of Tabasco sauce
½ c. oil	Dash of white pepper
1 tbsp. sugar	30 to 40 small fresh mushrooms
1 lg. clove of garlic, minced	Onion slices

Combine vinegar, oil, sugar, garlic, Tabasco sauce, white pepper and *2 tablespoons water* in covered jar; shake to mix well. Pour over mushrooms and onions in bowl. Marinate for 1 to 2 hours. Drain, reserving marinade for later use as dressing for tossed salad. Spoon mushrooms and onions into serving bowl.

Sharon M. Wilson, Pleasant Grove Grange, Oregon

GERMAN POTATO SALAD

Yields: 10 servings   Pan Size: 3 quart

5 lb. potatoes   **2½ tsp. salt**
¼ c. oil   **¾ c. vinegar**
½ onion, finely chopped   **2 tsp. sugar**

Cook potatoes in water to cover in saucepan until tender. Peel and slice while warm. Combine with oil, onion and salt in bowl; mix gently. Bring vinegar, sugar and *¾ cup water* to a boil in saucepan. Pour over potatoes; mix gently. Garnish with parsley or chopped chives. Let stand for 2 to 3 hours before serving.
Note: This recipe is from my German grandmother.

Beatrice K. Mottram, Passadunkeag Grange, Maine

PERFECT POTATO SALAD

Yields: 4 servings

2½ c. chopped cooked   **¼ c. sliced sweet pickle**
  potatoes   **1½ tsp. salt**
1 tsp. sugar   **1½ tsp. celery seed**
1 tsp. vinegar   **¾ c. mayonnaise**
½ c. chopped onion   **2 hard-boiled eggs, sliced**
½ c. chopped celery

Sprinkle potatoes with sugar and vinegar in bowl. Add onion, celery, pickle and seasonings; mix well. Add mayonnaise; mix lightly. Stir in sliced egg gently. Chill in refrigerator. Spoon into lettuce-lined salad bowl. Garnish with additional egg slices.

Charles E. Kruse
Director, Missouri Department of Agriculture

EASY POTATO SALAD

Yields: 6 servings

4 med. potatoes, peeled   **1 tsp. garlic powder**
1 lg. cucumber, sliced   **½ tsp. dillweed**
½ c. sour cream   **¼ tsp. salt**
½ c. plain yogurt   **⅛ tsp. pepper**
2 tsp. dried onion flakes

Cook potatoes in water to cover in saucepan until tender; cool. Slice potatoes. Mix with cucumber in bowl. Combine remaining ingredients in small bowl; mix well. Pour over potatoes; mix gently. Chill until serving time.

Louise Anderson, Lookout Mt. Grange, Oregon

SPINACH SALAD

Yields: 10 servings   Pan Size: blender

⅓ c. catsup
¼ c. vinegar
1 tbsp. Worcestershire sauce
¾ c. sugar
1 med. onion, chopped
2 tsp. salt
6 to 8 bunches spinach

1 can bean sprouts, drained
4 hard-boiled eggs, chopped
1 can sliced water chestnuts,
    drained
8 ounces bacon, crisp-fried,
    crumbled

Combine catsup, vinegar, Worcestershire sauce, sugar, onion and salt in blender container. Process until smooth. Mix remaining ingredients in salad bowl. Pour dressing over top; toss lightly to coat well.

C. Alan Pettibone
Director, Washington Department of Agriculture

HAWAIIAN SPINACH SALAD

Yields: 4 to 5 servings

1 bunch spinach, torn into
    bite-sized pieces
3 to 4 red or green apples,
    thinly sliced
4 to 8 oz. fresh mushrooms,
    sliced

4 oz. bacon, crisp-fried,
    crumbled
1 c. mayonnaise
¼ c. frozen orange juice
    concentrate, thawed

Combine spinach, apples, mushrooms and bacon in salad bowl; toss gently to mix well. Blend mayonnaise and orange juice concentrate in small bowl. Serve with salad.

Dorothy Chase Gawel, Kent Grange, Connecticut

SPINACH SALAD ORIENTALE

Yields: 4 servings

¼ c. peanut oil
2 tsp. soy sauce
1 tsp. vinegar
1 tsp. sesame seed

3 c. small spinach leaves
½ c. bean sprouts
½ c. chopped sliced water
    chestnuts

Combine peanut oil, soy sauce, vinegar and sesame seed in covered jar; shake well. Let stand at room temperature to blend flavors. Combine spinach, bean sprouts and water chestnuts in salad bowl; toss lightly. Add dressing; toss to coat well.

Harriet Guthrie, Mountain View Grange, Colorado

MARRIETTA'S TOMATO ASPIC

Yields: 4 servings   Pan Size: 4 cup

2 tbsp. unflavored gelatin	1 tbsp. sugar
2 c. mixed vegetable juice	½ tsp. basil
cocktail	2 hard-boiled eggs, finely
2 tbsp. lemon juice	chopped

Soften gelatin in a small amount of vegetable juice cocktail. Bring 1 cup vegetable juice cocktail, lemon juice and sugar to a boil in saucepan. Add gelatin; stir until gelatin dissolves. Add remaining vegetable juice cocktail, basil and eggs; mix gently. Pour into mold. Chill for 2 hours or until set, stirring several times. Unmold onto serving plate.

Ruth Lord, Rowley Grange, Massachusetts

ROTINI-VEGETABLE SALAD

Yields: 4 servings

8 oz. rotini	½ c. chopped broccoli
1 c. 1-in. pieces green beans	½ c. olives
½ c. chopped green pepper	2 tbsp. chopped garlic
½ c. chopped carrots	2 tsp. oregano
¼ c. chopped onion	½ c. Italian salad dressing
½ c. chopped summer squash	2 tomatoes, sliced

Cook rotini according to package directions; drain. Cool. Cook green beans in water in saucepan for 5 minutes; drain. Combine rotini, green beans, green pepper, carrots, onion, squash, broccoli, olives, garlic and oregano in bowl. Add salad dressing; mix well. Spoon into lettuce-lined salad bowl. Top with tomato slices.

Mrs. Allan Gaspar, Rowley Grange, Massachusetts

DUKE'S SALAD DRESSING

Yields: 3 cups   Pan Size: blender

1 can tomato soup	2 tbsp. Worcestershire sauce
⅓ c. vinegar	3 or 4 cloves of garlic, chopped
⅔ c. oil	½ tsp. paprika
⅔ c. sugar	1 tsp. salt
2 tbsp. mustard	

Combine all ingredients in blender container. Process until smooth. Store in covered container in refrigerator.

Delene Jarvi, Cobbosseecontee Grange, Maine

EXCELLENT MAYONNAISE DRESSING

Yields: 2 cups	Pan Size: double boiler

2 egg yolks	1 tsp. salt
2 tbsp. vinegar	½ c. flour
2 tbsp. lemon juice	1 tbsp. melted butter
1 tsp. dry mustard	1 c. oil
½ tsp. paprika	

Combine egg yolks, vinegar, lemon juice, dry mustard, paprika and salt in bowl; mix well. Blend flour, butter and *1 cup water* in double boiler. Cook for 10 minutes or until very thick, stirring constantly. Add oil and hot mixture to egg yolk mixture; beat until smooth. Store in covered jar in refrigerator.

Helen Speldrich, Irving Grange, Oregon

MOM'S SALAD DRESSING

Yields: 2 cups	Pan Size: 1 quart

¼ c. flour	1 tsp. salt
1 c. sugar	2 eggs
1 tsp. dry mustard	1 c. weak vinegar

Mix dry ingredients in saucepan. Blend in eggs and vinegar. Cook until thickened, stirring constantly.
Note: Makes enough dressing for 10 pounds potato salad.

Leone T. Baxter, Union Grange, Illinois

PAPAYA SEED DRESSING

Yields: 4 cups	Pan Size: blender

1 c. white wine vinegar	2 c. oil
½ c. sugar	1 sm. onion, minced
1 tsp. dry mustard	2 tbsp. fresh papaya seed
1 tsp. seasoned salt	

Combine vinegar, sugar, dry mustard and seasoned salt in blender container. Process until smooth. Add oil and onion gradually, processing constantly until smooth. Add papaya seed. Process until seed is the consistency of coarse pepper. Use as dressing for fruit salads and green salads or as marinade for spareribs and other meats.

Daisy Rathbun, Greenhorn Grange, California

Microwave Dishes

Microwave cooking is especially appealing for today's busy lifestyles. Equally good at cooking old favorites in half the time or specially developed recipes in minutes, the microwave oven simplifies food preparation, eliminating much of the constant supervision of conventional cooking. In addition, the serving dish can often be used as the cooking utensil, and microwaving requires less energy as well.

The microwave recipes in *The Glory of Cooking* showcase many of the foods for which microwave cooking is superior. Fish and shellfish stay juicy and tender with moist cooking and minimal handling. Vegetables retain more nutrients, fresher color, crisper texture, and better flavor because they cook faster with less added liquid. Sauces, measured, mixed, and cooked in the same large cup, require stirring only once or twice. Muffins, quick breads, and cakes are higher, lighter, and very tender. Candy is easy with very little stirring or watching. Even beef, pork, and chicken are juicier and leaner. All foods are fresh and tastier when reheated in the microwave. Of course, as with all major electronic appliances, microwave oven users should follow the manufacturer's instructions. However, you'll soon find that the possibilities are unlimited for easy, quick, cool, and delicious food preparation—the microwave way.

FILLET OF FISH AMANDINE

Yields: 2 to 3 servings   Pan Size: 8 inch

½ c. slivered almonds
½ c. butter
1 lb. fish fillets
1 tbsp. lemon juice

1 tsp. chopped parsley
½ tsp. salt
¼ tsp. dillweed
⅛ tsp. pepper

Microwave almonds and butter in glass dish on High for 6 minutes, stirring once. Remove almonds with slotted spoon, set aside. Dip fillets in butter, turning to coat; sprinkle with lemon juice, parsley and seasonings. Roll up and arrange in dish. Microwave, covered with waxed paper, on High for 4 minutes. Sprinkle with almonds. Microwave, covered, for 1 minute. Let stand for 4 minutes. Garnish with paprika or parsley sprigs.

Mary Buffington
National Director of Women's Activities

STROGANOFF CASSEROLE

Yields: 5 to 6 servings   Pan Size: 2 quart

1 lb. ground beef, crumbled
¼ c. chopped onion
2 cloves of garlic, minced
4 oz. medium noodles
1 c. sliced mushrooms

1   13-oz. can beef broth
⅛ tsp. pepper
8 oz. sour cream
2 tbsp. chopped parsley

Microwave ground beef, onion and garlic in glass casserole on High for 5 minutes, stirring once; drain. Stir in noodles, mushrooms, broth and pepper. Microwave, covered, on Medium for 22 minutes, stirring once. Let stand for 2 minutes. Blend in sour cream; sprinkle with parsley.

GLAZED CARROTS AND RAISINS

Yields: 4 servings   Pan Size: 1 quart

2 c. 1½-in. julienne carrots
2 tbsp. raisins
1 tbsp. butter

1 tbsp. brown sugar
½ tsp. grated lemon rind
⅛ tsp. salt

Microwave carrots and *1 tablespoon water* in covered glass casserole on High for 4½ to 5½ minutes or until tender-crisp, stirring once; drain. Add remaining ingredients; mix lightly. Microwave, covered, for 1 minute or until butter melts. Stir until carrots are evenly coated.

SAUTÉED MUSHROOMS

Yields: 2 to 4 servings   Pan Size: 8 inch

8 oz. mushrooms, sliced   **1 clove of garlic, minced**
¼ c. butter

Combine all ingredients in glass dish. Microwave on Medium-High for 4 minutes, stirring once.

GARDEN FRESH POTATOES

Yields: 5 to 6 servings   Pan Size: 1½ quart

1½ lb. new potatoes   **½ tsp. salt**
½ c. sour cream   **Dash of pepper**
¼ c. mayonnaise   **5 radishes, sliced**
3 green onions, sliced

Scrub potatoes; cut smaller ones into halves and quarter larger potatoes. Place in glass casserole. Add *2 tablespoons water*. Microwave, covered, on High for 8 to 10 minutes or until almost tender, stirring to turn and rearrange potatoes once. Let stand for several minutes; drain. Combine sour cream, mayonnaise, green onions, salt and pepper in bowl; blend well. Add to potatoes; mix lightly to coat. Arrange radishes over top.

CORN CHOWDER

Yields: 5 servings   Pan Size: 2 quart

4 slices bacon   **1 can cream of celery soup**
1 med. onion, chopped   **1¼ c. milk**
2 med. potatoes, peeled, cubed   **½ tsp. garlic salt**
1   17-oz. can corn, drained   **⅛ tsp. pepper**

Microwave bacon in paper towel-covered glass casserole on High for 3 to 4½ minutes or until crisp, turning dish once. Drain and crumble, reserving 2 teaspoons drippings. Mix reserved drippings, onion, potatoes and *¼ cup water*. Microwave, covered, for 4½ to 5 minutes or until potatoes are almost tender, stirring once. Add bacon and remaining ingredients. Microwave, covered, for 9 minutes or until heated to serving temperature, stirring once.

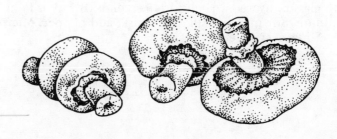

CRISP REFRIGERATOR PICKLES

Yields: 2 quarts	Pan Size: 1 quart

1 c. sugar	**4 c. thinly sliced cucumbers**
¾ c. white vinegar	**1 med. onion, sliced into rings**
½ tbsp. pickling salt	**1 green pepper, thinly sliced**
½ tbsp. celery seed	**1 sm. carrot**

Combine sugar, vinegar, pickling salt and celery seed in glass bowl. Microwave on High for 4½ minutes or until boiling, stirring once. Cool. Combine cucumbers, onion rings and green pepper in bowl. Slice carrot thinly with vegetable peeler. Add carrot to vegetables; toss lightly. Pack into sterilized jars. Add vinegar mixture; seal jars and shake. Refrigerate for 24 hours or longer before serving. May be refrigerated for up to 1 year.

BREAD PUDDING

Yields: 5 to 6 servings	Pan Size: 2 quart

4 slices bread, cubed	**Dash of salt**
¼ c. raisins	**2 c. milk**
3 eggs	**2 tbsp. butter**
½ c. packed brown sugar	**Cinnamon to taste**
1 tsp. vanilla extract	

Mix bread and raisins in casserole. Beat eggs, brown sugar, vanilla and salt in bowl. Microwave milk and butter in glass measure on High for 4½ minutes. Stir in egg mixture gradually. Pour over bread and raisins. Sprinkle with cinnamon. Microwave, covered with plastic wrap, on Medium for 14 minutes. Center will set as pudding cools.
Note: May substitute raisin bread. Use large eggs for best results.

BASIC WHITE SAUCE

Yields: 1 cup	Pan Size: 4 cup

1 c. milk	**2 tbsp. flour**
2 tbsp. butter	**Dash of pepper**

Microwave milk in glass measure on Medium-High for 2 minutes. Microwave butter in 2-cup glass measure on High for 45 seconds. Blend in flour. Microwave on High for 1 minute. Stir in milk with wire whisk; add pepper. Microwave on High for 3 minutes. Serve over vegetables.

SWEET AND SOUR PORK

Yields: 4 servings	Pan Size: 2 quart

1 8-oz. can pineapple chunks	1½ tsp. catsup
2 tbsp. brown sugar	1 lb. boneless pork shoulder,
2 tbsp. cornstarch	cut into ¾-in. cubes
¼ c. teriyaki sauce	2 med. green peppers,
3 tbsp. cider vinegar	cut into ¾-in. pieces

Drain pineapple, reserving juice. Mix brown sugar and cornstarch in glass casserole. Blend in reserved pineapple juice, teriyaki sauce, vinegar and catsup. Add pork and green pepper; mix well. Microwave, covered, on High for 5 minutes. Stir in pineapple chunks. Microwave, covered, on Medium for 12 to 15 minutes or until pork is cooked through, stirring once. Serve over rice.

Mrs. Robert Proctor, Manatee Grange, North Carolina

STEAK MAIN DISH

Yields: 2 servings	Pan Size: 9 inch

Flour	1 can mushroom soup
1 lb. steak	¼ c. dried onion
3 tbsp. oil	flakes

Pound flour into steak with meat mallet. Cut cross grain into 1-inch slices. Combine with oil in glass dish. Microwave on High for 3 to 4 minutes. Stir in soup and onion. Microwave, covered, for 4 to 5 minutes longer, stirring frequently. Test for tenderness. Microwave for 2 to 3 minutes longer or until tender, stirring frequently.

Florence Rasmussen, White Creek Grange, Washington

SWEET AND SOUR FISH FILLETS

Yields: 4 servings	Pan Size: 8 x 12 inch

1 lb. fresh fish fillets	¼ tbsp. dry mustard
1 8-oz. can pineapple chunks	2 tbsp. vinegar
3 tbsp. brown sugar	1 tbsp. soy sauce
1 tbsp. cornstarch	1½ oz. cashews

Arrange fillets in glass baking dish. Microwave, covered, on High for 5 minutes or until fish flakes easily; drain. Drain pineapple, reserving juice. Blend reserved juice, brown sugar, cornstarch, dry mustard, vinegar and soy sauce in glass bowl. Microwave for 1½ to 2 minutes or until thickened; stir until smooth. Stir in pineapple chunks and cashews. Spoon over fillets. Microwave for 1 to 2 minutes or until bubbly.

Carol Neff, Broad Hollow Grange, Illinois

SEAFOOD CASSEROLE

Yields: 6 servings	Pan Size: 9 inch

1 lb. fresh scallops	1 med. onion, chopped
1 lb. imitation crab legs	2 tbsp. butter
1 can cream of shrimp soup	2 c. bread crumbs
1 c. sour cream	2 tbsp. butter, melted
¼ c. dry vermouth	Parmesan cheese
½ tsp. dillweed	

Microwave scallops in glass dish on High for 3 to 4 minutes or until cooked through. Combine with crab in glass casserole. Combine soup, sour cream, wine and dillweed in bowl. Pour over seafood. Combine onion and 2 tablespoons butter in glass bowl. Microwave on High until transparent. Sprinkle over casserole. Sprinkle mixture of bread crumbs and 2 tablespoons melted butter over onions. Top with Parmesan cheese. Microwave until bubbly.

Virginia B. Grobusky
Secretary, South Carolina State Grange

CHICKEN BOLLINGER

Yields: 6 servings	Pan Size: 7 x 11 inch

½ c. butter	6 chicken breasts, skinned
½ c. fine bread crumbs	1 med. onion, chopped
3 tbsp. Parmesan cheese	1 4-oz. can mushrooms
1 tsp. each basil, oregano	drained
½ tsp. each garlic salt, paprika	1 tbsp. chopped parsley
¼ teaspoon each salt, pepper	¼ c. dry white wine

Microwave ½ cup butter on High in 9-inch glass dish for 45 seconds or until melted. Combine bread crumbs, cheese, basil, oregano, garlic salt, paprika, salt and pepper on waxed paper. Dip chicken into butter; roll in crumb mixture, coating well. Place in glass dish. Microwave for 6 to 6½ minutes per pound of chicken, turning chicken once. Let stand, covered with foil, for 10 minutes. Add onion to remaining butter. Microwave on High for 1 minute. Add mushrooms. Microwave for 1 minute. Stir in parsley. Microwave wine in glass measure for 30 seconds. Stir into mushroom mixture. Spoon over chicken.

Eleanor Bollinger, Smith Grange, Ohio

CHICKEN TARRAGON

Yields: 4 servings   Pan Size: 2 quart

   ¼ c. dry white wine   2 tsp. instant chicken bouillon
   1 tbsp. lemon juice   1 tsp. dried tarragon
   1 tbsp. cornstarch   4 chicken breast filets

Combine wine, lemon juice, cornstarch, bouillon, tarragon and *½ cup cold water* in glass baking dish. Microwave, uncovered, on High for 3 to 4 minutes or until thickened, stirring every minute. Add chicken, turning to coat well. Microwave, covered, for 5 to 7 minutes or until cooked through, turning once. Arrange chicken on serving plate; spoon sauce over top.

Steven D. Maurer
Director, Ohio Department of Agriculture

SPRING VEGETABLE MEDLEY

Yields: 4 servings   Pan Size: 1½ quart

   2 tbsp. butter   ⅛ tsp. pepper
   8 oz. fresh asparagus, cut   8 oz. fresh mushrooms, sliced
     into 2-in. pieces   1 med. tomato, cut into wedges
   ½ tsp. basil   ½ tsp. salt

Microwave butter in glass casserole on High for 30 seconds. Add asparagus, basil and pepper; toss lightly. Microwave, tightly covered, for 3 minutes. Add mushrooms; toss lightly. Microwave, covered for 3 minutes. Add tomato; toss lightly. Microwave, covered, for 3 minutes. Add salt. Let stand, covered, for 3 minutes.

FROSTED CAULIFLOWER

Yields: 6 servings

1 med. head cauliflower	**¾ c. shredded sharp Oregon**
½ c. mayonnaise	**Tillamook Cheddar cheese**
1 to 2 tsp. mustard	**Paprika**

Trim stem of cauliflower. Wrap in double layer of plastic wrap. Microwave on High for 6 to 9 minutes or until tender. Let stand for 5 minutes. Combine mayonnaise and mustard in glass measure. Microwave on High for 1 minute. Place cauliflower in serving dish. Spread mayonnaise mixture over cauliflower. Sprinkle with cheese. Microwave for 1 to 2 minutes or until cheese melts. Sprinkle with paprika.

Leonard Kunzman
Director, Oregon Department of Agriculture

SOUTHERN CREAMED CORN

Yields: 4 to 5 servings   Pan Size: 1 quart

10 ears fresh corn	**½ tsp. salt**
6 tbsp. butter	**¼ c. (or more) Florida milk**
1 tbsp. flour	

Cut kernels from corn ears; scrape cobs. Microwave butter on High in glass bowl for 30 seconds or until melted. Blend in flour and salt. Add corn and ¼ cup milk. Microwave, covered with plastic wrap, on High for 4 minutes. Stir corn and turn bowl 1 quarter turn. Microwave, covered, for 6 minutes longer or until tender, adding milk 1 tablespoon at a time if necessary to make of desired consistency. Let stand, covered, for 2 to 3 minutes before serving.

Doyle Conner
Commissioner, Florida Department of Agriculture

FLUFFY BLUEBERRY MUFFINS

Yields: 12 muffins   Pan Size: muffin

2 c. flour	**½ c. milk**
½ c. sugar	**½ c. oil**
1 tbsp. baking powder	**½ c. well-drained blueberries**
½ tsp. salt	**Cinnamon-sugar**
2 eggs, beaten	

Sift first 4 ingredients into bowl; make well in center. Add eggs, milk and oil; stir just until moistened. Stir in blueberries. Fill paper-lined muffin cups ½ full. Sprinkle with cinnamon-sugar. Microwave 6 at a time on Medium-High for 2½ to 4 minutes or until muffins test done.

Helen B. Davis, Waterbury Grange, Vermont

PEACH DUMPLINGS

Yields: 4 servings	Pan Size: 1½ quart

2 c. chopped fresh peaches	**½ tsp. baking powder**
½ c. each sugar, flour	**1 tbsp. oil**
1 tbsp. sugar	**¼ c. milk**

Mix peaches, ½ cup sugar and *½ cup water* in glass casserole. Microwave on High for 5 minutes. Combine flour, sugar, baking powder, oil and milk in bowl; mix until moistened. Drop by spoonfuls into hot peach mixture. Microwave, covered, for 3 to 5 minutes or until cooked through. Spoon peaches and syrup over dumplings.

Mary Ramm, Colton-Foothills Grange, Oregon

PEANUT BRITTLE

Yields: 2 pounds	Pan Size: 3 quart

1½ tsp. soda	**1 c. light corn syrup**
1 tsp. vanilla extract	**3 tbsp. melted butter**
1½ c. sugar	**1 lb. raw peanuts**

Heat greased baking sheet at 250 degrees in conventional oven. Mix soda, vanilla and *1 teaspoon water* in small bowl; set aside. Combine sugar, corn syrup and *1 cup water* in glass bowl; blend well. Microwave on High for 15 minutes or to 240 degrees on candy thermometer, soft-ball stage. Stir in butter and peanuts. Microwave on High for 20 minutes or to 300 degrees on candy thermometer, hard-crack stage, stirring occasionally with wooden spoon. Stir in soda mixture. Spread ¼ inch thick on heated baking sheet. Let stand until firm. Break into pieces. Store in airtight container.
Note: Use only microwave-safe candy thermometer.

Juanita Shearer, Yankton Grange, Oregon

RAISIN-BREAD PUDDING

Yields: 6 servings	Pan Size: 2 quart

4 c. cubed bread	**Dash of salt**
½ c. raisins	**2 c. milk**
3 eggs, beaten	**2 tbsp. margarine**
½ c. packed brown sugar	**Cinnamon to taste**
1 tsp. vanilla extract	

Mix bread and raisins in glass casserole. Beat eggs with brown sugar, vanilla and salt. Heat milk and margarine in glass measure on High for 4½ to 5 minutes. Beat into egg mixture gradually. Pour over bread and raisins. Sprinkle with cinnamon. Cover with waxed paper. Microwave on Medium for 12 to 14 minutes or until set. Cool.

Mary Ann Hartnett, Fruit Land Grange, Delaware

FROST AND BAKE FUDGE CAKE

Yields: 8 servings   Pan Size: 8 inch round

6 oz. semisweet chocolate chips	3 tbsp. shortening
⅔ c. sweetened condensed milk	1 egg
1 tsp. vanilla extract	⅔ c. milk
1⅓ c. buttermilk baking mix	1 tsp. vanilla extract
¾ c. sugar	½ c. chopped nuts

Microwave chocolate chips in 1-quart glass measure on High until melted. Add condensed milk, vanilla and *2 tablespoons water*; blend well. Pour into waxed paper-lined baking dish. Combine baking mix, sugar, shortening, egg and half the milk in mixer bowl. Beat for 1 minute. Add remaining milk and vanilla. Beat for 1 minute. Pour over chocolate layer. Microwave on High for 7½ minutes. Invert onto serving plate. Sprinkle with nuts.

Frances A. Hoffman, Northumberland Grange, Pennsylvania

VELVET SMOOTH CREAM PIE

Yields: 8 servings   Pan Size: 2 quart

¾ c. sugar	2 c. milk
6 tbsp. flour	1 tbsp. butter
¼ tsp. salt	1 tsp. vanilla extract
2 eggs	1 baked 9-in. pie shell

Combine sugar, flour and salt in deep glass bowl. Whisk in eggs and milk until smooth. Microwave on High for 8 minutes, stirring 3 times. Stir in butter and vanilla. Cool for 5 minutes. Pour into pie shell. Chill until set.
Note: May slice bananas into pie shell or stir 1 cup coconut into custard if desired.

Helen Edgar, Freeman Lake Grange, Idaho

PUMPKIN BARS

Yields: 24 servings   Pan Size: 8 x 12 inch

2 eggs	½ tsp. soda
½ c. oil	1 tsp. cinnamon
1 c. sugar	¼ tsp. each cloves, nutmeg,
1 c. pumpkin	ginger and salt
1 c. flour	½ c. chopped nuts
1 tsp. baking powder	¼ c. chopped dates

Beat eggs, oil, sugar and pumpkin in mixer bowl until smooth. Add sifted dry ingredients; mix lightly. Stir in nuts and dates. Pour into glass baking dish. Microwave on High for 8 to 10 minutes or until bars test done, turning pan occasionally. Cut into bars. Sprinkle with confectioners' sugar. Serve with whipped topping.

Mrs. Lister Endsley, Keene Hill Grange, Ohio

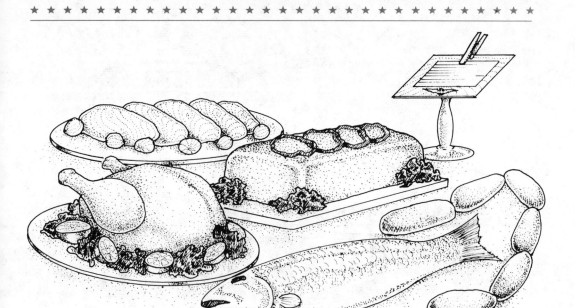

Main Dishes

The central focus of any menu is the entrée or main course, usually featuring juicy beef or pork, tender lamb or veal, succulent poultry or seafood. By far the most important element in many diets, there are enough cuts and kinds of these protein-rich foods to serve a different dish every day of the year. Long before written records were kept, man used cattle for food, domesticated pork, hunted chicken in Asian jungles, and fished the seas of the world. Although seafood has remained relatively unchanged over the years, modern meats and poultry bear little resemblance to the sinewy predecessors brought to the New World by ship. These supplemented the game and fish without which the earliest settlers might not have survived.

Some of our most delicious dishes were also brought to our shores by immigrants; however, our own specialties are equally rich and varied. Recipes from both a number of national and regional cuisines are included in *The Glory of Cooking*. Serve chops, roasts or ribs; shape savory meat loaves or balls; stretch with dumplings, vegetables, or pasta; roast, grill, or sauté; prepare hearty casseroles and stews or delicate crêpes and soufflés. Flavored with love and imagination, the main dish is truly the heart of every meal.

Beef

BEEF AND DUMPLING BAKE

Yields: 8 servings	Pan Size: 3 quart	Preheat: 350°

2 lb. 1-inch round steak cubes	⅓ c. milk
2 med. onions, sliced	2 tbsp. oil
1 can cream of chicken soup	2 tbsp. minced parsley
1 can onion soup	1½ c. flour
4 oz. mushrooms, sliced	1½ tsp. baking powder
1 tbsp. Worcestershire sauce	½ tsp. salt
⅓ c. flour	10 oz. frozen peas, thawed
1 egg	4 green pepper rings

Layer steak cubes and onion slices in casserole. Combine soups, mushrooms, Worcestershire sauce and ⅓ cup flour in bowl; mix well. Pour over onions. Bake, covered, for 2 hours. Combine egg, milk, oil and parsley in bowl; mix well. Sift 1½ cups flour, baking powder and salt together. Add to egg mixture; stir just until moistened. Layer peas over casserole. Arrange pepper rings in center. Drop dough by rounded teaspoonfuls around pepper rings. Bake, covered, at 400 degrees for 20 minutes or until dumplings are cooked through.

Richard and Barbara Grubb
Secretary, Pennsylvania Department of Agriculture

BUBBLE AND SQUEAK (ENGLAND)

Yields: 4 servings	Pan Size: 10 inch

1 med. onion, chopped	**1 c. chopped cooked beef**
2 tbsp. oil	**½ tsp. salt**
3 c. mashed cooked potatoes	**¼ tsp. pepper**
1 c. cooked chopped cabbage	

Sauté onion in oil in skillet until brown. Add remaining ingredients; mix well. Press mixture down firmly. Cook over medium-high heat until bottom is light brown; do not stir. Turn mixture over in several sections. Cook until brown. Serve immediately.

Linda Deyette, Mt. Holly Grange, Vermont

CORNISH PASTY (ENGLAND)

Yields: 1 serving	Pan Size: 10x15 inch	Preheat: 350°

1 recipe pie pastry	**¼ lb. (or more) steak cubes**
1 5 to 6-oz. potato, peeled, sliced	**Salt and pepper to taste**

Roll pastry dough into 8 or 9-inch circle on floured surface. Place potato and steak on half the circle. Sprinkle with salt and pepper. Fold dough in half to enclose filling. Dampen edges and seal; pierce top to vent. Place on baking sheet. Bake for 40 minutes to 1 hour or until brown. Miners in Cornwall carried pasties for lunch.

Lucy B. Streeter, Good Will Grange, Connecticut

DOWN-SOUTH MEAT PIE

Yields: 6 servings	Pan Size: 2½ quart	Preheat: 350°

2 lb. beef cubes	**3 c. canned tomatoes with juice**
2 tbsp. shortening	**½ c. drained corn**
1 c. chopped onion	**1¼ c. milk, scalded**
2 c. chopped celery	**¼ c. cornmeal**
½ c. chopped green pepper	**2 c. sifted flour**
3 tbsp. flour	**2¼ tsp. baking powder**
2 tsp. salt	**1 tsp. salt**
¼ tsp. each pepper, paprika	**¼ c. shortening**

Brown beef in 2 tablespoons shortening in skillet. Add onion, celery and green pepper. Cook until vegetables are tender. Stir 3 tablespoons flour, 2 teaspoons salt, ¼ teaspoon pepper and paprika into tomatoes. Add tomato mixture and corn to skillet; mix well. Pour into casserole. Bake, covered, for 30 minutes or until beef is almost tender. Pour hot milk over cornmeal in bowl; mix well. Cool. Sift remaining dry ingredients together twice in bowl. Cut in ¼ cup shortening until crumbly. Add cornmeal mixture; mix just until moistened. Drop by spoonfuls over casserole. Bake until brown.

Nellie Tucker, Elk Grove Grange, California

GREEN PEPPER STEAK

Yields: 4 servings   Pan Size: wok

1 lb. beef chuck or round
  steak, trimmed
¼ c. soy sauce
1 clove of garlic, chopped
1½ tsp. grated fresh ginger
¼ c. oil

½ c. each 1-in. squares red
  and green peppers
2 lg. stalks celery, thinly sliced
1 tbsp. cornstarch
2 tomatoes, cut into wedges

Slice beef cross grain ⅛ inch thick. Combine with soy sauce, garlic and ginger in bowl. Let stand for several minutes. Stir-fry beef mixture in hot oil in wok until tender. Add peppers and celery. Stir-fry for 10 minutes or until tender-crisp. Add mixture of cornstarch and *1 cup water*. Cook until thickened, stirring constantly. Add tomatoes. Cook until heated through.

Frances P. Caccamise, Gates Grange, New York

BEEF BURGUNDY (FRANCE)

Yields: 6 servings   Pan Size: 2 quart   Preheat: 350°

2 lb. 2-in. beef cubes
Butter
2 c. small whole onions
12 mushrooms
1 tsp. tomato paste
1 tbsp. flour

1 c. Burgundy
1 c. beef stock
1 tsp. salt
¼ tsp. pepper
¼ tsp. each marjoram, rosemary
  and thyme

Brown beef in a small amount of butter in skillet; remove with slotted spoon. Sauté onions and mushrooms in pan drippings. Stir in tomato paste and flour. Add wine, beef stock and seasonings; mix well. Combine with beef in casserole. Bake, covered, for 2 hours. Serve over rice or noodles.

Wayne A. Cawley
Secretary, Maryland Department of Agriculture

EASY BEEF STROGANOFF

Yields: 4 servings   Pan Size: 12 inch

1½ lb. round steak, cut into
  bite-sized pieces
3 tbsp. butter
1 med. onion, chopped

12 oz. mushrooms
½ c. sour cream
Salt and pepper to taste

Brown steak in butter in skillet. Add onion. Sauté for 3 minutes. Add mushrooms. Sauté for 3 minutes. Stir in sour cream and seasonings. Heat to serving temperature; do not boil. Serve over cooked noodles or rice.

Jeanne Davies
Master, Colorado State Grange

ROULADEN (GERMANY)

Yields: 4 servings	Pan Size: 12 inch	Preheat: 350°

1 ¼-in. thick round steak	Finely chopped onion
Mustard	Flour
Bacon slices	Salt and pepper to taste

Remove bone and fat from steak. Render fat in skillet. Cut steak into strips. Spread each strip with mustard. Top with bacon slice and sprinkle of chopped onion. Roll up strips, securing with toothpicks. Coat with mixture of flour and seasonings. Brown on all sides in drippings in skillet. Add a small amount of water. Bake, covered, for 1½ to 2 hours or until tender, adding additional water as necessary. Spoon into serving dish. *Note:* May simmer for 1½ to 2 hours if preferred.

Dr. and Mrs. Otis R. Bowen
Secretary, U.S. Department of Health and Human Services

BEEF BIRDS

Yields: 4 servings	Pan Size: 2 quart	Preheat: 300°

1½ lb. round steak	4 carrots, cut into strips
¼ c. flour	4 potatoes, peeled
1 tsp. salt	4 sm. onions
¼ tsp. pepper	1 can mushroom soup

Cut steak into 3x5-inch pieces. Coat with mixture of flour, salt and pepper. Place several carrot strips on each; roll to enclose filling and secure with toothpicks. Brown on all sides in a small amount of shortening in skillet. Place in casserole; add potatoes and onions. Top with soup. Bake, tightly covered, for 1½ hours or until steak and vegetables are tender.

BEEF STEW (ITALY)

Yields: 4 servings	Pan Size: 4 quart

1½ lb. 1-in. stew beef
3 tbsp. oil
1 lg. onion, chopped
⅔ c. chopped celery
2 cloves of garlic, minced
½ c. dry white wine

1 28-oz. can Italian
  tomatoes, chopped
½ c. minced parsley
1 tsp. rosemary
Salt and pepper to taste

Brown beef in oil in saucepan. Remove with slotted spoon. Sauté onion, celery and garlic in pan drippings. Add beef and remaining ingredients. Bring to a boil; reduce heat. Simmer, covered, for 1½ to 2 hours or until beef is tender.

Mary E. McDermott, Nauset Grange, Massachusetts

BEEF STEW WITH FRESH PARSLEY DUMPLINGS

Yields: 6 servings	Pan Size: stockpot

4 slices bacon, chopped
2 lb. beef chuck, cubed
⅓ c. flour
1 lg. onion, chopped
1 clove of garlic, crushed
1 can condensed beef bouillon
2 lg. tomatoes, peeled, seeded,
  chopped
12 peppercorns
3 whole cloves
6 tbsp. chopped parsley

½ bay leaf
¼ tsp. rosemary
4 carrots, peeled, chopped
1 med. rutabaga, peeled, chopped
1 lg. potato, peeled, chopped
1 tbsp. butter
1 c. flour
1½ tsp. baking powder
¼ tsp. salt
⅔ c. milk
2 tbsp. chopped parsley

Cook bacon in stockpot until light brown; drain on paper towels. Coat beef cubes with ⅓ cup flour. Cook over high heat in bacon drippings until brown. Add onion, garlic, bouillon, *1¼ cups water*, tomatoes and bacon. Add bouquet garni made of peppercorns, cloves, chopped parsley, bay leaf and rosemary. Simmer, covered, for 45 minutes. Add carrots, rutabaga, potato and *½ cup water*. Cook for 15 minutes longer. Remove bouquet garni. Cut butter into mixture of 1 cup flour, baking powder and salt in bowl until crumbly. Add milk and chopped parsley; beat until smooth. Drop by tablespoonfuls into stew. Simmer, covered, for 10 minutes. Remove dumplings. Pour stew into serving bowl; arrange dumplings on top.

Photograph for this recipe on page 67.

Recipes for this photograph on pages 30, 66, 128, 171.

FIVE-HOUR EASY BAKED STEW

Yields: 6 servings   Pan Size: roaster   Preheat: 250°

2 lb. stew beef	1 tsp. salt
1 c. chopped onion	½ tsp. pepper
1 c. chopped carrot	1 tbsp. sugar
1 c. chopped celery	2 tbsp. Minute tapioca
4 potatoes, chopped	1 can tomato soup

Layer ingredients in roaster in order listed. Do not mix. Pour *1 soup can water* over layers. Bake for 5 hours. Do not open oven during baking time.

Agnes DeLeon, Melrose Grange, Montana

BRAISED SIRLOIN TIPS

Yields: 6 servings   Pan Size: 10 inch

2 lb. sirloin tips	3 tbsp. soy sauce
1 tbsp. oil	⅛ tsp. garlic powder
⅓ c. cranberry juice cocktail	⅛ tsp. ginger
1 can beef consommé	Cornstarch

Cut beef into bite-sized pieces. Brown on all sides in oil in skillet. Add cranberry juice, consommé, soy sauce, garlic powder and ginger. Simmer for 1½ hours or until tender. Blend a small amount of cornstarch with a small amount of water. Stir into beef. Cook until thickened, stirring constantly.

Ray Moreau, Eastern Pomona Grange, New Hampshire

BEEF GOULASH (HUNGARY)

Yields: 6 to 8 servings   Pan Size: 4 quart

¼ c. butter	3 lb. lean beef cubes
¼ c. flour	1 c. drained chopped canned
2 c. beef broth	tomatoes
¼ tsp. Tabasco sauce	4 tsp. paprika
4 c. sliced onions	½ tsp. salt
2 cloves of garlic, minced	½ tsp. marjoram
¼ c. butter	1 bay leaf

Cook ¼ cup butter in saucepan until golden brown. Blend in flour. Cook over low heat until dark brown, stirring constantly. Stir in broth gradually. Cook until thickened, stirring constantly. Add Tabasco sauce; set aside. Sauté onions and garlic in ¼ cup butter in 4-quart saucepan until light brown. Add beef. Cook until brown, stirring frequently. Add tomatoes, reserved sauce and seasonings. Simmer, covered, for 1½ hours or until beef is tender, stirring occasionally. Remove bay leaf. Serve over noodles, spaetzle, mashed potatoes or rice.

Photograph for this recipe on page 68.

MARTY'S MEAT ROLL

Yields: 3 servings	Pan Size: 10x15 inch	Preheat: 450°

1½ c. chopped cooked roast beef	2 c. flour
2 tbsp. minced onion	4 tsp. baking powder
3 tbsp. beef gravy	½ tsp. salt
¼ tsp. salt	¼ c. shortening
⅛ tsp. pepper	¾ c. milk

Combine roast beef, onion, gravy, ¼ teaspoon salt and pepper in bowl; mix well. Sift flour, baking powder and ½ teaspoon salt into bowl. Cut in shortening until crumbly. Add milk; mix well. Roll ¼ inch thick on floured surface. Spread with beef mixture. Roll as for jelly roll. Cut into 1-inch slices. Place cut side up on greased baking sheet. Bake for 15 minutes or until brown. Serve with additional gravy.
Note: My Grandmother used this recipe for leftover roast beef.

Joann VanCise, New London Grange, Pennsylvania

FIREPLACE SIRLOIN

Yields: 6 servings

1 3 to 4-lb. sirloin steak, 2½-in. thick	Salt Melted butter

Build fire in fireplace 2 to 3 hours in advance to provide a deep hot bed of ashes. Remove hot embers from logs and arrange as cooking surface over ashes, placing logs to 1 side. Coat 1 side of steak completely with salt. Place salt side down on hot embers. Cook for 25 minutes. Remove from embers; brush off salt. Add fresh embers from logs to cooking surface. Coat other side of steak with salt. Place salt side down on embers. Cook for 20 minutes or to desired degree of doneness. Brush off salt. Place on serving plate; carve into thin slices. Dip slices in butter and place on bread. Serve with salad.

George Schultz
Secretary, U.S. Department of State

WRANGLER BEEF FOR SANDWICHES

Yields: 8 servings	Pan Size: 10 inch

¼ lb. onions, finely chopped	¾ tbsp. Worcestershire sauce
¼ clove of garlic, minced	2½ tsp. mustard
2½ tsp. shortening	Pinch each of cloves and pepper
¾ lb. cooked beef, thinly sliced	¼ tsp. celery salt
2½ tbsp. packed brown sugar	2¼ tsp. salt
1 6-oz. can tomato paste	2½ tbsp. vinegar

Sauté onions and garlic in shortening in skillet. Add beef, brown sugar, tomato paste, Worcestershire sauce, mustard and seasonings; mix well. Stir in vinegar and *10 tablespoons water*. Bring to a boil; reduce heat. Simmer for 15 minutes. Serve on sandwich buns.

Maleta O'Hern, Sanitaria Springs Grange, New York

SAUERBRATEN (GERMANY) Pot Roast

Yields: 8 servings	Pan Size: 4 quart

1 4 to 5-lb. pot roast	6 whole cloves
2 med. onions, thinly sliced	2 bay leaves
2 c. vinegar	Leaves of 3 to 4 stalks celery
2 tbsp. brown sugar	Flour
1 tbsp. salt	Shortening
¼ tsp. pepper	12 old-fashioned gingersnaps,
1 clove of garlic	crushed

Place roast in glass dish. Top with onion slices. Bring vinegar, brown sugar, salt, pepper and *2 cups water* to a boil in saucepan. Pour over roast. Place garlic, cloves, bay leaves and celery leaves in liquid. Chill, covered, for 4 to 5 days, turning roast each day. Remove roast; strain liquid and reserve. Coat roast with flour. Brown in a small amount of shortening in heavy saucepan. Add ½ cup reserved liquid. Cook, covered, over low heat for 3 to 4 hours or until tender, adding reserved liquid if needed. Remove roast to serving plate; cover with foil. Add enough reserved liquid to saucepan to measure 3 cups. Bring to a boil, stirring to deglaze. Add gingersnap crumbs. Cook over low heat until smooth, stirring constantly. Serve roast with gravy, applesauce and German potato pancakes.

Marian Moore, Volunteer Grange, Tennessee

EL PASO BEANS

Yields: 6 servings	Pan Size: 4 quart

1 lb. dried pinto beans	2 cloves of garlic, minced
1 lb. stew beef	1 tbsp. minced hot pepper
¼ lb. slab bacon	1 tsp. oregano
2 cans seasoned tomato sauce	Salt and pepper to taste
1 c. chopped onion	

Rinse beans. Combine with *6 cups cold water* in large saucepan. Simmer, covered, for 1½ hours. Add beef, bacon, tomato sauce, onion, garlic, hot pepper and oregano. Simmer for 1½ hours. Season to taste. Spoon into serving dish. Serve with corn bread.

Mary Dickerson, Decatur Grange, Virginia

BEEF TONGUE

Yields: 6 servings   Pan Size: Crock•Pot

1 fresh beef tongue	1 sm. onion, chopped
1 stalk celery, chopped	1 bay leaf
1 carrot, peeled, chopped	2 tbsp. salt

Wash beef tongue. Place in Crock•Pot with water to cover. Add remaining ingredients. Cook on Low for 7 to 9 hours. Remove beef and cool slightly; peel. Chill in refrigerator. Carve into slices. Good for sandwiches.

Edward F. Moody
Past Master, Kansas State Grange

JELLIED VEAL

Yields: 8 servings   Pan Size: stockpot

3 lb. veal shoulder and neck with bones	1 bay leaf
1 veal knuckle	1 tbsp. salt
1 calf's foot	1 tsp. pepper
2 whole cloves	Dash of cayenne pepper
1 onion	Dash of Worcestershire sauce
	8 hard-boiled eggs, sliced

Combine veal, veal knuckle, calf's foot, clove-studded onion, bay leaf, salt, pepper and water to cover in large stockpot. Bring to the boiling point; reduce heat. Simmer, covered, for 2 to 2½ hours or until meat is very tender. Remove meat with slotted spoon; chop into small pieces and reserve. Return bones to stockpot. Boil stock with bones, uncovered, for 30 minutes. Cool slightly. Strain stock. Stir in cayenne pepper and Worcestershire sauce. Press half the chopped veal, hard-boiled eggs and remaining veal into mold. Pour stock over layers, filling to rim. Chill for 12 hours or until firm. Unmold onto serving plate. Cut into slices.

Congressman Lindy Boggs
Member of Bicentennial Commission

VEAL SCALLOPS

Yields: 4 to 6 servings   Pan Size: 10 inch

1½ lb. veal scallops	1 c. dry bread crumbs
1 c. flour	1 c. butter
¼ tsp. salt	¼ c. lemon juice
⅛ tsp. pepper	1 lemon, thinly sliced
2 eggs, beaten	

Pound veal ⅛ inch thick with meat mallet. Mix flour, salt and pepper in bowl. Coat veal with flour mixture, eggs and bread crumbs. Brown several at a time in butter in hot skillet. Remove to warm platter. Add lemon juice to pan drippings in skillet. Cook for 2 to 3 minutes, stirring to deglaze skillet. Pour over scallops. Top with lemon slices.

Doris M. Olson, Eagle Cliff Grange, Washington

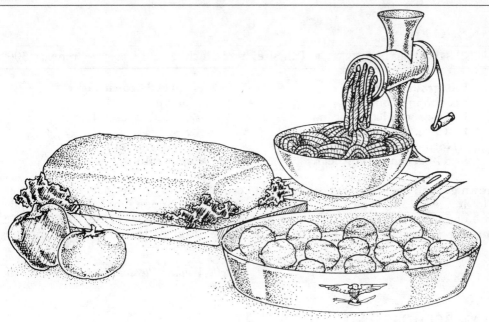

Ground Beef

BIERROCKS (GERMANY) Meat Pies

Yields: 8 servings	Pan Size: 9 x 13 inch	Preheat: 350°

2 pkg. dry yeast	7 to 8 c. flour
2 c. milk, scalded	2 lb. ground beef
3 tbsp. sugar	1 lb. bulk pork sausage
3 tbsp. shortening, melted	1 lg. onion, chopped
1 tbsp. salt	1 16-oz. can sauerkraut

Dissolve yeast in ¾ cup warm water in bowl. Add cooled milk, sugar, shortening, salt and 4 cups flour. Beat until smooth. Stir in enough additional flour to make easily handled dough. Knead on floured surface for 10 minutes or until smooth and elastic. Place in greased bowl, turning to grease surface. Let rise, covered, for 1 hour or until doubled in bulk. Brown ground beef and sausage in skillet, drain. Add onion and drained sauerkraut; mix well. Roll dough into two ¼-inch thick rectangles. Cut into 4-inch squares. Place large spoonful of ground beef mixture in center of each square. Fold corners to center to enclose filling; press to seal. Place in baking pan. Let rise, covered, until doubled in bulk. Bake for 20 minutes or until golden brown.

Kathleen McPhee, Klondike Piney Grange, Wyoming

RANCHO PIE

Yields: 8 to 10 servings	Pan Size: 9 x 13 inch	Preheat: 300°

1 lb. ground beef	⅔ c. packed brown sugar
1 c. chopped onions	1 c. catsup
1 16-oz. can baked beans	6 oz. grated mozzarella
1 15-oz. can Great	cheese
Northern beans	1 can refrigerator crescent
1 17-oz. can kidney beans	dinner rolls

Brown ground beef in skillet, stirring until crumbly. Add onions. Sauté until tender. Add drained beans, brown sugar and catsup; mix well. Spoon into baking dish. Bake for 45 minutes. Increase temperature to 425 degrees. Sprinkle cheese over casserole. Unroll crescent roll dough. Place on top of cheese, sealing edges. Bake for 10 minutes or until brown.

Stella Walker, Pleasant Grove Grange, Ohio

BEAN-BEEF CASSEROLE

Yields: 10 servings	Pan Size: 3 quart	Preheat: 350°

1½ lb. ground beef	2 tbsp. vinegar
1 sm. onion, chopped	3 tbsp. brown sugar
1 16-oz. can green beans	½ c. catsup
1 16-oz. can red kidney beans	½ tsp. dry mustard
1 16-oz. can pork and beans	½ tsp. salt

Brown ground beef in saucepan, stirring until crumbly; drain. Add remaining ingredients; mix well. Spoon into casserole. Bake for 30 minutes or until bubbly.

Enola Heydt, Henrietta Grange, New York

BARLEY HOT DISH

Yields: 10 to 12 servings	Pan Size: 4 quart	Preheat: 375°

1½ lb. ground beef	2 16-oz. cans tomatoes
1 c. chopped onion	¾ c. barley
½ c. chopped celery	½ bay leaf
3 tbsp. oil	1 tsp. marjoram
½ c. chopped green pepper	2½ tsp. salt
1 sm. can mushrooms	¼ tsp. pepper
1 can cream of mushroom soup	

Brown ground beef with onion and celery in oil in skillet, stirring frequently; drain. Add remaining ingredients and *2½ cups water.* Bring to a boil. Spoon into casserole. Bake for 1¼ hours, adding water as necessary to make of desired consistency.

Laurel Hamilton, Friend of Log Cabin Grange, Ohio

BARBECUED SAUERKRAUT AND BEEF

Yields: 6 to 8 servings	Pan Size: 9 x 9 inch	Preheat: 350°

1 lb. ground beef	1 lg. can sauerkraut, drained
2 tbsp. chopped onion	2 c. tomato juice
Salt and pepper to taste	¼ c. packed brown sugar

Brown ground beef with onion, salt and pepper in skillet, stirring until ground beef is crumbly; drain. Add sauerkraut; mix well. Stir in tomato juice and brown sugar. Spoon into greased baking dish. Bake for 1 hour or until of desired consistency. *Note:* May be prepared in electric skillet and simmered on 350 degrees for 1 hour.

Dorothy M. Becker, Bean Grange, Kansas

CABBAGE ROLLS (HUNGARY)

Yields: 6 to 8 servings	Pan Size: roaster	Preheat: 350°

1 lg. loose head cabbage	Salt to taste
2 c. rice	½ tsp. each Accent,
2 lb. ground beef	garlic salt and pepper
1 lg. onion, grated	1 lb. sauerkraut
3 eggs	1 lb. bacon, crisp-fried

Place cabbage leaves in boiling water for several minutes or until wilted. Cook rice according to package directions for 5 minutes; rinse and drain. Combine with next 7 ingredients in bowl; mix well. Roll by spoonfuls in cabbage leaves. Rinse and drain sauerkraut. Spread half the sauerkraut in roaster. Arrange cabbage rolls over top. Top with remaining sauerkraut. Sprinkle with crumbled bacon. Bake for 1½ hours.

Jean E. Thompson, Mt. Pleasant Grange, Pennsylvania

HAMBURGER HASH CHINESE-STYLE

Yields: 6 servings	Pan Size: 2 quart	Preheat: 350°

1 lb. ground beef	1 can cream of chicken soup
2 tbsp. oil	½ c. rice
2 med. onions, chopped	¼ c. soy sauce
1 c. thickly sliced celery	¼ tsp. pepper
1 can mushroom soup	1 can Chinese noodles

Brown ground beef in oil in skillet, stirring until crumbly; drain. Add next 7 ingredients and *1½ cups warm water*; mix well. Spoon into baking dish. Bake, covered, for 30 minutes. Bake, uncovered, for 30 minutes. Top with noodles. Bake for 15 minutes longer.

Leone Romine, Friend of Lookout Mt. Grange, Oregon

HAMBURGER STROGANOFF

Yields: 4 servings   Pan Size: 10 inch

    ½ c. minced onion   ½ tsp. pepper
    ½ c. butter   ½ tsp. paprika
    1 lb. ground beef   1 can golden mushroom soup
    2 tsp. salt   1 c. cottage cheese

Sauté onion in butter in skillet until golden. Add ground beef and seasonings. Cook until brown and crumbly; drain. Stir in soup and cottage cheese. Cook for 10 minutes or just until heated through. Serve on mashed potatoes, rice, noodles or toast.
Note: May stir in cooked noodles, place in casserole, top with cheese and bake at 325 degrees for 20 minutes.

Bonnie Aaron, Carbondale Grange, Kansas

OVEN CHOW MEIN

Yields: 6 to 8 servings   Pan Size: 2 quart   Preheat: 350°

    1 lb. ground beef   2 carrots, sliced
    2 tbsp. shortening   1 can sliced water chestnuts
    1 c. uncooked rice   1 can cream of mushroom soup
    1½ c. chopped onions   ⅓ c. soy sauce
    2 c. chopped celery   ½ tsp. each ginger, pepper

Brown ground beef lightly in shortening in skillet, stirring until crumbly; drain. Add remaining ingredients and *2 cups hot water*; mix well. Pour into casserole. Bake, covered, for 1 hour, stirring occasionally.

Peggy Striffler, San Diego Harbor Grange, California

EXTRA-GOOD HOMEMADE CHILI

Yields: 6 to 7 servings   Pan Size: 4 quart

    5 c. dried kidney beans   2 c. cooked whole tomatoes
    1 lb. ground beef   1 tsp. chili powder
    ½ lb. ground pork   1 tsp. (or more) cayenne pepper
    3 med. onions, chopped   2 tsp. salt
    ¼ c. chopped celery

Combine beans with water to cover in saucepan. Cook for 2½ hours or until beans are tender. Brown beef and pork lightly in skillet; drain. Add to beans with remaining ingredients. Simmer, covered, for 1 hour, stirring occasionally. Ladle into bowls.

Ida Grund, Round Butte Grange, Montana

HIGHTOWER'S AWFUL GOOD TEXAS CHILI

Yields: 8 servings	Pan Size: 5 to 6 quart

3 thick slices bacon	1 tbsp. each oregano,
3 lb. coarsely ground lean beef	salt and pepper
1 med. onion, finely chopped	1 12-oz. can dark Mexican beer
3 med. cloves of garlic, minced	4 to 8 dried red chili pods
1 6-oz. can tomato sauce	1 tbsp. Masa Harina
3 tbsp. cumin	Cayenne pepper to taste

Fry bacon in large cast-iron kettle until crisp. Remove bacon and reserve for another use. Sauté ground beef, onion and garlic in bacon drippings. Add tomato sauce, cumin, oregano, salt and pepper; mix well. Stir in beer. Remove from heat. Remove stems and seeds from chili pods. Combine with *3 cups water* in saucepan. Cook, covered, for 15 minutes. Pour into blender container; process until smooth. Stir into chili. Simmer for 1½ hours. Thicken with Masa Harina or thin with a small amount of water. Stir in cayenne pepper. Simmer for 30 minutes longer. Ladle into bowls.

Jim Hightower
Commissioner, Texas Department of Agriculture

TEXAS JAILHOUSE CHILI

Yields: 4 to 8 servings	Pan Size: Crock•Pot

4 to 5 lb. ground beef	1 to 2 tsp. white pepper
1½ to 3 tbsp. chopped green	1 to 2 tbsp. cumin
pepper	1 tbsp. paprika
2½ to 3 tbsp. chili powder	½ to 1 tsp. oregano
1 to 2 tbsp. crushed red pepper	1 tbsp. salt

Brown ground beef in skillet, stirring until crumbly; drain well. Combine with green pepper, seasonings and *1 cup water* in Crock•Pot. Cook on Low for 6 hours.

Ruth Gunn, Redwood Grange, Oregon

CROCK•POT BEAN DISH

Yields: 12 servings	Pan Size: Crock•Pot

1 lb. ground beef	2 15-oz. cans pork and beans
½ lb. bacon, chopped	1 c. catsup
1 c. chopped onion	¼ c. packed brown sugar
1 15-oz. can each kidney beans,	3 tbsp. white vinegar
butter beans and garbanzo	1 tbsp. liquid smoke
beans, drained	

Brown ground beef in skillet, stirring until crumbly; drain. Combine with remaining ingredients in Crock•Pot; mix well. Cook on Low for 4 to 6 hours.

Genevra Hess, Skyline Grange, Oregon

JOSEPH'S STUFFED GREEN PEPPERS (HUNGARY)

Yields: 8 servings	Pan Size: 2 quart	Preheat: 375°

1 med. onion, chopped	1 tbsp. Hungarian sweet
2 lg. cloves of garlic, chopped	paprika
1 tbsp. butter	¼ tsp. pepper
1 lb. lean ground beef	1 qt. jar sauerkraut
1 c. rice	4 lg. green peppers
1 egg, lightly beaten	2 c. tomato purée
2 bay leaves, crumbled	2 c. sour cream
1 tsp. basil	

Sauté onion and garlic in butter in skillet. Add to ground beef, rice, egg and seasonings in bowl; mix well. Drain sauerkraut, reserving 3 tablespoons liquid. Chop ⅓ of the sauerkraut very fine. Add finely chopped sauerkraut and reserved liquid to ground beef mixture. Cut tops from peppers and discard seed. Spoon ground beef mixture into peppers. Spread ⅓ of the sauerkraut in deep casserole. Place peppers upright in casserole. Spread remaining sauerkraut over peppers. Pour tomato purée over top. Bake, covered, for 1½ hours. Cut peppers into halves lengthwise. Place on serving plates. Stir sour cream into sauerkraut in casserole. Spoon over peppers.

Edna B. Johnson, Eastside Grange, Montana

MEXICAN EGGPLANT

Yields: 4 servings	Pan Size: 10 inch

1 lb. ground beef	1 tsp. oregano
¼ to ½ c. chopped onion	½ tsp. salt
1 tbsp. flour	1 sm. eggplant
½ c. chopped green pepper	Salt and pepper to taste
1 c. tomato sauce	1 c. shredded American cheese
½ to 1 tsp. chili powder	Parmesan cheese

Brown ground beef with onion in skillet, stirring frequently; drain. Stir in flour. Add green pepper, tomato sauce, chili powder, oregano and ½ teaspoon salt; mix well. Slice eggplant into ½-inch rounds; arrange over ground beef mixture. Simmer, covered, for 10 to 15 minutes or until eggplant is tender. Season with salt and pepper. Sprinkle with American cheese. Pass Parmesan cheese at serving time.

LaVeda Miles, Millbrook Grange, Illinois

CRANBERRY MEATBALLS

Yields: 6 to 8 servings	Pan Size: 10 inch	Preheat: 350°

2 lb. ground beef	⅛ tsp. pepper
1 c. bread crumbs	1 can cranberry sauce
1 sm. onion, grated	1 bottle of chili sauce
1½ tsp. salt	1 tbsp. lemon juice

Combine ground beef, bread crumbs, onion, salt, pepper and ¼ *cup water* in bowl; mix well. Shape into small balls. Brown in electric skillet. Combine cranberry sauce, chili sauce and lemon juice in bowl. Pour over meatballs. Simmer until meatballs are cooked through.

Madonna Monfort, Spencerville Grange, Ohio

MEATBALLS IN BEER

Yields: 4 servings	Pan Size: 3 quart
½ c. beer	¼ c. bread crumbs
½ c. catsup	1½ tsp. chopped onion
2 tbsp. vinegar	¼ tsp. horseradish
2 tbsp. Worcestershire sauce	Dash of Tabasco sauce
2 tbsp. sugar	2 tbsp. mayonnaise
Pepper to taste	⅛ tsp. nutmeg
½ lb. ground beef	½ tsp. pepper

Combine beer, catsup, vinegar, Worcestershire sauce, sugar and pepper to taste in saucepan; mix well. Simmer for 20 minutes. Mix remaining ingredients in bowl. Shape into meatballs. Brown in a small amount of oil in skillet; drain. Add meatballs to beer sauce. Simmer for 10 minutes.

Alene G. Grimes, Fairmont Grange, Oregon

KJOD KAKER (NORWAY) Meatballs

Yields: 6 to 8 servings	Pan Size: 10 inch
1 lb. ground beef	⅛ tsp. each nutmeg, allspice
¼ lb. ground pork	and ginger
1 egg, lightly beaten	Salt and pepper to taste
½ c. milk, scalded	Butter
1 tbsp. cornstarch	1 tbsp. (or more) flour
1 med. onion, minced	

Combine ground beef, ground pork, egg, milk and cornstarch in bowl; mix well. Add onion and seasonings; beat until well mixed. Shape into small balls. Brown in a small amount of butter in skillet. Add a small amount of water. Simmer until cooked through. Remove meatballs with slotted spoon. Add additional butter and flour to pan drippings. Cook until flour is browned, stirring constantly. Stir in enough water for medium gravy. Cook until thickened, stirring constantly. Return meatballs to gravy. Heat to serving temperature.

Clara Barsten, West Wenatchee Grange, Washington

MEATBALLS MACEDOINE (ITALY)

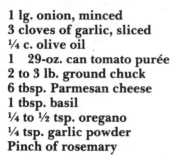

Yields: 8 to 12 servings   Pan Size: 8 quart

1 lg. onion, minced	1 tbsp. onion flakes
3 cloves of garlic, sliced	2 tbsp. salt
¼ c. olive oil	6 slices Italian bread
1 29-oz. can tomato purée	¼ c. olive oil
2 to 3 lb. ground chuck	1 35-oz. can whole tomatoes
6 tbsp. Parmesan cheese	2 lg. onions, sliced
1 tbsp. basil	2 lb. green peppers, sliced
¼ to ½ tsp. oregano	1 lb. mushrooms, sliced
¼ tsp. garlic powder	Butter
Pinch of rosemary	

Sauté 1 onion and 1 clove of garlic in ¼ cup olive oil in saucepan. Add tomato purée and *2 to 3 cups water*; mix well. Simmer for 1 to 2 hours, stirring frequently. Combine crumbled ground chuck, Parmesan cheese, basil, oregano, garlic powder, rosemary, onion flakes and salt in bowl; mix well. Add enough water to make of desired consistency. Soak bread in water. Squeeze out excess water and mash. Add to ground chuck mixture; mix well. Shape into balls. Brown in ¼ cup olive oil in skillet. Remove with slotted spoon. Drain excess pan drippings. Add tomatoes to skillet. Cook for 20 to 30 minutes, mashing with fork. Add tomatoes and meatballs to simmered sauce. Simmer for 30 minutes longer. Cook 2 onions and green peppers in covered skillet until wilted. Sauté mushrooms in butter in skillet for 5 to 6 minutes. Cook, covered, for 2 minutes longer. Add onions, green peppers, and sautéed mushrooms to sauce. Simmer for 45 minutes. Serve on crusty Italian bread.

John Lombardi, Friend of Pittsfield Grange, Massachusetts

MEATBALL SANDWICHES

Yields: 6 servings

1½ lb. ground beef	2 c. stewed tomatoes
½ c. soft bread crumbs	2 tbsp. brown sugar
¼ c. raisins	6 lg. rolls
¼ c. golden raisins	3 tbsp. butter, softened
1 egg, beaten	3 tbsp. German mustard
Salt and pepper to taste	

Mix first 5 ingredients and seasonings in bowl. Shape into 6 meatballs; place in casserole. Add tomatoes and brown sugar. Bake for 45 minutes. Split rolls; scoop out slightly. Spread with butter and mustard. Place meatball in each; spoon sauce over top.

ORIENTAL MEATBALLS

Yields: 6 servings	Pan Size: electric skillet

1½ lb. ground beef	¼ c. packed brown sugar
1½ c. soft bread crumbs	½ tsp. ginger
2 tbsp. chopped onion	1 tbsp. cornstarch
1 egg, beaten	¼ tsp. salt
⅓ c. milk	¼ c. vinegar
¼ tsp. dry mustard	1 tbsp. soy sauce
1½ tsp. salt	1 lg. tomato, cut into 8
⅛ tsp. pepper	wedges
2 tbsp. shortening	1 med. green pepper, cut
1 13-oz. can pineapple chunks	into strips

Combine ground beef, bread crumbs, onion, egg, milk, dry mustard, 1½ teaspoons salt and pepper in bowl; mix well. Shape into 18 meatballs. Brown in shortening in electric skillet. Pour off drippings. Drain pineapple, reserving ½ cup juice. Mix brown sugar, ginger, cornstarch and ¼ teaspoon salt in saucepan. Stir in reserved pineapple juice, vinegar and soy sauce. Cook until thickened, stirring constantly. Pour over meatballs. Cook for 5 minutes. Add tomato wedges, green pepper and pineapple. Cook until heated through.

Mrs. Raymond Hertel, Rock Creek Grange, Illinois

MEAT LOAF ROLL

Yields: 10 to 12 servings	Pan Size: 10 x 15 inch	Preheat: 325°

2 lb. ground beef	½ stick margarine
1 c. cracker crumbs	10 to 12 slices bread, cubed
½ c. milk	1 tbsp. chopped onion
2 eggs, slightly beaten	½ tsp. salt
2 tsp. salt	Dash of pepper
¼ tsp. pepper	½ tsp. poultry seasoning
1 tsp. prepared mustard	½ can Cheddar cheese soup
1 tbsp. catsup	¼ c. milk
1 c. chopped celery	3 oz. cheese, shredded

Combine ground beef and next 7 ingredients in bowl; mix well but do not overmix. Cook celery in water to cover in saucepan until tender. Cool partially; add margarine. Combine with bread cubes, onion, ½ teaspoon salt, dash of pepper and poultry seasoning in bowl; toss lightly. Pat ground beef mixture into 12x15-inch rectangle on heavy foil. Spread with bread mixture. Roll as for jelly roll from short side; seal ends. Wrap in foil; place in baking pan. Bake for 2 hours. Turn back foil. Bake for 30 minutes longer or until brown. Remove to serving plate. Heat soup, milk and cheese in saucepan over low heat, stirring frequently. Serve with meat roll.
Note: Roll may be frozen before baking. Allow extra time for baking.

Mrs. Elmer W. Franks, Valley College Grange, Ohio

FAMILY MEAT LOAF

Yields: 6 to 8 servings	Pan Size: 10 inch	Preheat: 350°

1½ lb. ground beef	½ tsp. each dry mustard,
1 c. dry bread crumbs	celery salt
1¼ c. milk	¼ tsp. each sage, pepper
¼ c. minced onion	1 tsp. salt
1 egg	⅛ tsp. garlic powder
1 tbsp. Worcestershire sauce	1 8-oz. can tomato sauce

Combine all ingredients except tomato sauce in bowl; mix well. Shape into loaf in shallow ungreased baking pan. Bake for 40 minutes. Pour tomato sauce over top. Bake for 20 minutes longer.
Note: May substitute ground venison or meat loaf mixture for ground beef.

Bonnie L. Brown, Shavers Creek Grange, Pennsylvania

MEAT LOAF SUPREME

Yields: 8 servings	Pan Size: 9 x 13 inch	Preheat: 350°

1½ lb. lean ground beef	½ tsp. oregano
½ lb. lean pork sausage	¼ tsp. salt
2 eggs, beaten	4 slices ham
¾ c. bread crumbs	1½ c. shredded mozzarella
½ c. tomato juice	cheese
2 tbsp. minced parsley	

Combine ground beef, pork sausage, eggs, bread crumbs, tomato juice, parsley and seasonings in bowl; mix well. Pat into 10 x 12-inch rectangle on waxed paper. Arrange ham over beef mixture to within 1 inch of edges. Sprinkle with cheese. Roll from short side as for jelly roll; seal edges. Place seam side down in baking dish. Bake for 1¼ hours or until cooked through.

Marie Thelen
Michigan Director of Women's Activities

POLPETTONE CON PATATE (ITALY)
Meat Loaf with Potato Filling

Yields: 6 servings	Pan Size: 10 inch	Preheat: 350°

1 c. bread crumbs	Salt and pepper to taste
1 lb. chopped lean beef	4 tbsp. olive oil
2 tsp. chopped parsley	2 c. mashed cooked potatoes
½ c. Parmesan cheese	1 tsp. chopped parsley
2 eggs, beaten	8 oz. mozzarella cheese,
1 sm. onion, minced	sliced

Reserve 2 tablespoons bread crumbs. Combine remaining bread crumbs with beef, 2 teaspoons parsley, Parmesan cheese, eggs, onion, salt, pepper and ½ *cup water* in bowl; mix well. Oil baking dish with 1 tablespoon olive oil. Sprinkle with reserved crumbs. Press half the beef mixture into prepared dish. Mix mashed potatoes with 1 teaspoon parsley in bowl. Layer potatoes and mozzarella cheese over beef layer. Top with remaining beef mixture; press edges to seal. Brush with 3 tablespoons olive oil. Bake for 30 minutes or until brown.

Mary E. Campbell, Sams Valley Grange, Ohio

SKILLET LASAGNA

Yields: 8 servings   Pan Size: electric skillet

2 lb. lean ground beef	5 c. medium uncooked noodles
¼ c. oil	1 tbsp. each basil, oregano
1 onion, chopped	and parsley flakes
1 green pepper, chopped	1 tsp. salt
4 8-oz. cans tomato sauce	8 oz. mozzarella cheese, shredded
1 lb. small curd cottage cheese	

Brown ground beef in oil in skillet, stirring until crumbly. Add onion and green pepper. Sauté for several minutes; drain. Spread evenly in skillet. Layer half the tomato sauce, cottage cheese, noodles, mixture of seasonings and remaining tomato sauce over ground beef mixture. Pour *1 cup water* over layers. Bring to a boil over high heat; reduce heat. Simmer for 30 to 35 minutes. Sprinkle with mozzarella cheese. Simmer, covered, for 10 minutes or until cheese melts.

Ella Wilbur, Lawsville Grange, Pennsylvania

MACARONI CASSEROLE

Yields: 8 servings   Pan Size: 9 x 13 inch   Preheat: 375°

8 oz. macaroni	2 cans tomato soup
4 tsp. salt	1 c. milk
6 slices bacon, chopped	1 tsp. oregano
½ c. chopped onion	1 tsp. salt
½ c. canned chopped	¼ tsp. pepper
mushrooms	1½ c. shredded Cheddar
1 lb. ground beef	cheese

Stir macaroni into *6 cups boiling water* and 4 teaspoons salt in saucepan. Boil rapidly for 2 minutes, stirring constantly. Remove from heat. Let stand, covered, for 5 minutes. Cook bacon in skillet until partially cooked. Add onion and mushrooms. Sauté for 5 minutes. Add ground beef. Cook until browned and crumbly, stirring frequently. Stir in soup, milk and seasonings. Rinse macaroni with warm water; drain well. Layer macaroni, sauce and cheese ½ at a time in greased baking dish. Bake for 20 minutes or until bubbly.

Shirley Zeek, Lincoln Grange, Oregon

NOODLE BOWL CASSEROLE

Yields: 8 servings	Pan Size: 3 quart	Preheat: 350°

1 lb. ground beef
1 can tomato sauce
1 can whole tomatoes
16 oz. cottage cheese
8 oz. sour cream

8 oz. cream cheese,
   softened
5 green onions, chopped
½ green pepper, chopped
1 pkg. medium noodles

Brown ground beef in skillet, stirring until crumbly; drain. Add tomato sauce and tomatoes. Simmer for 15 minutes. Combine cottage cheese, sour cream, cream cheese, onions and pepper in bowl; mix well. Cook noodles in boiling salted water in saucepan until tender; drain. Layer half the noodles, cheese mixture, remaining noodles and sauce in greased casserole. Chill for 24 hours. Bake for 30 minutes. Reduce temperature to 300 degrees. Bake for 1 to 1½ hours longer or until brown.

Helen Shoemaker
National Grange Assistant Youth Director

TALLARIATE (GREECE) Ground Beef-Noodle Casserole

Yields: 10 to 12 servings	Pan Size: 9x13 inch	Preheat: 325°

2 to 3 lb. ground beef
1 lg. onion, chopped
1 green pepper, chopped
3 cloves of garlic, crushed
1 can tomatoes
1½ c. tomato juice
1 c. drained whole kernel corn

1 c. sliced ripe olives
2 c. grated cheese
1 tbsp. sugar
1 to 2 tbsp. chili powder
Salt and pepper to taste
1 lb. egg noodles, cooked
2 c. grated cheese

Brown ground beef with onion, green pepper and garlic in skillet, stirring frequently; drain. Add tomatoes, tomato juice, corn, olives, 2 cups cheese, sugar, seasonings and noodles; mix well. Spoon into baking dish. Let stand in refrigerator for 3 hours to overnight. Pour *1 cup cold water* over top. Bake for 40 minutes. Sprinkle with 2 cups cheese. Bake for 5 minutes longer or until cheese melts.

Violet Morrow, Garden Home Grange, Colorado

CHEESY NOODLE CASSEROLE

Yields: 8 servings	Pan Size: 2½ quart	Preheat: 350°

8 oz. wide noodles
2 c. shredded Cheddar cheese
¾ c. cottage cheese
⅓ c. sour cream
1 tbsp. poppy seed
1 can tomato soup

1 tsp. salt
¼ tsp. pepper
1 lb. ground beef
⅓ c. chopped onion
⅓ c. chopped green pepper
3 tbsp. margarine

Cook noodles according to package directions; drain. Add 2 cups Cheddar cheese, cottage cheese, sour cream and poppy seed; mix well. Stir in soup, salt and pepper. Pour into greased casserole. Brown ground beef with onion and green pepper in margarine, stirring frequently; drain. Spoon over noodle mixture. Top with additional Cheddar cheese if desired. Bake for 35 to 45 minutes or until bubbly.

Kathy Netto, Zion-Oak Grange, Arkansas

RAVIOLI (ITALY)

Yields: 12 servings   Pan Size: 12 quart

½ lb. ground beef	½ c. Parmesan cheese
½ lb. pork sausage	Salt and pepper to taste
1 sm. onion, finely chopped	3 eggs, lightly beaten
½ clove of garlic, chopped	1 recipe Ravioli Dough
2 tsp. chopped parsley	1 recipe Ravioli Sauce
1 c. cooked chopped spinach	Parmesan cheese
½ c. bread crumbs	

Brown ground beef and sausage with onion, garlic and parsley in skillet, stirring frequently. Put through food grinder. Combine with spinach, bread crumbs, ½ cup Parmesan cheese, salt and pepper in bowl; mix well. Add enough egg to bind. Drop mixture by teaspoonfuls 2 inches apart onto 1 rectangle Ravioli Dough. Top with remaining dough. Press around mounds of filling to form squares. Cut squares apart with pastry cutter. Drop into 8 quarts boiling salted water in large saucepan. Cook for 15 to 20 minutes; drain. Place in serving bowl. Pour Ravioli Sauce over top. Sprinkle with additional Parmesan cheese.

Ravioli Dough

3 c. flour	2 eggs
¼ tsp. salt	2 tbsp. butter

Sift flour and salt into bowl; make well in center. Place eggs and butter in well; mix thoroughly. Add about *1 cup warm water* gradually to make stiff dough. Knead on floured surface until smooth. Let rest, covered, for 10 minutes. Divide into 2 portions. Roll each portion into thin rectangle on floured surface.

Ravioli Sauce

1½ lb. ground beef	2 sm. cans mushrooms
1 lg. onion, chopped	2 tsp. chopped parsley
3 cloves of garlic, minced	1 tsp. each rosemary, allspice
¼ c. olive oil	½ tsp. each celery salt, thyme
¼ c. tomato paste	3 tbsp. Worcestershire sauce
4 med. cans tomato sauce	

Brown ground beef with onion and garlic in olive oil in saucepan, stirring frequently. Stir in tomato paste blended with *1½ cups hot water*. Add remaining ingredients; mix well. Simmer for 2 to 3 hours, adding water as necessary for desired consistency.

Kathy Ransdell, Harstine Grange, Washington

BACHELOR'S SPAGHETTI

Yields: 4 servings	Pan Size: 4 quart

1 to 2 lb. ground beef	**Spaghetti**
Tomato sauce	**Salt and pepper to taste**

Brown ground beef in skillet, stirring until crumbly; drain. Stir in tomato sauce. Simmer to desired consistency. Cook spaghetti in boiling water in saucepan for 15 minutes; drain. Add sauce; mix well. Season to taste.

William J. Bennett
Secretary, U.S. Department of Education

ONE-STEP TAMALE PIE

Yields: 6 servings	Pan Size: 7x12 inch	Preheat: 350°

1 lb. ground beef	**1 12-oz. can whole kernel**
1 c. chopped onion	**corn, drained**
2 cloves of garlic, minced	**½ c. sliced ripe olives**
2 8-oz. cans tomato sauce	**Hot pepper sauce to taste**
1 c. milk	**1 tbsp. chili powder**
2 eggs, lightly beaten	**2 tsp. salt**
¾ c. yellow cornmeal	

Brown ground beef with onion and garlic in skillet, stirring frequently; drain. Add remaining ingredients; mix well. Pour into greased baking dish. Bake for 40 to 45 minutes or until knife inserted in center comes out clean. Cut into squares.

Pamela Donovan, Ada Grange, Oregon

SPAGHETTI PIE

Yields: 6 servings	Pan Size: 10 inch	Preheat: 350°

6 oz. spaghetti	**¼ c. chopped green pepper**
2 tbsp. butter	**1 8-oz. can tomatoes, chopped**
⅓ c. Parmesan cheese	**1 6-oz. can tomato paste**
2 eggs, well beaten	**1 tsp. sugar**
1 c. cottage cheese	**1 tsp. oregano**
1 lb. ground beef	**½ tsp. garlic salt**
½ c. chopped onion	**½ c. shredded mozzarella cheese**

Cook spaghetti according to package directions; drain. Add butter, Parmesan cheese and eggs; mix well. Shape as for crust in buttered pie plate. Spread with cottage cheese. Brown ground beef with onion and green pepper in skillet, stirring frequently; drain. Stir in tomatoes, tomato paste, sugar, oregano and garlic salt. Cook until heated through. Spoon into prepared pie plate. Bake for 20 minutes. Sprinkle with mozzarella cheese. Bake for 5 minutes longer or until cheese melts.

Tina A. Brigham, River Side Grange, Michigan

POOR MAN'S STEAK

Yields: 6 servings	Pan Size: Dutch oven	Preheat: 350°

3 lb. ground beef	**1 green pepper, chopped**
1 c. bread crumbs	**1 tbsp. salt**
1 c. milk	**Flour**
1 onion, chopped	**1 can mushroom soup**

Combine ground beef, bread crumbs, milk, onion, green pepper and salt in bowl; mix well. Press into 10x15-inch pan. Chill overnight. Cut into serving pieces. Coat well with flour. Brown on both sides in a small amount of oil in Dutch oven. Top with soup. Bake for 1 hour.

Grace M. Moody, Olathe Grange, Kansas

CABBAGE PATCH STEW AND DUMPLINGS

Yields: 6 to 8 servings	Pan Size: 4 quart

1 lb. ground beef	**1 15-oz. can kidney beans**
2 med. onions, chopped	**1½ tsp. chili powder**
1½ c. coarsely chopped	**1 tsp. salt**
cabbage	**¼ tsp. pepper**
1 med. zucchini, peeled,	**1 c. flour**
thinly sliced	**2 tsp. baking powder**
¼ c. chopped celery	**½ tsp. salt**
4 c. canned tomatoes	**½ c. milk**

Brown ground beef in saucepan, stirring until crumbly; drain. Add onions, cabbage, zucchini and celery. Sauté until lightly browned. Stir in tomatoes, kidney beans with liquid, chili powder, 1 teaspoon salt, pepper and *1 cup water*. Bring to a boil; reduce heat. Simmer for several minutes. Combine flour, baking powder and ½ teaspoon salt in bowl. Stir in milk. Drop by teaspoonfuls into stew. Cook, covered, for 12 minutes; do not remove cover during cooking.

Mrs. Irvin Bittner, White Deer Grange, Pennsylvania

KIDNEY BEAN STEW

Yields: 4 servings	Pan Size: 3 quart

4 or 5 slices bacon	**1 c. chopped carrots**
½ to 1 lb. ground beef	**1 can kidney beans**
1 sm. onion, chopped	**3 tbsp. catsup**
1 c. chopped potatoes	

Fry bacon in saucepan until crisp; drain on paper towel. Brown ground beef in bacon drippings, stirring until crumbly; drain. Add remaining ingredients, crumbled bacon and *1½ cups water*; mix well. Simmer for 1 hour, stirring occasionally.

Arden Fitch, Olivesburg Grange, Ohio

LUBEE (LEBANON) Green Beans and Lamb

Yields: 3 to 4 servings   Pan Size: 3 quart

1 to 1¼ lb. 1-in. lamb cubes	1 can tomato purée
1 lg. onion, sliced	1 sm. can tomato sauce
1 clove of garlic, chopped	2 lb. green beans, cut into halves
¼ c. butter	Allspice, cinnamon, salt and
1 can tomatoes, chopped	pepper to taste

Brown lamb with onion and garlic in butter in saucepan. Add tomatoes, tomato purée, tomato sauce and *1 cup water*; mix well. Cook until lamb is tender. Add beans and seasonings. Cook until beans are tender. Serve with rice.

Helen Massabny
Friend of the National Grange, Arlington Virginia

LAMB CHOPS AND YOGURT

Yields: 6 servings   Pan Size: grill

6 to 12 lamb chops, 1-in. thick	1 c. yogurt
2 tbsp. lemon juice	½ c. finely chopped onion
Paprika, pepper and salt to taste	1 clove of garlic, minced
1 tsp. garlic powder	

Sprinkle lamb chops with lemon juice. Let stand for several minutes. Sprinkle with paprika, pepper and salt. Place in glass dish. Pour mixture of yogurt, onion and garlic over lamb. Marinate for 8 hours or longer. Grill over hot coals.

Candace Burke, South Buffalo Grange, Pennsylvania

WARAK INIB MIHSHEE (SYRIA) Grape Leaf Rolls

Yields: 6 servings   Pan Size: 2 quart

50 fresh grape leaves	4 lamb bones
1 lb. lamb, finely chopped	1 tsp. salt
1 c. rice, rinsed	Juice of 2 lemons
Salt and pepper to taste	

Soak grape leaves in hot water to cover in bowl for 15 minutes. Combine lamb, rice and salt and pepper to taste in bowl; mix well. Drain grape leaves and pat dry; remove stems. Place 1 tablespoon lamb mixture in center of each leaf. Fold stem end over filling and roll leaf to enclose filling. Place bones in saucepan. Arrange rolls in rows over bones, alternating direction of rows in each layer. Sprinkle with 1 teaspoon salt. Place inverted plate on rolls. Fill pan with water to level of plate. Simmer, covered, for 25 minutes. Add lemon juice. Simmer, covered, for 10 minutes longer or until tender. *Note:* May substitute pickled grape leaves for fresh and omit soaking step.

Fannie Glazier, Guenoc Grange, California

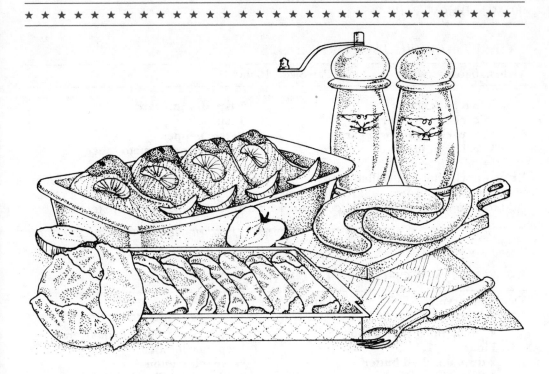

Pork

BARBECUED SPARERIBS

Yields: 6 to 8 servings	Pan Size: Dutch oven	Preheat: 350°

3 to 4 lb. spareribs	2 tbsp. lemon juice
1 onion, finely chopped	2 tbsp. Worcestershire sauce
½ c. chopped celery	3 tbsp. brown sugar
1 clove of garlic, minced	1 tsp. dry mustard
2 c. catsup	2 tsp. salt
¼ c. vinegar	½ tsp. pepper

Brown spareribs in Dutch oven. Combine onion, celery, garlic, catsup, vinegar, lemon juice, Worcestershire sauce, brown sugar, dry mustard and seasonings in bowl; mix well. Pour over spareribs. Bake for 1¼ hours or until spareribs are tender.

Ginny Mangel, Eureka Grange, Pennsylvania

SKILLET BARBECUED PORK CHOPS

Yields: 6 to 8 servings	Pan Size: 10 inch

6 to 8 pork chops	**1 tsp. dry mustard**
⅔ c. chopped celery	**1 tsp. salt**
¼ c. packed brown sugar	**¼ tsp. pepper**
¼ c. lemon juice	**4 8-oz. cans tomato sauce**

Brown pork chops in skillet over medium heat for 5 minutes on each side; drain. Sprinkle celery, brown sugar, lemon juice and seasonings evenly over pork chops. Add tomato sauce. Simmer, covered, for 1 hour or until pork chops are tender.

Kathleen L. Pritchett, Norwich Grange, Connecticut

BRAISED PORK CHOPS WITH GRAPEFRUIT

Yields: 4 servings	Pan Size: 12 inch

4 1-in. thick pork chops	**2 fresh pears, cut into quarters**
Flour	**1 tsp. marjoram**
2 tbsp. unsalted butter	**¼ tsp. cinnamon**
1 tbsp. oil	**Sections of 2 Florida grapefruit**
2 sm. onions, sliced into rings	

Coat pork chops with flour. Brown on both sides in butter and oil in skillet over medium heat. Remove pork chops. Sauté onion rings in pan drippings. Add pork chops, pears and *½ cup water*. Sprinkle with marjoram and cinnamon. Simmer for 1¼ hours or until chops are tender and sauce is thick. Add grapefruit sections. Simmer until heated through.

Photograph for this recipe on page 136.

PORK CHOPS AND CARROTS COUNTRY-STYLE

Yields: 4 to 8 servings	Pan Size: 9 x 13 inch	Preheat: 350°

8 med. carrots, cut into	**½ tsp. pepper**
** julienne strips**	**8 thin pork chops**
¼ c. flour	**2 tbsp. lard**
¼ tsp. thyme	**1 lg. onion, cut into 8 slices**
1½ tsp. salt	

Arrange carrots in baking dish. Combine flour, thyme, salt and pepper in bowl. Dip pork chops in flour mixture, coating well. Brown in lard in skillet. Place on carrots. Place 1 onion slice on each pork chop. Pour *⅓ cup water* into dish. Bake, covered with foil, for 40 to 50 minutes or until tender.

Blanche Rice, Hamburg Grange, New York

PORK CHOP-APPLE BAKE

Yields: 6 servings   Pan Size: 9 x 13 inch   Preheat: 325°

6 pork chops
¼ tsp. seasoned salt
⅛ tsp. marjoram
1 med. onion, sliced

3 to 4 apples, cut into halves
¼ c. packed brown sugar
1 c. sour cream

Brown pork chops on both sides in skillet. Sprinkle with seasoned salt and marjoram. Layer onion slices and pork chops in casserole. Arrange apples around pork chops. Sprinkle with brown sugar. Bring sour cream just to the simmering point in saucepan. Pour over chops. Bake, covered, for 1½ hours or until tender.

Lois G. Thorpe, Middlebury Grange, Vermont

PORK CHOPS SUPREME

Yields: 6 servings   Pan Size: 9 x 12 inch   Preheat: 325°

6 pork chops
6 thin slices lemon

2 c. packed brown sugar
1 c. catsup

Arrange pork chops in ungreased baking dish. Place 1 slice lemon on each chop. Top with brown sugar and catsup. Bake, covered, for 1 hour and 25 minutes. Bake, uncovered, for 15 minutes longer.

Ralph Daub, Henlopen Grange, Delaware

STROODLES

Yields: 6 servings   Pan Size: heavy 8 quart

6 pork chops
6 med. potatoes, peeled,
**   sliced**
3 c. flour

2 tsp. baking powder
½ tsp. salt
1 egg
Bacon drippings

Brown pork chops on both sides in skillet. Place pork chops, potatoes and water to cover in heavy saucepan. Combine remaining ingredients in bowl. Add enough water to make stiff dough. Roll and stretch thin on floured surface. Brush with bacon drippings. Roll as for jelly roll. Cut into 1½-inch slices. Arrange over pork chops and potatoes. Cook, covered, for 30 minutes or until pork chops and potatoes are tender and dumplings are steamed through.

June Urban, Rockwood Grange, Oregon

PORK CHOPS AND WILD RICE

Yields: 8 servings	Pan Size: 9 x 13 inch	Preheat: 350°

8 oz. wild rice	1 c. minced onion
8 1 to 1½-inch thick lean	2 cans cream of mushroom soup
pork chops	3 tbsp. Sherry or Sauterne
Salt and pepper to taste	

Wash rice in sieve under running water. Combine with *3 cups water* and 1½ teaspoons salt in saucepan. Cook for 15 minutes; drain. Place in baking dish. Sprinkle pork chops with salt and pepper. Brown on both sides in a small amount of oil in skillet. Arrange over rice. Sauté onion in pan drippings in skillet; drain drippings. Add soup, *1 cup water* and wine; mix well. Bring to a boil, stirring to deglaze skillet. Pour over pork chops. Bake, covered, for 1 to 1½ hours or until pork chops are tender.

Howard C. Richards, Secretary
Wisconsin Department of Agriculture, Trade and Consumer Protection

HONEYED PORK CHOPS

Yields: 6 servings	Pan Size: 10 inch

6 ¾-in. thick pork chops	2 tbsp. shortening
2 tbsp. flour	2 grapefruit, sectioned
2 tsp. salt	¼ tsp. nutmeg
⅛ tsp. pepper	1 tbsp. honey

Coat pork chops with mixture of flour, salt and pepper. Brown on both sides in shortening in skillet. Add *¼ cup water*. Simmer, tightly covered, for 45 minutes. Sprinkle with nutmeg; arrange grapefruit over top. Drizzle with honey. Simmer, tightly covered, for 15 minutes longer.

HAWAIIAN PORK CHOPS

Yields: 4 servings	Pan Size: 9 inch	Preheat: 250°

4 loin pork chops
Salt and pepper to taste
Flour

4 slices pineapple
4 pitted prunes
4 carrots

Season pork chops with salt and pepper; coat with flour. Arrange in baking pan. Place 1 slice pineapple and 1 prune on each pork chop. Place carrots between pork chops. Pour *⅓ cup water* into pan. Bake, covered, for 1½ hours. Remove pork chops to warm platter. Thicken pan juices with additional flour. Pour over pork chops.

Christine Kearne, Yucaipa Valley Grange, California

PORK CHOP-VEGETABLE CASSEROLE

Yields: 6 to 8 servings	Pan Size: 9 x 13 inch	Preheat: 350°

3 c. mixed chopped
   vegetables
2 c. uncooked rice

8 pork chops
3 bouillon cubes
1 med. onion, sliced

Combine chopped vegetables and rice in baking dish; mix well. Brown pork chops on both sides in skillet. Arrange over vegetables. Add bouillon cubes and *4 cups water* to skillet, stirring to dissolve bouillon and deglaze skillet. Pour over casserole. Arrange onion slices over top. Bake, covered, for 1 hour.

Roberta Gibbs, Kamiah Grange, Idaho

CREOLE PORK STEAKS

Yields: 4 to 6 servings	Pan Size: 10 inch

4 to 6 pork steaks
1 stalk celery, sliced
2 c. tomato sauce
1 c. uncooked brown rice

2 tbsp. brown sugar
¼ to ½ tsp. basil
1 tsp. salt

Trim steaks. Grease skillet with trimmings. Brown steak on both sides over medium heat. Add celery. Sauté lightly; drain. Add remaining ingredients and *1½ cups water*; mix well. Simmer, covered, for 40 minutes or until tender.

E. Mae Thompson, Powell Butte Grange, Oregon

PORK TENDERLOIN FLORENTINE

Yields: 6 servings	Pan Size: 9 x 13 inch	Preheat: 325°

2 ¾-lb. pork tenderloins
1 clove of garlic, crushed
8 oz. cream cheese, softened
10 oz. frozen spinach, thawed,
    drained

3 med. carrots, cut into
    julienne strips, cooked
1 chicken bouillon cube
1 tbsp. flour
1 tsp. Dijon-style mustard

Place tenderloins side by side with thick portions at opposite ends. Slice almost through each tenderloin lengthwise. Arrange cut sides up, overlapping long sides slightly to form rectangle. Pound to even thickness with meat mallet. Spread with garlic,cream cheese and spinach. Arrange carrots lengthwise on spinach. Roll up from wide side; tie with string at 2-inch intervals. Place in baking pan. Dissolve bouillon cube in *1 cup hot water*. Pour into pan. Bake for 1 hour or until tender. Blend flour and *¼ cup water* with pan juices in saucepan. Cook until thickened, stirring constantly. Stir in mustard. Serve with sliced tenderloin.

Julie Heberer, Turkey Hill Grange, Illinois

ROAST PORK WITH ORANGE GLAZE

Yields: 8 servings	Pan Size: roaster	Preheat: 325°

1 4 to 5-lb. double-loin
    pork roast, boned, rolled, tied
1 clove of garlic

1 c. Smucker's sweet orange
    marmalade
1 1-in. piece gingerroot

Place roast fat side up on rack in roaster. Bake for 2 hours. Combine garlic, marmalade, and gingerroot in saucepan. Cook over low heat until bubbly. Brush on roast. Bake to 170 degrees on meat thermometer, brushing several times with marmalade mixture.

Photograph for this recipe on page 101.

TOUCHE (FRANCE) Pork Pie

Yields: 6 servings	Pan Size: 10 inch	Preheat: 350°

1 3-lb. pork roast
1 can green peas, drained
6 med. potatoes, chopped
3 med. onions, chopped

⅓ c. milk
3 tbsp. butter
½ tsp. salt
1 recipe 2-crust pie pastry

Cook roast in water to cover in saucepan until tender. Drain and chop. Mix with peas in bowl. Cook potatoes and onions in water to cover in saucepan until tender; drain. Mash with milk, butter and salt. Layer half the potato mixture, pork mixture and remaining potatoes in pastry-lined pie plate. Top with remaining pastry; seal edge and cut vents. Bake for 1 hour or until brown.

Bonita M. Carter, Friend of Holden Grange, Maine

TOURTIERE (FRANCE) Meat Pie

Yields: 6 servings	Pan Size: 10 inch	Preheat: 450°

2 lb. lean pork	¼ tsp. each nutmeg, allspice
1 lb. round steak	¼ tsp. pepper
½ c. finely chopped onion	2½ c. bread crumbs
1 tbsp. salt	1 recipe 2-crust pie pastry

Grind pork and steak together. Combine with onion, seasonings and *1 cup water* in saucepan. Cook over medium heat for 30 minutes, stirring frequently; remove from heat. Stir in crumbs. Cool. Pour into pastry-lined plate. Top with remaining pastry, sealing edge and cutting vents. Bake for 30 minutes or until brown.

Irene V. Lannon, Anthony Grange, Rhode Island

MEATBALLS (DENMARK)

Yields: 6 servings	Pan Size: 10 inch

1½ lb. ground pork	2 tsp. salt
1 egg	2 tbsp. butter
½ c. seasoned dry bread crumbs	2 tbsp. flour
1 tbsp. grated onion	¼ tsp. pepper
2 tsp. grated lemon rind	1 c. milk

Combine first 5 ingredients and 1 teaspoon salt in bowl; mix well. Shape into 1-inch balls. Brown several at a time in butter in skillet. Drain, reserving 2 tablespoons drippings. Blend flour, pepper and 1 teaspoon salt into drippings. Stir in milk and *1 cup water* gradually. Cook until thickened, stirring constantly. Add meatballs. Simmer until heated through.

Ray Moreau, Eastern Pomona Grange, New Hampshire

SAUERKRAUT-PORK ROLL

Yields: 5 servings	Pan Size: 9 x 13 inch	Preheat: 350°

1 lb. ground fresh pork	Dash of pepper
½ c. dry bread crumbs	1 16-oz. can sauerkraut, drained
1 egg, lightly beaten	¼ c. chopped onion
½ tsp. Worcestershire sauce	5 slices bacon
1 tsp. salt	

Combine ground pork, bread crumbs, egg, Worcestershire sauce, salt and pepper in bowl; mix well. Pat into 7x10-inch rectangle on waxed paper. Mix sauerkraut and onion in bowl. Spread over pork mixture. Roll as for jelly roll. Place in baking dish. Arrange bacon over top. Bake for 1 hour or until cooked through.

Bunny Kuhl, Rocksprings Grange, Ohio

CABBAGE ROLLS

Yields: 10 servings   Pan Size: 12 inch

1 head cabbage
3 to 4 lb. ground pork
1 onion, chopped
2 cloves of garlic, crushed
1 egg
1 c. cooked barley
Salt and pepper to taste

1 onion, sliced
4 8-oz. cans tomato sauce
¼ to ½ c. milk
Sugar to taste
Flour
Milk

Steam cabbage for 45 minutes. Separate leaves carefully. Combine pork, chopped onion, garlic, egg, barley, salt and pepper in bowl; mix well. Spoon onto cabbage leaves; roll to enclose filling. Brown rolls lightly in a small amount of oil in skillet. Arrange onion rings over rolls. Pour tomato sauce over top. Simmer, covered, for 45 minutes. Remove rolls to warm serving plate. Add ¼ to ½ cup milk to skillet, stirring to deglaze. Stir in sugar and mixture of enough flour and milk to thicken to desired consistency. Cook until thickened, stirring constantly. Spoon over cabbage rolls. Serve with boiled potatoes.

Irene Homolka
Oregon Director of Women's Activities

ORIENTAL SWEET AND SOUR PORK

Yields: 3 to 4 servings   Pan Size: large skillet

½ c. flour
2 eggs, lightly beaten
½ tsp. salt
1 lb. lean pork, cut into
   bite-sized pieces
Oil for deep frying
1 green pepper, coarsely chopped

1 c. pineapple chunks
1 lg. carrot, sliced
1 clove of garlic, minced
2 tbsp. vinegar
1½ tbsp. sugar
1 tbsp. honey
1 tbsp. cornstarch

Mix flour, eggs and salt in bowl until smooth. Dip pork in batter, coating well. Deep-fry in oil for 10 minutes; drain on paper towel. Combine with green pepper, pineapple, carrot, garlic and *½ cup water* in skillet. Cook, covered, for 10 minutes. Blend vinegar, sugar, honey, cornstarch and *½ cup water* in bowl. Stir into pork mixture. Cook for 5 minutes or until thickened. Simmer until pork is tender.

Doris Mills, California Grange, Arkansas

SPECIAL SAUSAGE TOPPING

Yields: 6 servings   Pan Size: 9 inch

1 lb. sweet Italian sausages,
  peeled, sliced
1 red pepper, sliced
1 green pepper, sliced
1 onion, chopped

1 tbsp. curry powder
2 tbsp Dijon justard
1½ c. dry white wine
8 oz. mushrooms, sliced
1 c. sour cream

Brown sausages in skillet. Add peppers and onion. Cook for 5 minutes. Stir in curry powder and mustard. Cook for 5 minutes longer. Add wine. Cook until slightly thickened, stirring frequently. Stir in mushrooms and sour cream. Heat to serving temperature. Serve over hot baked potatoes.

Photograph for this recipe on page 102.

ITALIAN SAUSAGE SKILLET

Yields: 4 to 6 servings   Pan Size: 12 inch

6 Italian sausages
2 tbsp. oil
1 med. onion, chopped
1 med. green pepper, chopped
12 oz. wide noodles, cooked
½ c. milk

2 c. shredded Monterey
  Jack cheese
½ c. Parmesan cheese
Salt and pepper to taste
Fresh parsley, chopped

Slice sausages ½-inch thick. Sauté in oil in skillet until partially cooked. Add onion and green pepper. Sauté until sausage is cooked through; drain. Add noodles, milk and cheeses. Cook until cheeses melt, stirring constantly. Add seasonings and parsley.

Jackie Allen, Stonyford Grange, California

ITALIAN SAUSAGE AND VEGETABLES WITH PASTA

Yields: 6 servings   Pan Size: 12 inch

1 lb. Italian link sausage
1 c. sliced onion
½ c. sliced green pepper
1 clove of garlic, minced
3 tbsp. oil
4 c. sliced small zucchini
1 c. sliced carrots, cooked

1   4-oz. can mushrooms, drained
2 c. canned tomatoes
1   8-oz. can tomato sauce
1 bay leaf
1½ c. pasta, cooked
1 c. shredded mozzarella cheese

Simmer sausage in water in saucepan for 10 minutes; drain. Cut into 1-inch slices. Sauté onion, green pepper and garlic in oil in skillet. Add zucchini. Simmer for 5 minutes. Add next 6 ingredients; mix well. Simmer for 15 minutes; remove bay leaf. Pour sauce over pasta in serving dish. Top with mozzarella cheese.

Carole Zimmerman, Ackley Grange, Pennsylvania

SAUSAGE JAMBALAYA

Yields: 12 servings	Pan Size: 6 quart

1 lb. hard Italian sausage, thinly sliced	2 c. canned tomatoes
1½ c. chopped onions	2 bay leaves, crumbled
½ c. chopped celery	½ tsp. thyme
½ c. chopped green pepper	2 tsp. salt
8 scallions, chopped	2 c. chopped cooked ham
2 cloves of garlic, crushed	2 tbsp. chopped parsley
	3 c. uncooked rice

Sauté sausage, onions, celery, green pepper, scallions and garlic lightly in shortening in saucepan. Add tomatoes and seasonings; mix well. Simmer for 10 to 15 minutes. Add ham, parsley, rice and *4 cups water*. Simmer, covered, for 30 minutes or until liquid is absorbed.

Liz Lidstrom, Friend of Lookout Mt. Grange, Oregon

RED CABBAGE AND SAUSAGE

Yields: 6 servings	Pan Size: large skillet

3 sm. tart apples, peeled, sliced	⅛ tsp. cloves
2 qt. sliced red cabbage	1 tsp. salt
¼ c. lemon juice	1 sm. tart apple, sliced
3 tbsp. brown sugar	6 smoked Polish sausages

Combine 3 apples, cabbage, lemon juice, brown sugar, cloves, salt and *1 cup water* in large skillet. Simmer, covered, for 30 minutes. Add 1 apple and raisins; mix well. Arrange sausage over top. Simmer, covered, for 15 minutes longer.

Eleanor Moe, Wintersburg Grange, California

DO-AHEAD SAUSAGE FONDUE

Yields: 8 servings	Pan Size: 8x12 inch	Preheat: 300°

8 slices bread, cubed	4 eggs
2 c. shredded sharp American cheese	2¼ c. milk
1½ lb. link sausage, cut into thirds	¾ tsp. dry mustard
	1 can cream of mushroom soup
	½ c. milk

Spread bread cubes in buttered baking dish. Sprinkle with cheese. Brown sausage in skillet; drain on paper towel. Arrange on cheese. Beat eggs, 2¼ cups milk and dry mustard in bowl. Pour over layers. Chill overnight. Blend soup and ½ cup milk in bowl. Pour over casserole. Bake for 1½ hours or until set.

Lois M. Mecklenburg, Bluestem Grange, Washington

SAUSAGE, CHEESE AND EGG CASSEROLE

Yields: 4 servings	Pan Size: 7x11 inch	Preheat: 350°

1 lb. bulk sausage	1 tsp. dry mustard
6 eggs	2 slices bread, crumbled
2 c. milk	1 c. grated cheese
1 tsp. salt	1 sm. onion, chopped

Brown sausage in skillet, stirring until crumbly; drain. Beat eggs with milk, salt and dry mustard in bowl. Add sausage, bread crumbs, cheese and onion; mix well. Pour into greased baking dish. Refrigerate for several hours to overnight. Bake for 45 minutes. Cut into squares. Serve hot.

Tom Smith, River Side Grange, Michigan

SCRAPPLE (GERMANY)

Yields: 6 servings	Pan Size: loaf/skillet

1 lb. pork sausage	1 or 2 eggs, beaten
4 c. chicken broth	Flour
1½ c. yellow cornmeal	Oil
Salt to taste	

Brown sausage in skillet, stirring until crumbly; drain. Bring chicken broth to a boil in saucepan. Stir in cornmeal and salt. Cook for several minutes, stirring constantly. Add sausage. Cook for 20 minutes or until of desired consistency, stirring frequently. Pour into loaf pan. Chill in refrigerator. Invert onto plate. Cut into slices. Dip each slice into egg; coat with flour. Fry in a small amount of oil in skillet until brown on both sides.

Cecelia Willette, Swaukteanaway Grange, Washington

SPINACH-RICE-SAUSAGE CASSEROLE

Yields: 4 servings	Pan Size: 1½ quart	Preheat: 350°

2 c. chopped drained spinach	1 c. minced celery
1 c. cooked rice	1 egg
8 oz. bulk pork sausage	Salt and pepper to taste
1 lg. onion, minced	1 c. grated cheese

Combine spinach, rice, sausage, onion, celery, egg and seasonings in bowl; mix well. Place in casserole. Bake for 20 minutes. Sprinkle with cheese. Bake until golden.

Edith E. Berry, Upper Sound Grange, Washington

SAUSAGE-PEANUT PILAF

Yields: 4 servings	Pan Size: 1 quart	Preheat: 350°

1 lb. bulk pork sausage	1 can mushroom soup
1 c. chopped celery	¼ c. chopped green pepper
½ c. chopped onion	½ c. chopped salted peanuts
1 c. cooked rice	

Brown sausage in skillet, stirring until crumbly. Add celery and onion. Sauté for 3 minutes; drain. Add rice, soup and green pepper; mix well. Pour into casserole. Sprinkle with peanuts. Bake for 30 minutes.

Beatrice K. Mottram, Passadumkeag Grange, Maine

VIOLA'S HAM LOAVES

Yields: 6 to 8 servings	Pan Size: 9 x 9 inch	Preheat: 350°

1 lb. smoked ham	2 eggs
2 lb. pork sausage	1 c. milk
1 c. cracker crumbs	1 can tomato soup

Put ham and sausage through food grinder together. Combine with cracker crumbs, eggs and milk in bowl; mix well. Shape into 2 loaves. Place in baking dish. Blend soup with *½ soup can water*. Pour over loaves. Bake for 1½ hours.

Viola McConkey, Millbrook Grange, Illinois

HAM LOAVES

Yields: 10 servings	Pan Size: 9 x 13 inch	Preheat: 350°

1½ lb. ground ham	½ tsp. salt
1 lb. ground chuck	⅛ tsp. pepper
2 eggs	¾ c. packed brown sugar
1 c. milk	1 tsp. dry mustard
1 c. cracker crumbs	¼ c. vinegar

Combine ground ham, ground chuck, eggs, milk, cracker crumbs, salt and pepper in bowl; mix well. Shape into 10 individual loaves. Place on rack in baking pan. Add enough water to cover bottom of pan. Bake for 30 minutes. Combine brown sugar, dry mustard and vinegar in small bowl; mix well. Pour over loaves. Bake for 1 hour longer, basting every 20 minutes and adding water to sauce if necessary.

Marjorie Gongaware, Harrold Grange, Pennsylvania

Recipes for this photograph on pages 94, 151, 289.

GLAZED HAM BALLS

Yields: 6 servings	Pan Size: 9 x 12 inch	Preheat: 350°

1 lb. ground ham	½ c. milk
8 oz. ground fresh pork	1 9-oz. can crushed pineapple
¾ c. soft bread crumbs	⅓ c. packed brown sugar
2 tbsp. chopped onion	1 tsp. vinegar
2 eggs, beaten	2 to 3 tbsp. mustard

Combine ground ham, ground pork, bread crumbs, onion, eggs and milk in bowl; mix well. Shape into 1½-inch balls. Place in baking dish. Combine remaining ingredients in bowl; mix well. Pour over ham balls. Bake for 45 minutes.

Tammy Marstall, Carbondale Grange, Kansas

HAM AND GREEN BEAN CASSEROLE

Yields: 6 servings	Pan Size: 2 quart	Preheat: 350°

2 c. chopped potatoes	½ c. milk
1 c. sliced carrots	1½ c. thinly sliced ham
2 c. cut green beans	½ c. bread crumbs
⅓ c. finely chopped onion	1 to 2 tbsp. butter
1 can cream of mushroom soup	

Cook vegetables in a small amount of water in saucepan until tender-crisp; drain. Heat soup and milk to the boiling point in saucepan. Add vegetables. Alternate layers of ham and vegetables in casserole. Sprinkle with bread crumbs; dot with butter. Bake for 30 minutes.

Mrs. Frank Dieffenbach, Marion Grange, Pennsylvania

HAM MOUSSE

Yields: 4 to 6 servings	Pan Size: 4 cup mold

2 c. chopped boiled ham	1 tsp. gelatin
Pinch of dry mustard	1 c. concentrated meat stock
Pinch of cayenne pepper	½ c. whipping cream, whipped

Put ham through meat grinder twice. Combine with dry mustard and cayenne pepper. Soften gelatin in stock in saucepan. Bring to a boil, stirring until gelatin dissolves. Mix with ham. Chill until partially set. Fold in stiffly whipped cream. Spoon into mold. Chill until firm. Unmold onto serving plate.
Note: This recipe is from a 1908 cookbook. Chicken, veal, lamb, salmon or lobster may be substituted for ham.

Dee Haynes Goldner, Wallingford Grange, Connecticut

Recipes for this photograph on pages 97, 111, 156.

COUNTRY OVERNIGHT SOUFFLÉ

Yields: 8 to 12 servings   Pan Size: 9 x 13 inch   Preheat: 350°

16 slices bread, crusts trimmed	1 c. chopped tomato
Butter, softened	6 eggs
10 slices Cheddar cheese	3 c. milk
10 thin slices cooked ham	½ tsp. Worcestershire sauce
1½ c. chopped mushrooms	½ tsp. finely chopped chives
1 lg. onion, minced	½ tsp. dry mustard
1 c. chopped black olives	1 c. dry bread crumbs
1 c. chopped green pepper	½ c. melted butter

Spread 1 side of bread slices with butter. Place 8 slices buttered side down in greased baking dish. Layer cheese, ham, mushrooms, onion, olives, green pepper and tomato over bread. Place remaining bread slices buttered side up on top. Beat eggs, milk, Worcestershire sauce, chives and dry mustard with wire whisk in bowl. Pour over layers. Chill, covered, overnight. Mix bread crumbs with melted butter in bowl. Sprinkle over soufflé. Bake for 1 hour.

Lois G. Crum, Cedar Hill Grange, New Mexico

HAM AND CHEESE DELIGHT

Yields: 8 servings   Pan Size: 8 x 8 inch   Preheat: 325°

8 slices bread, crusts trimmed	2 c. grated cheese
Butter, softened	3 eggs, slightly beaten
2 c. ground cooked ham	2 c. milk
2 tbsp. prepared mustard	Salt and pepper to taste

Spread bread with butter; cut into halves diagonally. Layer bread, mixture of ham and mustard and cheese ½ at a time in baking pan. Beat eggs with milk and seasonings. Pour over layers. Chill for 1 hour to overnight. Bake until set.

Laura Ingram, Quinault Grange, Washington

BAKED SANDWICH

Yields: 6 servings   Pan Size: 12 x 18 inch   Preheat: 300°

12 slices bread, crusts trimmed	Butter, softened
8 oz. Swiss cheese, sliced	4 eggs
Mustard	3 c. milk
8 oz. sliced ham	½ tsp. salt

Place 6 slices bread in buttered baking dish. Layer cheese over bread. Brush with mustard. Arrange ham over cheese. Butter 1 side of remaining bread slices. Place buttered side up over ham. Beat eggs, milk and salt in bowl until smooth. Pour over sandwiches. Chill in refrigerator overnight. Bake for 1 hour.

Nancy McKenzie, Friend of Rockwell Grange, Oregon

HAM AND NOODLES

Yields: 8 servings	Pan Size: 9 x 13 inch	Preheat: 350°

16 oz. small egg noodles	1 tsp. salt
½ c. chopped onion	⅛ tsp. pepper
½ c. chopped green pepper	1 c. sour cream
½ c. chopped celery	1 tsp. lemon juice
¼ c. butter	1 c. bread crumbs
2 lb. ham, chopped	¼ c. melted butter
1 tsp. parsley flakes	

Cook noodles in boiling salted water in saucepan; drain. Sauté onion, green pepper and celery in ¼ cup butter in saucepan. Add noodles, ham, parsley flakes, salt and pepper; mix well. Stir in sour cream and lemon juice. Spoon into buttered baking dish. Top with mixture of bread crumbs and melted butter. Bake for 30 minutes.

Beulah I. Pearson
Kansas Director of Women's Activities

HAM AND ORANGE CURRIED RICE FOR-A-CROWD

Yields: 50 servings	Pan Size: Dutch oven	Preheat: 375°

2 lg. green peppers, chopped	10 lb. chopped cooked ham
1 lg. onion, chopped	7 c. uncooked rice
1½ c. butter	½ c. grated orange rind
1½ c. packed brown sugar	6 c. orange juice
1 tbsp. curry powder	

Sauté green peppers and onion in butter in Dutch oven. Add brown sugar, curry powder and ham; mix well. Bake for 20 minutes. Cook rice according to package directions just until tender-firm. Add rice, orange rind and orange juice to ham mixture; mix well. Bake, covered, for 30 minutes. Bake, uncovered, for 30 minutes.

Mitzi Furst, Hopewell Grange, Illinois

SKILLET GERMAN PIZZA

Yields: 4 servings	Pan Size: 10 inch

3 med. potatoes, peeled, grated	⅛ tsp. pepper
½ c. chopped onion	3 eggs, slightly beaten
½ c. chopped green pepper	½ c. shredded sharp
2 c. julienne ham	Cheddar cheese
¼ tsp. salt	

Mix first 6 ingredients in bowl. Heat oil in skillet. Pat potato mixture into skillet. Cook, covered, over low heat until tender. Pour eggs over potato mixture. Cook for 10 minutes or until eggs are set. Top with cheese. Cook for 2 minutes.

Florence E. Williamson, Bottle Run Grange, Pennsylvania

HAM CASSEROLE

Yields: 12 servings   Pan Size: 9 x 13 inch   Preheat: 350°

1½ lb. cooked ham, chopped	2 c. medium white sauce
4 c. chopped potatoes, cooked	½ c. grated sharp cheese
4 onions, chopped, cooked	Buttered bread crumbs
16 oz. frozen peas, cooked	

Layer ham, potatoes, onions, peas, white sauce, cheese and bread crumbs in greased baking dish. Bake for 45 minutes.

Madaline L. Hanman, Shavers Creek Grange, Pennsylvania

ART'S MCKENZIE RIVER BOILED BEANS

Yields: 6 servings   Pan Size: 6 quart

2 c. dried pinto beans	Salt to taste
2 slices ¼-in. thick ham, chopped	¼ tsp. pepper
3 tbsp. catsup	3 lg. onions, cut into quarters

Soak beans in water to cover in saucepan; drain. Bring *1 quart water* to a boil in saucepan. Add beans, ham, catsup, salt and pepper. Bring to a boil; reduce heat. Simmer for 1 hour, stirring frequently. Add water if necessary to cover beans. Add onions. Cook for 1 hour longer or until tender but not mushy.
Note: May substitute other dried beans if desired.

Arthur V. Olson, Walterville Grange, Oregon

FRIED SALT PORK AND MILK GRAVY

Yields: 4 servings   Pan Size: 10 inch

1 lb. salt pork, thinly sliced	1 qt. milk
Flour	

Place salt pork in skillet with a small amount of cold water. Bring to a boil. Drain on paper towel. Coat pork well with flour; shake to remove excess. Brown in skillet until crisp. Remove to serving plate. Stir enough flour into pan drippings to make gravy of desired consistency. Add milk. Cook until thickened. Serve with pork.

Mrs. Marion F. Ryan, Malone Grange, New York

Seafood

FISHERMAN'S FISH CASSEROLE (RUSSIA)

Yields: 10 to 12 servings	Pan Size: 2 quart	Preheat: 350°

1 lb. fish fillets
¼ c. butter, melted
¼ c. flour
2 c. milk
1 tsp. salt
¼ tsp. white pepper

¾ tsp. nutmeg
1 c. fine bread crumbs
¼ c. butter, melted
1 c. rice, cooked
2 tbsp. chopped onion
¼ tsp. nutmeg

Poach fish in water to cover in saucepan over low heat. Drain and flake. Blend ¼ cup butter and flour in saucepan. Add milk gradually. Cook until thickened, stirring constantly. Stir in salt, pepper and ¾ teaspoon nutmeg. Toss bread crumbs with ¼ cup butter. Toast lightly. Layer ⅓ of the rice, ⅓ of the fish, ½ of the onion, ½ of the bread crumbs and ⅓ of the white sauce in greased casserole. Repeat layers. Top with remaining rice, fish and sauce. Sprinkle with ¼ teaspoon nutmeg. Bake for 45 minutes or until bubbly.

Katherine E. Langworthy, Fabuis Grange, Michigan

FISH ITALIANO

Yields: 4 servings	Pan Size: 7x11 inch	Preheat: 350°

2 tbsp. margarine	1 tsp. Worcestershire sauce
1 onion, thinly sliced	¼ c. Parmesan cheese
1½ lb. red snapper fillets	½ tsp. paprika
½ c. mayonnaise	½ tsp. salt
2 tbsp. lemon juice	Oregano and parsley to taste

Melt margarine in baking dish. Layer onion and fillets in dish. Combine next 6 ingredients in bowl; mix well. Pour over fish fillets. Sprinkle with oregano and parsley. Bake for 35 to 40 minutes or until fish flakes easily.

Esther F. Russell, Rainbow Valley Grange, California

FLOUNDER STUFFED WITH CRAB MEAT

Yields: 4 servings	Pan Size: 9 x 13 inch	Preheat: 400°

1 lb. crab meat	¼ tsp. Old Bay seasoning
1 egg, lightly beaten	Dash of hot pepper sauce
¼ c. chopped green pepper	2 lb. flounder fillets
2 tbsp. milk	2 tbsp. oil
1 tsp. mayonnaise	Paprika to taste
1 tsp. dry mustard	

Combine first 8 ingredients in bowl; mix well. Wash flounder and pat dry. Cut into 8 uniform-sized serving pieces. Place 4 pieces flounder skin side down in baking pan. Spoon crab mixture onto flounder. Cover with remaining flounder. Brush with oil; sprinkle with paprika. Bake for 20 minutes or until fish flakes easily.

Tom and Debby Kean
Governor of New Jersey

POACHED SALMON

Yields: 6 to 8 servings	Pan Size: 6 quart

1 lg. onion, sliced	3 or 4 whole cloves
1 lemon, thinly sliced	5 peppercorns
3 tbsp. rock salt	1 bay leaf
5 lg. sprigs parsley	6 to 8 1-in. salmon steaks

Combine first 7 ingredients with 4 quarts water in saucepan. Bring to a boil; reduce heat. Simmer for 30 minutes. Add salmon. Simmer for 8 to 10 minutes or until fish flakes easily. Remove to serving plate. Garnish with additional parsley. Serve with drawn butter, rice and buttered green beans.

Ruth Hanes, Garcia Grange, California

SALMON STEAKS

Yields: 2 servings	Pan Size: 9 inch

2 salmon steaks	**¾ c. diagonally sliced asparagus**
Salt and pepper to taste	**¾ c. sliced fresh mushrooms**
3 tbsp. oil	**½ tsp. lemon rind**
¼ tsp. grated gingerroot	

Season salmon with salt and pepper. Brown in 2 tablespoons oil in skillet. Cook for a total of 10 minutes per inch of thickness. Sauté green onion and gingerroot in 1 tablespoon oil in small skillet for 30 seconds. Add asparagus, mushrooms, lemon rind and *2 tablespoons water*. Simmer, covered, for 2 minutes. Spoon vegetables over salmon on serving plate. Garnish with lemon slices.

BAKED SOLE

Yields: 8 servings	Pan Size: 9 x 13 inch	Preheat: 325°

8 sole fillets	**Parmesan cheese**
Salt and pepper to taste	**2 cans cream of shrimp soup**
3 tomatoes, thinly sliced	**Seasoned bread crumbs**
1 lg. onion, thinly sliced	

Season sole with salt and pepper. Layer half the sole, tomatoes and onion in baking dish. Sprinkle with Parmesan cheese. Add layers of remaining sole, tomatoes and onion. Top with soup and bread crumbs. Bake for 1 hour or until fish flakes easily.

John H. Sununu
Governor of New Hampshire

SWORDFISH IN FOIL

Yields: 4 servings   Pan Size: 9 x 13 inch   Preheat: 425°

1 c. sliced mushrooms	1 tsp. dillseed
1 onion, thinly sliced	1½ lb. swordfish steaks
2 tbsp. chopped green pepper	Flour
1 tbsp. chopped parsley	Salt to taste
2 tbsp. melted butter	4 slices tomato
2 tbsp. lemon juice	4 sm. bay leaves
½ tsp. vegetable salt	

Combine first 8 ingredients in bowl. Spread half the mixture in foil-lined baking dish. Coat swordfish with flour. Arrange in prepared dish. Sprinkle with salt. Top with tomato slices, bay leaves and remaining mushroom mixture. Bake, covered with foil, for 40 minutes. Remove bay leaves.

Mary C. Durkee, Saratoga Grange, New York

CAMPSIDE TROUT

Yields: 4 servings   Pan Size: 10 inch

4 12-in. trout	1 egg, beaten
Flour	1 c. finely crushed cornflakes
Salt and pepper to taste	¼ c. each butter, olive oil

Clean trout; remove heads. Pat dry with paper towels. Coat with mixture of flour, salt and pepper. Dip in egg; roll in cornflake crumbs, coating well. Brown in butter and oil in skillet over high heat for 4 minutes on each side; reduce heat to medium. Cook, covered, for 3 minutes longer or until fish flakes easily.

George E. Myers, Centre Hill Grange, Pennsylvania

TUNA QUICHE

Yields: 6 servings   Pan Size: 10 inch   Preheat: 375°

1 10-in. pie shell	3 eggs, lightly beaten
1 can solid-pack white tuna	1½ c. half and half
½ c. grated Swiss cheese	Salt, pepper and nutmeg
1 tbsp. chopped chives	to taste

Bake pie shell until partially baked. Rinse tuna under cold running water; drain. Flake into pie shell. Sprinkle with cheese and chives. Combine remaining ingredients in bowl; mix well. Pour over tuna. Bake for 45 minutes or until knife inserted in center comes out clean. Let stand for 15 minutes before serving.

Mr. and Mrs. Caspar Weinberger
Secretary, U.S. Department of Defense

HOT TUNA PUFFS

Yields: 6 servings   Pan Size: baking sheet

6 slices bread	**½ tsp. Worcestershire sauce**
1 7-oz. can tuna, drained	**½ c. mayonnaise**
2 tsp. minced onion	**1 egg, beaten**
1 tsp. mustard	**¼ c. shredded cheese**

Toast bread lightly on 1 side. Combine tuna, onion, mustard, Worcestershire sauce and ¼ cup mayonnaise in bowl; mix well. Spread on untoasted side of bread. Mix remaining mayonnaise, egg and cheese in bowl. Spread over tuna mixture. Place on baking sheet. Broil on lowest rack until topping is light brown and puffy.

Thelma Palmer, Winthrop Grange, Maine

CREAMY TUNA TOPPING

Yields: 4 servings   Pan Size: 1 quart

2 tbsp. butter, melted	**¼ tsp. hot pepper sauce**
3 tbsp. flour	**2 7-oz. cans tuna**
2½ c. milk	**¼ c. chopped black olives**
½ tsp. dry mustard	**¼ c. chopped pimento**

Combine butter and flour in saucepan; mix well. Cook over medium heat for 3 minutes, stirring constantly. Remove from heat. Stir in milk gradually. Cook until thickened, stirring constantly. Add mustard and hot pepper sauce. Drain and flake tuna. Fold tuna, olives and pimento into hot sauce.

Photograph for this recipe on page 102.

TUNA ST. JACQUES

Yields: 6 servings   Pan Size: 6 ramekins   Preheat: 450°

3 green onions, chopped	**Finely chopped parsley**
4 oz. fresh mushrooms, chopped	**2 cans white tuna, drained**
3 tbsp. butter	**2 tbsp. Parmesan cheese**
1 can cream of chicken soup	**⅓ c. bread crumbs**
½ c. dry vermouth	**1 tbsp. melted butter**
White pepper to taste	

Sauté green onions and mushrooms in 3 tablespoons butter in skillet. Bring soup, vermouth and pepper to a boil in saucepan; blend well. Stir half the sauce into mushroom mixture. Spoon mushroom sauce into buttered ramekins. Top with parsley and tuna. Spoon remaining sauce over tuna. Mix cheese and bread crumbs. Sprinkle over tops. Drizzle with melted butter. Bake for 10 minutes or until browned.

Christel H. Laselle, Londonderry Grange, Vermont

CANADIAN SEAFOOD CASSEROLE

Yields: 10 to 12 servings	Pan Size: 2 quart	Preheat: 350°

1 c. noodles
1 lb. scallops
1 can lobster
1 can crab meat
1 can baby clams
1 can shrimp
1 can mushrooms
1 can mushroom soup

1 sm. onion, chopped
1 green pepper, chopped
½ c. chopped celery
1 tbsp. soy sauce
Salt, pepper and garlic
   salt to taste
Buttered bread crumbs
Paprika

Cook noodles according to package directions for 5 minutes; drain and rinse. Parboil scallops in water to cover in saucepan; drain. Combine scallops with undrained lobster, crab meat, clams, shrimp, mushrooms and soup in saucepan. Cook until heated through, stirring constantly. Add onion, green pepper, celery, soy sauce and seasonings; mix well. Stir in noodles. Spoon into casserole. Sprinkle with crumbs and paprika. Bake for 1 hour.

Paul McQuaid, Anthony Grange, Rhode Island

DEVILED CLAMS

Yields: 8 servings	Pan Size: clam shells/baking sheet	Preheat: 350°

2 c. minced clams
½ c. minced onion
⅓ c. chopped green pepper
⅓ c. chopped celery
1½ c. dry bread crumbs
1 c. heavy cream

2 tbsp. melted butter
2 tsp. mustard
1½ tsp. salt
Pepper to taste
Parmesan cheese
Bacon slices, cut into halves

Combine first 10 ingredients in bowl; mix well. Spoon into clam shells. Place on baking sheet. Bake for 20 minutes. Sprinkle generously with Parmesan cheese. Top with bacon slices. Bake until bacon is crisp.

Grace Seidel, Henlopen Grange, Delaware

CLAM CASSEROLE

Yields: 4 servings	Pan Size: 1½ quart	Preheat: 350°

2 cans minced clams with
   liquid
9 saltine crackers, crushed

2 eggs, lightly beaten
½ c. melted butter
1½ c. milk

Combine all ingredients in bowl; mix well. Spoon into baking dish. Bake for 45 minutes or until bubbly.

Irene Pipicello, Acorn Grange, Maine

CLAM PIE

Yields: 8 servings	Pan Size: 8 x 12 inch	Preheat: 350°

12 lg. clams
2 sm. potatoes, chopped
2 hard-boiled eggs, sliced

Salt and pepper to taste
1 recipe 2-crust pie pastry

Mince clams in bowl, reserving liquid. Add potatoes, eggs, salt and pepper. Stir in a small amount of water if necessary to make of desired consistency. Spoon into pastry-lined baking dish. Top with remaining pastry, sealing edge and cutting steam vents. Bake for 1½ hours.

Mrs. Glendon Miller, Cumberland Grange, New Jersey

CRAB CASSEROLE

Yields: 4 servings	Pan Size: 1½ quart	Preheat: 350°

8 oz. crab meat
1 c. cooked rice
5 hard-boiled eggs, chopped
1½ c. mayonnaise
1 6-oz. can evaporated milk

½ tsp. salt
Dash of pepper
¼ tsp. red pepper
½ c. shredded Cheddar cheese

Combine crab meat, rice and eggs in bowl. Add mayonnaise, evaporated milk, salt, pepper and red pepper; mix well. Spoon into casserole. Sprinkle cheese on top. Bake for 20 minutes. Serve as main dish or hot appetizer.

Gerald L. Baliles
Governor of Virginia

ERMA'S CRAB CASSEROLE

Yields: 4 servings	Pan Size: 1 quart	Preheat: 350°

¼ c. butter
2 tbsp. Worcestershire sauce
5 tbsp. flour
¼ tsp. dry mustard
½ tsp. salt

⅛ tsp. pepper
2 c. milk
¾ c. grated sharp cheese
1 lb. back-fin crab meat
1 slice bread, crumbled

Melt butter with Worcestershire sauce in double boiler. Blend in flour, dry mustard, salt and pepper. Stir in milk gradually. Cook until thickened, stirring constantly. Add cheese, stirring until cheese melts. Stir in crab meat. Spoon into casserole. Top with crumbs. Bake for 30 minutes.

Erma Connally, Henlopen Grange, Delaware

CRAB IMPERIAL

Yields: 8 servings	Pan Size: 8 x 12 inch	Preheat: 350°

2 lb. crab meat	2 tsp. salt
1 green pepper, chopped	1½ tbsp. pepper
4 pimentos, minced	Mayonnaise
2 eggs, beaten	Paprika
1⅓ c. mayonnaise	

Combine crab meat, green pepper, pimentos, eggs, 1⅓ cups mayonnaise, salt and pepper in bowl; mix well. Spoon into baking dish. Spread thin layer of mayonnaise over top. Sprinkle with paprika. Bake for 20 minutes.

Shirley Millman, Henlopen Grange, Delaware

COLONIAL OYSTER AND HAM PIE

Yields: 4 servings	Pan Size: 1½ quart	Preheat: 350°

1 med. onion, chopped	½ c. white wine
2 tsp. butter	½ c. milk
1 pt. fresh oysters	1½ c. chopped cooked ham
½ c. butter, melted	2 c. green peas
½ c. flour	

Sauté onion in 2 teaspoons butter in skillet; set aside. Drain oysters, reserving ½ cup liquid. Blend ½ cup melted butter and flour in saucepan. Stir in reserved oyster liquid, wine and milk. Cook until thickened, stirring constantly; remove from heat. Add oysters, ham, peas and sautéed onion; mix well. Spoon into casserole. Bake for 15 minutes.

Richard W. Riley
Governor of South Carolina

SCALLOPED SCALLOPS

Yields: 6 servings	Pan Size: 4 quart	Preheat: 350°

¼ c. milk	1 sm. onion, sliced
2 med. potatoes	1 lb. sea scallops
½ tsp. salt	3 med. potatoes
½ tsp. pepper	Butter
½ c. flour	Milk

Pour ¼ cup milk in buttered casserole. Slice 2 potatoes into casserole. Sprinkle with half the salt and pepper and ⅓ of the flour. Layer onion, scallops and ⅓ of the flour over potatoes. Slice remaining potatoes over scallops. Sprinkle with remaining flour, salt and pepper. Dot with butter. Add enough milk to almost cover layers. Bake, loosely covered, for 1¼ hours. Bake, uncovered, for 15 minutes or until light brown.

Miriam Pinheiro, North Attleboro Grange, Massachusetts

SHRIMP-STUFFED BAKED AVOCADOS

Yields: 6 servings	Pan Size: baking sheet	Preheat: 350°

3 tbsp. flour
½ tsp. salt
⅛ tsp. pepper
¼ c. butter, melted
1½ c. milk
1 egg, lightly beaten
1 c. chopped cooked shrimp

¾ c. chopped celery, partially
cooked
3 lg. avocados
3 tbsp. lemon juice
½ tsp. salt
Grated cheese

Blend flour, ½ teaspoon salt and pepper into melted butter in saucepan. Stir in milk gradually. Cook until thickened, stirring constantly. Stir a small amount of hot mixture into egg; stir egg into hot mixture. Cook until thickened, stirring constantly. Stir in shrimp and celery. Peel avocados; cut lengthwise into halves. Sprinkle with lemon juice and ½ teaspoon salt. Spoon shrimp mixture into avocados. Sprinkle with cheese. Place on baking sheet. Bake for 15 minutes. Broil for 3 to 4 minutes if desired. *Note:* May substitute crab, lobster or chicken for shrimp.

Mary Click, DeSabla Grange, California

SHRIMP FETTUCINI

Yields: 6 servings	Pan Size: 3 quart	Preheat: 350°

1 med. white onion,
chopped
1 med. yellow onion,
chopped
1 stick butter
2 lb. shrimp, peeled

2 tsp. chopped fresh
parsley
1 c. half and half
16 oz. Velveeta jalapeño
cheese
1 pkg. fettucini

Sauté onions in butter in skillet until transparent. Add shrimp and parsley. Cook over low heat for 5 minutes. Add half and half. Cook for several minutes, stirring constantly. Reserve 3 slices cheese; chop remaining cheese. Stir chopped cheese into shrimp mixture. Cook until cheese melts, stirring constantly. Cook fettucini according to package directions; drain. Combine with sauce in casserole; mix well. Place cheese slices on top. Bake for 10 minutes or until cheese melts.

Bob Odom
Commissioner, Louisiana Department of Agriculture

CREOLE PICKLED SHRIMP

Yields: 2 servings   Pan Size: 1 quart

½ c. vinegar	2 tsp. paprika
1 c. oil	2 tsp. salt
1 tbsp. mustard	2 c. cooked shrimp
1 tbsp. mustard seed	1 c. sliced pickling onions

Bring vinegar, oil, mustard, mustard seed, paprika and salt to a boil in saucepan. Cook for 5 minutes. Layer shrimp and onions in bowl. Pour vinegar mixture over top. Chill for 8 hours or longer.

Hazel Mecham, Pleasant Grove Grange, Oregon

SHRIMP AND RICE CASSEROLE

Yields: 8 to 10 servings   Pan Size: 9 x 13 inch   Preheat: 350°

½ c. chopped celery	1 c. rice, cooked
½ c. chopped green pepper	1 can tomato soup
1 lg. onion, chopped	1 tsp. Worcestershire sauce
1 stick margarine	Salt and pepper to taste
3 lb. shrimp, cooked, peeled	1 lb. sharp Cheddar cheese,
1 lg. can sliced mushrooms,	grated
drained	

Sauté celery, green pepper and onion in margarine in skillet. Combine with shrimp, mushrooms, rice, soup, Worcestershire sauce, salt, pepper and ⅔ of the cheese in bowl; mix well. Spoon into baking dish. Sprinkle remaining cheese on top. Bake for 45 minutes.

D. Leslie Tindal
Commissioner, South Carolina Department of Agriculture

SCAMPI

Yields: 2 servings   Pan Size: 6 inch

1 med. onion, chopped	2 tbsp. oil
1 sm. green pepper, chopped	1½ c. wine
1 4-oz. can mushrooms,	Juice of 1 lemon
drained	12 med. shrimp
1 stalk celery, chopped	Garlic to taste
2 tbsp. butter	

Sauté vegetables in butter and oil in skillet for 5 minutes. Add remaining ingredients. Bring to a boil. Cook for 5 minutes or just until shrimp test done.

Shari Corwin, Five Mile Prairie Grange, Washington

Poultry

BARBECUED MARINATED CHICKEN

Yields: 4 servings   Pan Size: grill

¼ c. oil	1 tsp. cumin
¼ c. soy sauce	1 tsp. oregano
1 tbsp. lemon juice	2 tsp. salt
2 cloves of garlic, minced	1 tsp. pepper
2 tsp. curry powder	4 chicken breast fillets
2 tsp. grated gingerroot	8 tsp. melted butter

Combine oil, soy sauce, lemon juice, garlic and seasonings in shallow dish; mix well. Add chicken; coat well. Chill, covered, for 3 hours or longer. Grill over hot coals for 5 minutes on each side. Remove to serving plate. Brush with melted butter. Garnish with mint.

Mrs. Lee Finkenbinder, Mifflin Grange, Pennsylvania

FRYPAN BARBECUED CHICKEN

Yields: 8 servings	Pan Size: electric skillet	Preheat: 340°

1 c. catsup	1 c. flour
½ c. packed brown sugar	½ tsp. chili powder
1 tbsp. onion flakes	1 tsp. salt
2 tbsp. Worcestershire sauce	¼ tsp. pepper
2 tbsp. mustard	2 fryers, cut into quarters
½ c. Burgundy	⅓ c. olive oil

Bring first 6 ingredients to a boil in saucepan. Simmer for several minutes. Mix flour, chili powder, salt and pepper in bag. Add chicken; shake to coat well. Brown on both sides in hot olive oil in skillet. Pour sauce over chicken. Simmer, covered, for 45 minutes or until tender, basting occasionally.

Georgia Lovegren, Clatskanie Grange, Oregon

MAPLE-BARBECUED CHICKEN

Yields: 6 to 8 servings	Pan Size: grill

½ c. oil	½ tsp. Tabasco sauce
¾ c. vinegar	1 tbsp. salt
½ c. thick maple syrup	3 chickens, split

Combine first 5 ingredients and *¼ cup water* in bowl; mix well. Place chicken halves skin side up on grill. Cook for 20 to 30 minutes or until brown on bottom. Turn chicken; brush with sauce. Cook for 30 to 40 minutes longer or until tender, turning frequently and brushing with sauce.

Blanche B. Dowd, Beacon Light Grange, Vermont

LONE RANGER CHICKEN

Yields: 4 servings	Pan Size: 9 x 13 inch	Preheat: 400°

1 broiler, cut into quarters	1 tbsp. sugar
1 8-oz. can tomato sauce	½ tsp. mustard
1 sm. onion, chopped	½ tsp. garlic powder
2 tbsp. soy sauce	

Wash chicken; pat dry. Arrange in buttered baking dish. Combine remaining ingredients in bowl; mix well. Spoon over chicken; coating well. Bake for 1 hour or until chicken is tender.

Louise M. Pratt, Obwebutuck Grange, Connecticut

CHICKEN CRÊPES

Yields: 4 servings	Pan Size: 9 x 13 inch	Preheat: 325°

1 c. sliced fresh mushrooms
6 tbsp. butter, melted
¼ c. flour
¼ tsp. pepper
2 c. milk

2 tsp. instant chicken
  bouillon
2 c. chopped cooked chicken
8 lg. crêpes
½ c. toasted sliced almonds

Sauté mushrooms in 2 tablespoons butter in small skillet. Blend ¼ cup butter, flour and pepper in saucepan. Cook for 1 minute, stirring constantly. Stir in milk and bouillon gradually. Cook until thickened, stirring constantly. Add sautéed mushrooms and chicken. Heat through. Place about ½ cup filling in center of each crêpe; fold sides to center overlapping slightly. Place in baking dish. Sprinkle with almonds. Bake for 10 minutes.

CALIFORNIA SECRET

Yields: 2 to 4 servings	Pan Size: Crock•Pot

1 chicken, cut up
4 8-oz. cans tomato sauce
3 tbsp. oil
1 c. chopped green chilies
1 med. onion, chopped
2 cloves of garlic, minced

¼ tsp. liquid smoke
2 bay leaves
¼ tsp. nutmeg
⅛ tsp. cloves
1 tsp. salt
½ tsp. pepper

Combine all ingredients in Crock•Pot; mix well. Cook until chicken is tender.

David and Lois Austin
California State Grange

BOILED POTPIE

Yields: 8 servings   Pan Size: 4 quart

3 lb. chicken pieces	1 c. peas
¼ tsp. rosemary	2 c. flour
2 tsp. salt	2 tbsp. oil
3 potatoes, peeled, chopped	1 egg
1 c. whole kernel corn	2 tbsp. chopped parsley
½ to 1 c. chopped onion	Salt and pepper to taste

Cook chicken with rosemary and 1 teaspoon salt in water to cover in saucepan. Remove chicken; bone and chop. Add enough water to broth to measure 2 quarts. Add vegetables. Bring to a boil. Combine flour, 1 teaspoon salt, oil and egg in bowl. Add enough water to make easily handled dough; mix well. Roll thin on floured surface. Cut into squares. Drop into simmering broth. Add parsley, seasonings to taste and chicken. Simmer, covered, for 20 to 30 minutes or until vegetables are tender, stirring occasionally.

Elizabeth Norris, Royal Grange, Pennsylvania

CHICKEN AND DUMPLINGS

Yields: 4 to 6 servings   Pan Size: 5 quart

1 fryer, cut up	1 bay leaf
½ tsp. salt	2 c. flour
¼ tsp. pepper	1 tbsp. baking powder
1 c. sliced onions	2 tbsp. chopped parsley
1 c. sliced celery	1 tsp. salt
½ c. carrot sticks	½ c. milk
2 c. chicken broth	⅓ c. mayonnaise

Sprinkle chicken with ½ teaspoon salt and pepper. Combine with vegetables, chicken broth, bay leaf and *3 cups water* in saucepan. Bring to a boil; reduce heat. Simmer, covered, for 45 minutes. Remove bay leaf. Combine flour, baking powder, parsley and 1 teaspoon salt in bowl. Stir in milk and mayonnaise. Drop by tablespoonfuls over chicken. Simmer for 10 minutes longer.

Florence Brown, Litchfield Grange, New York

CHICKEN AND HOMEMADE NOODLES

Yields: 6 to 8 servings   Pan Size: stockpot

2 eggs, beaten	1 med. onion, chopped
¼ c. milk	4 tsp. salt
¾ tsp. salt	2 tsp. pepper
2 c. (about) flour	3 carrots, thinly sliced
2 2½ to 3-lb. fryers, cut up	2 tbsp. flour

Combine eggs, milk and ¾ teaspoon salt in bowl; mix well. Add 2 cups flour or enough to make a stiff dough. Divide into 2 portions. Roll each portion very thin on floured surface. Let stand for 20 minutes. Roll dough up loosely. Slice at ¼-inch intervals. Unroll strips; cut into desired lengths. Let stand for 2 hours to dry. Combine chicken with *about 8 cups water* or enough to cover, onion, 4 teaspoons salt and pepper in stockpot. Bring to a boil; reduce heat. Simmer, covered, for 1 hour or until tender. Remove chicken and cool. Bone chicken. Bring broth to a boil. Add noodles and carrots. Simmer, covered, for 10 minutes. Stir in chicken. Blend 2 tablespoons flour with *¼ cup cold water*. Add to noodles. Cook until thickened, stirring constantly.

Delores H. Clocker, Barberton Grange, Washington

CHICKEN PAPRIKA (HUNGARY)

Yields: 4 servings	Pan Size: 10 inch

3 lb. fryer, cut up	1 tbsp. paprika
2 onions, finely chopped	1 tsp. salt
3 tbsp. shortening	1 c. sour cream

Wash chicken; pat dry. Brown onions lightly in shortening in skillet. Add paprika and chicken. Sprinkle with salt. Cook until chicken is lightly browned on both sides. Reduce heat. Simmer, covered, for 1 hour or until tender. Pour sour cream over chicken. Cook until heated through; do not boil. Serve over hot noodles.

Kathryn E. Ruff, Hillstown Grange, Connecticut

CHICKEN CURRY (INDIA)

Yields: 4 to 5 servings	Pan Size: 12 inch

2 med. onions, sliced	⅓ c. butter
2 or 3 cloves of garlic, minced	1 lg. fryer, cut up
1 piece fresh gingerroot, chopped	1 tomato, sliced
1 to 3 tbsp. curry powder	1 c. chicken broth
1 tbsp. chili powder	1 c. cottage cheese
	Salt to taste

Sauté first 5 ingredients in butter in skillet until light brown. Add chicken. Cook for 15 minutes. Add remaining ingredients. Simmer for 40 minutes or until chicken is tender, adding a small amount of additional broth if necessary. Serve with rice.

Verl Woods, Rickreall Grange, Oregon

CHICKEN JAMBALAYA

Yields: 4 servings   Pan Size: 7 quart

1 3 to 4-lb. fryer, cut up	6 Creole smoked sausages,
2 tbsp. oil	sliced
4 c. chopped onion	3½ tsp. salt
¾ c. chopped green pepper	½ tsp. freshly ground pepper
¾ c. sliced green shallot tops	¼ tsp. cayenne pepper
1 tbsp. finely minced garlic	½ tsp. chili powder
3 tbsp. finely minced parsley	2 bay leaves, crushed
½ c. finely chopped lean	¼ tsp. each thyme, basil
baked ham	⅛ tsp. each cloves, mace
1 lb. lean pork, cubed	1½ c. rice

Brown chicken in oil in stockpot, turning to brown evenly. Remove pieces when brown. Add vegetables, parsley, ham and pork. Cook over medium heat for 15 minutes or until brown, stirring frequently. Add sausage and seasonings. Cook for 5 minutes, stirring frequently. Add chicken, rice and *3 cups water*; mix gently. Bring to a boil; reduce heat. Simmer, covered, for 35 minutes, stirring occasionally. Increase heat to medium. Cook, uncovered, for 10 minutes, stirring frequently.

Wilma Corbin, Pleasant Valley Grange, Washington

JAMBALAYA

Yields: 10 to 12 servings   Pan Size: stockpot

1 5 to 6-lb. chicken, cut up	2 c. chopped green onions
Salt and pepper to taste	2 to 3 c. chopped green peppers
½ c. bacon drippings	1 can Ro-Tel tomatoes
1 lb. hot sausage	5 c. rice
1 lb. mild sausage	1 tsp. garlic powder

Cut chicken into bite-sized pieces. Season with salt and pepper. Brown in bacon drippings in stockpot. Add sausage. Cook until sausage is brown. Remove chicken and sausage. Add green onions and green peppers. Cook until brown. Add Ro-Tel. Simmer until golden brown. Add chicken, sausage and *10 cups water*. Bring to a boil. Add rice and garlic powder. Simmer, covered for 30 minutes. Stir mixture. Simmer for 15 minutes longer.

Charlene Knox, Bethlehem Grange, Ohio

MUSHROOM AND CHICKEN ITALIENNE

Yields: 6 to 8 servings   Pan Size: 4 quart

1 c. chopped onion	5 tbsp. butter
1½ c. rice	1 lb. fresh mushrooms, sliced
3 tbsp. butter	1 tbsp. flour
1 can condensed chicken broth	1 16-oz. can tomatoes, mashed
½ c. chopped onion	½ tsp. sugar
½ c. chopped green pepper	1 tsp. salt
1 clove of garlic, minced	⅛ tsp. pepper
	4 c. chopped cooked chicken

Sauté 1 cup onion and rice in 3 tablespoons butter in saucepan. Add broth and *2 cups water*. Simmer, covered, for 25 minutes or until liquid is absorbed. Sauté ½ cup onion, green pepper and garlic in 5 tablespoons butter in saucepan. Add mushrooms. Sauté for 5 minutes. Stir in flour, tomatoes, sugar and seasonings. Simmer for 10 minutes. Add chicken. Cook until heated through. Spoon over rice in serving dish.

Betty Therrien, Obwebetuck Grange, Connecticut

BATTER CHICKEN PIE

Yields: 6 servings   Pan Size: 9 x 13 inch   Preheat: 450°

2½ c. broth	2 tsp. baking powder
1 chicken, cooked, boned	1 tsp. salt
1 stick margarine	1 tsp. pepper
1 c. flour	1 c. milk

Pour broth over chicken in baking dish. Dot with margarine. Blend remaining ingredients in bowl. Pour over chicken; do not stir. Bake for 25 minutes.

Mrs. Charles Hooker, Old Richmond Grange, North Carolina

CHICKEN PIE

Yields: 8 servings   Pan Size: 9 x 13 inch   Preheat: 400°

½ c. chopped onion	1 c. drained canned peas
⅓ c. margarine	1 6-oz. can sliced mushrooms, drained
⅓ c. flour	
1½ tsp. salt	¼ c. chopped pimento
3 c. chicken broth	4 oz. noodles, cooked
4 c. chopped cooked chicken	1 recipe biscuits

Sauté onion in margarine in saucepan. Stir in flour and salt. Add broth gradually. Cook until thickened, stirring frequently. Add chicken, vegetables and noodles. Spoon into baking dish. Top with biscuits. Bake until biscuits are light brown.

Ruby Plank, Monroe Grange, Ohio

SWISS CHICKEN QUICHE

Yields: 6 servings	Pan Size: 9 inch	Preheat: 425°

1 unbaked pie shell
1 c. shredded Swiss cheese
2 tbsp. flour
1 tbsp. instant chicken
  bouillon

2 c. chopped cooked chicken
3 eggs, beaten
1 c. milk
¼ c. chopped onion
2 tbsp. chopped green pepper

Prick pie shell with fork. Bake for 8 minutes. Reduce temperature to 350 degrees. Toss cheese with flour and bouillon granules in bowl. Add remaining ingredients; mix well. Pour into pie shell. Bake for 40 to 45 minutes or until set. Let stand for 10 minutes before serving.

Ruth Wunderlich, Salt Valley Grange, Nebraska

BRUNSWICK STEW

Yields: 6 servings	Pan Size: stockpot

1 6-lb. chicken, cut up
2 lg. onions, sliced
2 bay leaves
2 stalks celery, chopped
3 or 4 med. potatoes, chopped

3 to 4 c. cut corn
1 tbsp. each sugar, salt
1 tsp. pepper
4 c. chopped fresh tomatoes
1 to 2 c. canned lima beans

Cook chicken in *2½-quarts water* with onions, bay leaves and celery for 2 hours or until tender. Remove chicken; bone and chop. Add potatoes, corn and seasonings to stock. Cook until potatoes are tender. Add remaining vegetables and chicken. Simmer for 15 minutes.

Agnes Johnson, Livingston Grange, New Jersey

POULTRY STEW WITH DOUGH BOYS

Yields: 8 servings	Pan Size: 6 quart

1 fryer, cut up
2 c. chopped potatoes
1 c. chopped carrots
1 lg. onion, chopped

1 stalk celery, chopped
Poultry seasoning to taste
2 c. flour
½ tsp. each salt, sage

Combine chicken with *3 quarts water* in stockpot. Cook until very tender. Add vegetables and poultry seasoning. Cook until vegetables are tender. Combine flour, salt and sage in bowl. Add *1 cup water*; mix well. Roll very thin on floured surface. Cut into 2-inch squares. Drop into simmering stew, adding water if needed to cover dumplings. Cook, covered, for 10 to 15 minutes. Ladle into soup bowls, discarding bones.

Evelyn B. Pond, Wilmot Grange, New Hampshire

BREAST OF CHICKEN VAL DOSTANA (ITALY)

Yields: 4 servings	Pan Size: 9 x 13 inch	Preheat: 350°

4 chicken breast filets	1 clove of garlic,
3 tbsp. flour	finely chopped
Salt and pepper to taste	½ c. 35% cream
¼ c. olive oil	¼ c. chicken stock
¼ c. white wine	2 tbsp. chopped fresh parsley
¼ c. Brandy	¼ c. white wine
4 oz. Fontina cheese, sliced	¼ c. Brandy
6 lg. fresh mushrooms, sliced	1 tbsp. butter
½ lg. onion, finely chopped	1 tbsp. Parmesan cheese

Cover chicken with plastic wrap. Flatten with meat mallet. Coat filets with flour; season with salt and pepper. Sauté in olive oil in skillet until golden brown. Arrange filets in baking pan. Pour ¼ cup wine and ¼ cup Brandy on top. Place Fontina cheese on top. Bake for 20 minutes. Sauté mushrooms, onion and garlic in pan drippings until golden. Add cream, chicken stock, parsley, ¼ cup wine, ¼ cup Brandy, butter and Parmesan cheese. Simmer for 10 minutes. Pour over chicken. Serve chicken hot with sautéed asparagus.

Elena Buonpane, Forks Prairie Grange, Washington

HONEY-DIPPED CHICKEN

Yields: 5 servings	Pan Size: 9 x 13 inch	Preheat: 375°

1 egg	Salt and pepper to taste
¼ c. honey	1 chicken, cut up
½ c. pecan meal	Melted butter
½ c. bread crumbs	

Beat egg and honey in small bowl. Combine pecan meal, crumbs and seasonings in bag. Dip chicken in honey mixture; coat well with crumbs. Arrange in baking dish. Drizzle with melted butter. Bake for 1 hour or until tender.

Mary I. Grafton, Pleasant Hill Grange, Ohio

CHICKEN AND CUCUMBER

Yields: 4 servings	Pan Size: 1½ quart	Preheat: 400°

1 whole chicken breast	2 tsp. oil
2½ tbsp. soy sauce	1 lb. fresh peas, shelled
1 sm. onion, chopped	½ c. consommé
¾ tsp. ginger	½ unpeeled cucumber
8 oz. mushrooms, sliced	1 tbsp. cornstarch

Marinate thinly sliced chicken in mixture of soy sauce, onion and ginger. Sauté mushrooms in oil in covered skillet for 5 minutes. Remove mushrooms. Add chicken mixture, peas and consommé. Cook, covered, for 10 minutes. Cut cucumber in half lengthwise; slice ¼ inch thick. Add cucumber and mixture of cornstarch and *2 tablespoons water* to skillet; mix well. Cook until thickened, stirring constantly. Add mushrooms. Pour into casserole. Bake for 5 minutes.

Ralph W. Durkee, Saratoga Grange, New York

CHICKEN POT ROAST

Yields: 4 servings	Pan Size: 4 quart

4 chicken breasts	4 med. potatoes, peeled
Flour	8 carrots
Salt and pepper to taste	2 med. onions, quartered
1 tsp. crushed garlic	½ c. Rosé
¼ c. olive oil	2 tbsp. oregano
2 tbsp. butter	Cornstarch

Coat chicken with mixture of flour, salt and pepper. Brown on all sides with garlic in olive oil and butter in heavy saucepan. Add vegetables, wine and *2 cups water*. Sprinkle with oregano. Simmer for 1 to 1½ hours or until chicken is tender. Remove chicken and vegetables to serving dish. Thicken sauce to desired consistency with cornstarch. Serve over chicken.

Jayne Maniche, Friend of Riverside Grange, Ohio

FIFTEEN-MINUTE CHICKEN

Yields: 6 servings	Pan Size: 10 inch

4 chicken breasts	Salt and white pepper to taste
Flour	3 tbsp. raspberry vinegar
¼ c. butter	1 tbsp. chopped parsley
1 tbsp. fresh rosemary	

Bone chicken; cut into pieces. Roll chicken pieces several at a time in flour; shake to remove excess flour. Melt butter over high heat in skillet. Add chicken. Stir-fry for 3 to 5 minutes or until cooked through. Add rosemary, salt and pepper. Add vinegar, stirring to deglaze skillet. Sprinkle with parsley. Serve over brown rice.
Note: May substitute lemon juice, orange juice, Sherry or other wine for raspberry vinegar if desired.

Michael N. Castle
Governor of Delaware

CORNY CHICKEN

Yields: 4 servings	Pan Size: Crock•Pot

4 or 5 chicken breast filets	1 c. sliced mushrooms
1 tsp. salt	1 c. drained whole kernel corn
½ tsp. paprika	½ c. chopped onion
1 c. tomato sauce	½ c. chopped green pepper
1 c. canned stewed tomatoes	1 clove of garlic, crushed

Place chicken in Crock•Pot. Sprinkle with salt and paprika. Pour tomato sauce over top. Add vegetables and garlic; mix well. Cook on Medium for 8 hours.

Kathy Ward, Friend of Princeton Grange, Idaho

ITALIAN CHICKEN BREAST

Yields: 4 servings	Pan Size: 2 quart

3 chicken breasts, boned, chopped	1 lg. tomato, cut into quarters
2 c. sliced mushrooms	1 clove of garlic, minced
1 lg. onion, chopped	1 tbsp. olive oil
1 green pepper, sliced	Salt and pepper to taste
	½ c. cooking Sherry

Sauté chicken, mushrooms, onion, green pepper, tomato and garlic in olive oil in skillet until chicken is tender; do not brown. Sprinkle with salt and pepper. Simmer, covered, for 15 minutes. Add Sherry. Heat to serving temperature. Serve over homemade noodles.

Addie Fife, Clatskanie Grange, Oregon

STUFFED CHICKEN BREAST ATHENIA

Yields: 4 servings   Pan Size: 12 inch

4 chicken breasts, split, skinned, boned	½ tsp. salt
	¼ tsp. pepper
2 tbsp. crumbled feta cheese	1 egg, beaten
1 tbsp. chopped walnuts	2 tbsp. milk
1 tbsp. chopped parsley	2 tbsp. olive oil
¾ c. flour	2 tbsp. butter

Cut pocket in each chicken breast cutlet. Mix cheese, walnuts and parsley. Spoon 1 tablespoon into each cutlet; press edge to seal. Coat with mixture of flour, salt and pepper. Dip in mixture of egg and milk. Coat with remaining flour mixture. Place on waxed paper-lined plate. Chill in refrigerator. Heat olive oil and butter in skillet over medium heat until foam subsides. Add cutlets. Cook until brown. Reduce heat; turn cutlets. Cook until brown and tender.

Barbara McGrosso, Ramona Grange, California

WEST COAST CHICKEN SAUTÉ

Yields: 4 servings   Pan Size: 10 inch

4 chicken breast filets	¼ c. dry white wine
Flour	1 c. sliced fresh mushrooms
2 tbsp. oil	2 tbsp. chopped parsley
2 tbsp. melted butter	½ tsp. rosemary
¾ c. orange juice	

Flatten chicken breast filets with meat mallet. Coat lightly with flour. Brown in mixture of oil and butter in skillet. Add remaining ingredients. Simmer for 5 minutes or until chicken is tender. Place chicken on warm serving platter. Simmer pan juices until slightly thickened. Spoon over chicken. Garnish with orange sections and avocado slices.

Photograph for this recipe on page 67.

AFRICAN CHICKEN (AFRICA)

Yields: 8 servings   Pan Size: Dutch oven   Preheat: 325°

2 chickens, cut up, skinned	1 c. melted butter
1 tsp. salt	2 cloves of garlic, chopped
½ tsp. pepper	4 lg. onions, sliced
6 tomatoes, sliced	1 pkg. fresh spinach

Arrange chicken in Dutch oven. Sprinkle with salt and pepper. Place tomato slices on chicken. Drizzle with butter. Layer garlic and onions over tomatoes. Bake, covered, for 1½ hours. Add spinach. Cook, covered, on stove top for 3 to 5 minutes or until spinach is tender. Serve over rice.

Bess Farrance, Henlopen Grange, Delaware

ALMOND CHICKEN CASSEROLE

Yields: 4 to 6 servings	Pan Size: 9 x 12 inch	Preheat: 375°

1 8-oz. can pineapple chunks in heavy syrup	¾ c. almonds, toasted
Chicken stock	⅔ c. Sherry
3 c. chopped cooked chicken	¼ c. soy sauce
2 stalks celery, diagonally sliced	¼ c. cornstarch
1 green pepper, cut into 1-in. pieces	1 tsp. ginger
	½ tsp. garlic powder
	1 sm. tomato, cut into wedges
	2 tbsp. sliced green onions

Drain pineapple, reserving syrup. Add enough chicken stock to measure 2 cups liquid. Combine pineapple, chicken, celery, green pepper and almonds in bowl; mix well. Mix pineapple syrup mixture with Sherry, soy sauce, cornstarch, ginger and garlic powder in bowl; stir to dissolve cornstarch. Pour over chicken mixture; mix well. Spoon into baking dish. Bake for 40 to 45 minutes or until thickened and bubbly, stirring occasionally. Add tomato wedges. Sprinkle with green onions. Bake for 5 minutes longer. Serve with rice.

Deborah Wing, Halcyon Grange, Maine

BAKED CHICKEN AND CABBAGE (HUNGARY)

Yields: 6 servings	Pan Size: two 9 x 13 inch	Preheat: 400°

1 2½ to 3-lb. broiler-fryer, cut up	2 apples, sliced
3 tbsp. melted butter	1 tbsp. grated lemon rind
Salt and pepper to taste	2 tsp. caraway seed
1 sm. head cabbage, sliced	1 tsp. sugar
½ c. sliced onions	2 c. shredded Swiss cheese

Brush chicken with butter. Sprinkle with salt and pepper. Place in baking dish. Bake for 45 to 55 minutes or until chicken is tender. Combine cabbage, onions and apples in baking dish. Sprinkle with mixture of lemon rind, caraway seed and sugar. Bake, covered, for 30 to 35 minutes or until cabbage is tender. Sprinkle with 1 cup cheese. Arrange baked chicken on top; drizzle pan drippings over chicken. Sprinkle with remaining 1 cup cheese. Bake until cheese melts. Garnish with chopped parsley.

Eleanor Gunser, Middletown Grange, Pennsylvania

CHICKEN CASSEROLE

Yields: 6 to 8 servings   Pan Size: 1½ quart   Preheat: 350°

1 sm. onion, chopped
½ c. chopped celery
¼ c. margarine
4 c. chicken-flavored
  stuffing mix

1½ c. hot chicken broth
1½ to 2 c. chopped
  cooked chicken
¼ c. salted cashews

Sauté onion and celery in margarine in skillet. Combine with stuffing mix and broth in bowl; mix well. Layer stuffing mixture and chicken ½ at a time in casserole. Top with cashews. Bake for 45 minutes or until brown.

Iola Y. Elliott
Ohio Director of Women's Activities

CHICKEN AND DRESSING CASSEROLE

Yields: 12 to 15 servings   Pan Size: 9 x 13 inch   Preheat: 350°

½ c. butter, melted
¾ c. flour
½ tsp. salt
6 c. stock
4 c. soft bread crumbs
6 eggs, beaten
6 tbsp. butter
½ c. chopped onion

¼ c. chopped celery
¼ c. parsley
¼ tsp. sage
¼ tsp. curry powder
1 4 to 5-lb. chicken,
  cooked, boned
Bread crumbs

Blend ½ cup butter, flour and salt in saucepan. Add stock gradually. Cook for 5 minutes or until thickened, stirring constantly. Combine next 8 ingredients in bowl; mix well. Spoon into buttered baking dish. Arrange chicken over dressing. Pour sauce over top. Sprinkle with additional bread crumbs. Bake for 45 minutes.

Elizabeth Watson, Buell Grange, Oregon

CREAM CHICKEN CASSEROLE WITH POPPY SEED

Yields: 6 servings   Pan Size: 1½ quart   Preheat: 350°

1 c. sour cream
1 can cream of chicken soup
1 c. cracker crumbs

1 stick of margarine, melted
1 tsp. poppy seed
1 chicken, cooked, boned

Combine sour cream and soup in bowl; mix well. Mix cracker crumbs, margarine and poppy seed in small bowl. Layer chicken, sour cream mixture and crumb mixture in casserole until all ingredients are used, ending with crumb mixture. Bake for 30 minutes or until bubbly.

Agnes Dixon, Rocksprings Grange, Ohio

CHICKEN AND HAM LASAGNA

Yields: 6 to 8 servings	Pan Size: 9 x 13 inch	Preheat: 350°

¼ c. melted butter	1 3-oz. can mushrooms,
⅓ c. flour	drained
1 tbsp. minced onion	8 oz. lasagna noodles, cooked
⅛ tsp. garlic powder	2 c. chopped cooked chicken
⅛ tsp. pepper	10 oz. frozen asparagus
2 c. chicken broth	6 oz. mozzarella cheese,
1 c. milk	shredded
½ c. Parmesan cheese	6 oz. thinly sliced ham

Blend butter and flour in saucepan. Stir in onion, garlic powder, pepper, broth and milk. Cook until bubbly, stirring constantly. Stir in Parmesan cheese and mushrooms. Place half the noodles in baking dish. Layer chicken, asparagus, 1 cup mozzarella and ⅓ cup sauce over noodles. Add layers of ham, remaining noodles and remaining sauce. Sprinkle with remaining ½ cup mozzarella cheese. Bake at 350 degrees for 35 minutes. Let stand for 10 minutes before serving.

Priscilla Stuart, Summit Park Grange, Washington

CHICKEN PARMESAN

Yields: 8 servings	Pan Size: 9 x 13 inch	Preheat: 350°

1 c. French bread crumbs	½ tsp. salt
¾ c. grated Parmesan cheese	⅛ tsp. pepper
¼ c. chopped parsley	8 chicken legs and thighs
1 clove of garlic, minced	1 c. melted butter

Combine first 6 ingredients in shallow dish. Dip chicken in butter; coat with crumbs. Arrange in single layer in baking pan. Sprinkle with any remaining butter and crumbs. Bake for 1 hour or until chicken is tender.

Evelyn Ruckman, Morgan Hill Grange, California

CHICKEN TERIYAKI

Yields: 6 servings	Pan Size: 9 x 13 inch	Preheat: 350°

¼ c. soy sauce	¼ c. honey
¼ c. sweet wine	½ tsp. each salt, garlic salt
¼ c. sugar	1 2 to 3-lb. fryer, cut up

Combine soy sauce, wine, sugar, honey and seasonings in bowl; mix well. Let stand for 30 minutes. Add chicken. Marinate for 1 hour. Drain, reserving marinade. Arrange chicken in baking dish. Bake for 40 to 45 minutes or until chicken is tender, basting frequently with marinade.

Kim Peterson, Sauvies Island Grange, Oregon

CHICKEN TETRAZZINI

Yields: 12 servings   Pan Size: 3 quart   Preheat: 350°

1 6-lb. hen	3½ c. chicken broth
1 lg. onion, minced	1 c. heavy cream
1 lg. green pepper, minced	3 tbsp. dry Sherry
8 oz. mushrooms, chopped	1½ c. mixed Swiss and Parmesan
4 oz. pimento, chopped	cheese
6 tbsp. butter	Salt and pepper to taste
5 tbsp. flour	1 lb. thin spaghetti, cooked

Stew chicken until tender. Remove skin and bones. Cut chicken into bite-sized pieces. Sauté onion, green pepper, mushrooms and pimento in 2 tablespoons butter in skillet until tender; set aside. Blend ¼ cup butter and flour in saucepan. Stir in broth gradually. Cook over low heat until slightly thickened, stirring constantly. Stir in warmed cream. Cook for 1 minute. Stir in Sherry and ¾ cup cheese. Cook until cheese melts. Add sautéed vegetables. Combine half the sauce with spaghetti in casserole. Make well in center. Combine remaining sauce and chicken. Spoon into well. Sprinkle with remaining cheese. Bake for 30 minutes or until golden.

Mrs. Robert Proctor, Manatee Grange, North Carolina

EASY CHICKEN TETRAZZINI

Yields: 10 to 12 servings   Pan Size: 10 x 10 inch   Preheat: 225°

2 c. chopped onions	1 can cream of chicken soup
2 c. celery	6 oz. spaghetti
1 tbsp. shortening	1 can cream of mushroom soup
1 tbsp. margarine	3 oz. Parmesan cheese
2 c. chopped cooked chicken	Salt and pepper to taste
2½ c. chicken broth	

Sauté onions and celery in shortening and margarine in electric skillet. Layer remaining ingredients on top. Cook for 1 hour, stirring gently several times. Cheese should remain on top.

Marie J. Setzler, Seneca County Union Grange, Ohio

HOT CHICKEN SALAD

Yields: 12 to 15 servings   Pan Size: 9 x 13 inch   Preheat: 350°

3 c. chopped cooked chicken	⅓ c. lemon juice
2 cans cream of chicken soup	1 can water chestnuts
3 c. cooked rice	1 c. salad dressing
½ c. chopped onion	Crushed potato chips
2 c. chopped celery	

Combine first 8 ingredients in bowl; mix well. Spoon into baking dish. Bake for 30 minutes. Top with potato chips. Bake for 20 minutes longer.

Margaret Rice, Narcisse Grange, Washington

KING OF CHICKEN CASSEROLE

Yields: 6 servings   Pan Size: 3 quart

3 c. chopped cooked chicken	1 16-oz. can peas
5 c. chicken broth	1 tsp. thyme
1 c. chopped green and red peppers	1 tsp. sage
	1 tsp. oregano
1 c. chopped onion	1 tsp. celery seed
2 cans golden mushroom soup	1 8-oz. package egg noodles
	Salt and pepper to taste

Combine chicken, broth, peppers, onion, soup and peas in saucepan. Bring to a boil. Cook until peppers and onion are tender. Add seasonings. Cook on medium heat for 5 minutes. Add noodles; remove from heat. Let stand, covered, for 15 to 20 minutes or until noodles are tender. Season to taste.

Betty King, Berea Grange, North Carolina

SWEET AND SOUR CHICKEN

Yields: 4 to 6 servings   Pan Size: 9 x 13 inch   Preheat: 400°

2½ to 3 lb. chicken pieces	2 tsp. soy sauce
2 c. catsup	¾ tsp. pepper
2 tbsp. Worcestershire sauce	1 c. drained crushed pineapple
1 tbsp. brown sugar	

Arrange chicken in baking dish. Combine remaining ingredients in bowl; mix well. Spoon over chicken. Bake for 1 hour or until chicken is tender.

Erna Ruttenbur, Divide Grange, Montana

SWEET AND SOUR CHICKEN WINGS

Yields: 4 servings   Pan Size: 9 x 13 inch   Preheat: 350°

18 to 24 chicken wings	1 c. cider vinegar
1 c. cornstarch	½ c. catsup
3 eggs, beaten	1½ c. sugar
2 to 3 c. oil for frying	2 tbsp. soy sauce

Disjoint chicken wings; discard tips. Combine with water to cover in saucepan. Boil for 15 to 20 minutes or until tender. Drain, reserving ½ cup broth. Roll chicken in cornstarch, coating well; dip into eggs. Deep-fry in hot oil until light brown; drain. Place chicken in baking dish. Combine remaining ingredients and reserved broth in saucepan. Bring to a boil, mixing well. Pour over chicken. Bake for 45 minutes. Let stand for several minutes before serving.
Note: May make ahead, cool completely and serve as buffet or appetizer dish.

Karen Moir
Idaho Director of Women's Activities

BAJA CALIFORNIA CHICKEN

Yields: 8 servings	Pan Size: 9 x 13 inch	Preheat: 350°

8 chicken breast filets
Seasoned salt and pepper
  to taste
¼ c. olive oil

¼ c. tarragon vinegar
2 cloves of garlic, crushed
⅔ c. dry Sherry

Sprinkle chicken with seasoned salt and pepper. Mix olive oil, vinegar and garlic in skillet. Add chicken. Sauté until golden brown, turning frequently. Remove chicken to baking dish. Pour Sherry over chicken. Bake for 10 minutes.

Nancy Reagan
The White House

CHICKEN-CHEESE CASSEROLE

Yields: 6 to 8 servings	Pan Size: 9 x 13 inch	Preheat: 350°

5 or 6 chicken breasts,
  cooked, chopped
1 sm. onion, chopped
½ c. chopped celery
½ c. chopped green pepper

Chopped pimento
2 c. mayonnaise
1 c. half and half
¾ c. grated Cheddar cheese
1 can chow mein noodles

Combine chicken with next 7 ingredients in bowl; mix well. Spoon into baking dish. Top with noodles. Bake for 30 minutes.

Alberta Cross, Brandywine Grange, Maryland

CHICKEN ENCHILADAS

Yields: 6 servings	Pan Size: 11 x 15 inch	Preheat: 350°

18 corn tortillas
3 cans cream of chicken soup
1 can chopped green chilies
1 lg. onion, minced
½ tsp. cayenne pepper
1 tsp. chili powder

4 whole chicken breasts,
  cooked, chopped
1 lb. Cheddar cheese,
  grated
1 lb. Monterey Jack cheese,
  grated

Fry tortillas using package directions; drain and tear into pieces. Combine soup, chilies, onion and seasonings in bowl. Layer tortillas, chicken, soup mixture and cheese in greased baking pan until all ingredients are used. Bake for 35 to 40 minutes or until brown and bubbly.

Eleanor K. Grant, Poe Valley Grange, Oregon

Recipes for this photograph on pages 18, 149, 153, 158, 188.

CHICKEN GEM

Yields: 6 servings	Pan Size: 9 x 13 inch	Preheat: 350°

3 chicken breasts	**¼ c. flour**
1 onion, sliced	**1 c. sliced fresh mushrooms**
Salt and pepper to taste	**2 c. (scant) milk**
1 c. rice	**1 tbsp. curry powder**
¼ c. butter, melted	**½ c. mayonnaise**

Cook chicken with onion, salt, pepper and water to cover in saucepan. Drain and bone chicken, reserving 2 cups broth. Cook rice in reserved broth in saucepan until tender. Layer rice and chicken in baking dish. Blend butter and flour in saucepan. Cook for 2 minutes, stirring constantly. Add mushrooms. Sauté for 1 minute. Stir in milk. Cook over medium heat until thickened, stirring constantly. Add curry powder and salt and pepper to taste. Remove from heat. Stir in mayonnaise. Pour over chicken. Bake for 20 to 25 minutes or until bubbly.

Shirley Holt, Platte Grange, Michigan

HERBED CHICKEN IN FOIL

Yields: 4 servings	Pan Size: baking sheet	Preheat: 450°

1 tbsp. butter	**2 tsp. marjoram**
1 onion, sliced	**2 tbsp. chopped parsley**
2 c. cooked rice	**1 tsp. salt**
4 lg. chicken breast filets	**Dash of pepper**
Kitchen Bouquet	**½ c. dry white wine**
1 can mushroom soup	

Butter 4 squares of aluminum foil. Layer several slices onion, ½ cup rice and 1 chicken filet on each square. Brush chicken with Kitchen Bouquet. Combine soup, marjoram, parsley, salt and pepper in bowl; mix well. Spoon over chicken. Spoon 2 tablespoons wine over each filet. Seal foil. Place on baking sheet. Bake for 1 hour.

William E. Brock
Secretary, U.S. Department of Labor

CHICKEN REUBEN

Yields: 6 servings	Pan Size: 9 x 13 inch	Preheat: 375°

4 whole boned chicken	**1 qt. sauerkraut**
breasts	**8 oz. Swiss cheese, sliced**
Salt to taste	**Thousand Island dressing**

Place chicken in baking dish. Sprinkle with salt. Layer sauerkraut, cheese and dressing over chicken. Bake for 1 hour.

Janie Dennis, Richland Grange, Ohio

Recipes for this photograph on pages 90, 139, 157.

CHICKEN AND ASPARAGUS

Yields: 6 servings	Pan Size: 3 quart	Preheat: 375°

¼ c. dry white wine
¼ c. blue cheese
1 can cream of mushroom
  soup
½ tsp. salt

¼ tsp. pepper
6 chicken breasts
2 tbsp. flour
3 tbsp. oil
1 lb. fresh asparagus spears

Combine wine, cheese, soup, salt and pepper in shallow baking dish; mix well. Roll chicken in flour; coat well. Brown on both sides in oil in skillet. Arrange chicken in soup mixture, spooning soup over top. Arrange asparagus around chicken. Bake, covered, for 30 minutes or until asparagus and chicken are tender.

Jean Kitchen, Blooming Valley Grange, Michigan

CHICKEN AND ASPARAGUS CASSEROLE

Yields: 4 servings	Pan Size: 9 x 9 inch	Preheat: 375°

4 chicken breast filets
1½ tsp. MSG
¼ tsp. pepper
½ c. oil
20 oz. frozen asparagus, cooked

1 can cream of chicken soup
½ c. mayonnaise
1 tsp. lemon juice
½ tsp. curry powder
1 c. shredded sharp cheese

Sprinkle chicken with MSG and pepper. Brown on both sides in oil in skillet for 6 minutes. Layer asparagus and chicken in baking dish. Combine soup, mayonnaise, lemon juice and curry powder in bowl; mix well. Pour over chicken. Sprinkle with cheese. Bake, covered with foil, for 30 minutes.

Sandra Treichler, Fleetwood Grange, Pennsylvania

VEGETABLE CHICKEN STRATA

Yields: 8 servings	Pan Size: 9 x 13 inch	Preheat: 350°

8 slices whole wheat bread
2 c. shredded Swiss cheese
1 lg. package frozen mixed
  vegetables, thawed
16 frozen breaded chicken
  breast strips

6 eggs
2 c. milk
½ tsp. nutmeg
½ tsp. salt
¼ tsp. pepper
¼ c. Parmesan cheese

Layer half the bread, Swiss cheese and vegetables, all the chicken strips and remaining bread, Swiss cheese and vegetables in greased baking dish. Whisk eggs, milk and seasonings together in bowl. Pour over layers. Sprinkle with Parmesan cheese. Chill for 3 hours to overnight. Bake for 1 hour or until knife comes out clean.

Pearl Buell, Klondike-Piney Grange, Wyoming

PARTY CHICKEN

Yields: 8 servings	Pan Size: 9 x 13 inch	Preheat: 250°

1 to 2 pkg. dried beef	2 cans mushroom
8 slices bacon	soup
8 chicken breast filets	½ pt. sour cream

Spread dried beef in baking dish. Wrap bacon slice around each filet. Place in prepared dish. Pour mixture of soup and sour cream over top. Bake for 3 hours.

Gloria O. Abbott, Union Grange, Maine

STUFFED CORNISH HENS ORLANDO

Yields: 4 servings	Pan Size: 9 x 13 inch	Preheat: 350°

¼ c. finely chopped celery	1 tsp. orange rind
½ c. finely chopped onion	3 Florida oranges,
1 clove of garlic, crushed	peeled, chopped
1 tsp. tarragon	1 8-oz. can water chestnuts,
1 tbsp. unsalted butter	chopped
2 c. toasted whole wheat	4 Rock Cornish game hens
bread cubes	½ c. Florida orange juice

Sauté first 4 ingredients in butter in skillet until onion is tender. Combine sautéed vegetables, bread cubes, orange rind, oranges and water chestnuts in bowl; mix lightly. Stuff each game hen lightly with 1 cup stuffing. Place in baking dish. Bake for 1 hour or until tender, basting with orange juice every 15 minutes.

Photograph for this recipe on page 136.

POLYNESIAN LIVERS WITH BEAN SPROUTS

Yields: 2 servings	Pan Size: 12 inch

1 lb. chicken livers	¼ tsp. ginger
2 med. green peppers, seeded	1 c. canned juice-pack
1 can bean sprouts, drained	pineapple cubes
¾ c. chicken bouillon	1 can mushrooms
2 oz. onion, chopped	2 tbsp. cider vinegar
1 tsp. salt	1 tbsp. cornstarch
Pepper to taste	

Bring 4 cups water to a boil in skillet. Add chicken livers. Cook for 1 minute; drain. Cut peppers into 1-inch pieces. Add peppers, bean sprouts, bouillon, onion, salt, pepper and ginger to livers. Cook, covered, for 10 minutes. Add pineapple and undrained mushrooms. Stir in vinegar and mixture of cornstarch and *3 tablespoons water*. Cook until thickened, stirring constantly.

Dot Nickerson, Jacksonville Grange, Maine

BREADED TURKEY PATTIES

Yields: 40 to 45 patties	Pan Size: 3 baking sheets	Preheat: 350°

6 lb. ground turkey	2 tsp. celery salt
3 c. bread crumbs	1 tsp. each salt and pepper
6 eggs	1 tsp. poultry seasoning
1 tsp. seasoning salt	5 c. bread crumbs
1 tbsp. onion powder	12 eggs, beaten

Combine turkey, 3 cups bread crumbs, 6 eggs and seasonings in bowl; mix well. Shape into balls; flatten into patties. Coat with remaining crumbs, beaten eggs, then crumbs again. Place on baking sheets. Bake at 350 degrees for 30 minutes.

Betty Shaffer, Atascadero Grange, California

GOLDEN CHEDDAR TURKEY BAKE

Yields: 6 servings	Pan Size: 6 x 10 inch	Preheat: 325°

3 c. chopped cooked turkey	1 tbsp. lemon juice
1½ c. sliced celery	1 tsp. salt
1 c. cubed Cheddar cheese	1½ c. cornflake crumbs
¾ c. salad dressing	2 tbsp. melted butter
¼ c. toasted slivered almonds	1 med. tomato, sliced
¼ c. chopped onion	

Combine first 8 ingredients in bowl; mix lightly. Spoon into baking dish. Sprinkle mixture of cornflake crumbs and butter over top. Bake for 35 minutes. Top with tomato slices. Bake for 5 minutes longer. Garnish with additional cheese.

Marie Holmes, Progressive Grange, Vermont

TURKEY ROULETTES

Yields: 3 to 6 servings	Pan Size: 9 x 13 inch	Preheat: 425°

2 c. flour	1 to 2 c. chopped cooked
1 tbsp. baking powder	turkey
¾ tsp. salt	2 to 3 tbsp. gravy
¼ c. shortening	1 tbsp. minced green pepper
⅔ to ¾ c. milk	1 tsp. minced onion

Sift first 3 ingredients together into bowl. Cut in shortening. Add enough milk to make soft dough. Knead on lightly floured surface. Roll into 9 x 18-inch rectangle. Combine remaining ingredients in bowl. Spread on dough. Roll as for jelly roll from wide side; seal edge. Cut into 1-inch slices. Arrange cut side up in well-greased baking pan. Bake for 15 to 20 minutes. Serve with hot gravy. Garnish with parsley.

Elizabeth Clogston, Rowley Grange, Massachusetts

Vegetables and Side Dishes

A colorful display of fresh vegetables is as much a feast for the eye as sun-ripened tomatoes, peas straight from the pod, or corn minutes from the garden are for the taste. With so many climate and soil variations in this country, almost all the world's vegetables grow within our borders. And because of rapid transportation and refrigeration, the supermarket has a vegetable wonderland any time of year. In every season, an abundance of vegetables—picked from the garden or not— is available to add color and texture to our menus and nutrients to our diets.

The vegetable and side-dish recipes gathered in *The Glory of Cooking* include a number which were favorites in old-world households, as well as many which would have been familiar in Colonial kitchens. They are as delicious today as then, when growing seasons were short and root cellars ample. In addition, many recipes feature new combinations that taste and look wonderful together, unusual side dishes to complement the main course, or mixtures of vegetables and side-dish ingredients for the best of both. If the harvest has been especially plentiful, look for other ideas using vegetables in accompaniments, soups, salads, breads, and even desserts elsewhere in this book. Seasoned and sauced with flair, stir-fried or braised to perfection, vegetables can be so attractive and tempting that everyone, even reluctant vegetable fans, will enjoy them.

PENNSYLVANIA DUTCH-STYLE GREEN BEANS

Yields: 4 servings   Pan Size: 9 inch

1 16-oz. can green beans	¼ tsp. dry mustard
2 or 3 slices bacon	¼ tsp. salt
1 sm. onion, sliced	1 tbsp. brown sugar
2 tsp. cornstarch	1 tbsp. vinegar

Drain beans, reserving ½ cup liquid. Fry bacon in skillet until crisp. Drain and crumble, reserving 1 tablespoon bacon drippings. Sauté onion lightly in bacon drippings. Stir in cornstarch, dry mustard, salt and reserved bean liquid. Cook until thickened, stirring constantly. Stir in brown sugar, vinegar and beans. Cook until heated through. Spoon into serving dish. Top with crumbled bacon.

Ada B. Milburn, Lexington Grange, Kansas

CHICKEN-FRIED GREEN BEANS

Yields: 4 servings   Pan Size: 10 inch

½ c. flour	⅛ tsp. pepper
3 tbsp. cornmeal	1 16-oz. can green beans,
½ tsp. garlic powder	drained
¼ tsp. salt	3 tbsp. butter

Combine first 5 ingredients in plastic bag or container; mix well. Add beans. Shake to coat well. Cook in butter in skillet over high heat for 10 minutes or until coating is brown and crunchy. Serve drizzled with additional butter if desired.

Mrs. J. W. Hildreth Sr., Olathe Grange, Kansas

BAKED BEANS WITH MAPLE SYRUP

Yields: 8 servings   Pan Size: stockpot/3 quart   Preheat: 300°

1½ lb. dried navy beans	½ c. maple syrup
½ c. chopped onion	1 tsp. dry mustard
4 oz. salt pork, cubed	1 tsp. salt
½ c. packed brown sugar	

Wash beans. Bring beans and *12 cups water* to a boil in stockpot. Simmer for 2 minutes; remove from heat. Let stand, covered, for 1 hour to overnight. Simmer beans, covered, for 1 hour or until tender. Drain, reserving liquid. Combine beans, 1½ cups reserved liquid and remaining ingredients in casserole. Bake, covered, for 3½ to 4 hours, stirring occasionally and adding additional reserved bean liquid if necessary.

Sandy Turner, Statesville Grange, Tennessee

BUCKAROO BEANS

Yields: 4 servings	Pan Size: Crock•Pot

2 c. dried pinto beans	2 6-oz. cans tomato paste
2 med. onions, chopped	1 tsp. dry mustard
2 green peppers, chopped	1 tbsp. chili powder
2 cloves of garlic, chopped	½ tsp. oregano
4 slices bacon	1 tbsp. salt
¼ c. packed brown sugar	1 bay leaf

Soak beans in water to cover overnight. Drain. Combine with remaining ingredients and *4 cups water* in Crock•Pot. Cook on Low for 8 to 10 hours or until beans are tender. Remove bay leaf.

Emma DuVall, Little Bear Grange, Wyoming

BROCCOLI CASSEROLE

Yields: 6 servings	Pan Size: 1½ quart	Preheat: 350°

2 tbsp. butter, melted	8 oz. cream cheese, softened
1 tbsp. flour	2 pkg. frozen chopped broccoli,
Salt and pepper to taste	cooked, drained
1 c. milk	Bread crumbs

Blend butter, flour, salt and pepper in saucepan. Stir in milk gradually. Cook until thickened, stirring constantly. Add cream cheese; mix until smooth. Combine with broccoli in casserole; mix gently. Bake for 20 minutes. Sprinkle with bread crumbs. Broil for several minutes until brown.

Alta M. Berry, Obwebetuck Grange, Connecticut

BROCCOLI-RICE PUFF

Yields: 3 to 4 servings	Pan Size: 9 inch	Preheat: 350°

1½ c. hot cooked rice	3 oz. skim milk
3 oz. sharp Cheddar cheese, grated	¾ c. canned sliced mushrooms, drained
1 egg, lightly beaten	5 oz. frozen chopped broccoli
Salt to taste	Pepper to taste
2 eggs	

Combine rice, ½ of the cheese, 1 egg and salt in bowl; mix well. Press into pie plate to form crust. Beat 2 eggs in bowl. Add skim milk, mushrooms, broccoli, salt and pepper; mix well. Spoon into prepared plate. Bake for 20 minutes. Sprinkle with remaining cheese. Bake for 10 minutes longer.

Mary White, David Crockett Grange, Texas

ROTKRAUT (GERMANY) Red Cabbage

Yields: 4 to 6 servings   Pan Size: 10 inch

4 slices bacon, chopped
1 med. onion, sliced
1 sm. head red cabbage, sliced
2 to 3 apples, peeled, chopped

¼ c. cider vinegar
2 tbsp. sugar
Salt to taste

Sauté bacon and onion in skillet until transparent. Add cabbage. Sauté until transparent. Add apples and 2 tablespoons vinegar. Stir in *1 cup hot water*. Simmer, covered, for 30 to 40 minutes; do not overcook. Add remaining vinegar, sugar and salt; mix well. Spoon into serving dish. Serve with beef, venison or fish.

Pearl D. Orient, New Alexandria Community Grange, Pennsylvania

SKILLET CABBAGE

Yields: 10 servings   Pan Size: 10 inch

Bacon drippings
4 c. chopped cabbage
2 lg. onions, sliced
2 c. chopped celery
2 tomatoes, chopped

1 green pepper, sliced
  into rings
2 tbsp. sugar
¾ tsp. salt
¼ tsp. pepper

Heat bacon drippings in skillet over low heat. Add remaining ingredients. Cook, covered, for 5 to 10 minutes or until tender-crisp, stirring occasionally. Spoon into serving dish.

Roma Hunter, Sodom Grange, Ohio

KULSKI Z KAPUSTA PO POLSKI (POLAND) Noodles and Cabbage

Yields: 6 to 8 servings   Pan Size: 12 inch

¼ c. chopped onion
¼ c. butter
4 c. chopped cabbage
1 tsp. caraway seed

½ tsp. salt
⅛ tsp. pepper
8 oz. noodles, cooked
½ c. sour cream

Sauté onion in butter in skillet. Add cabbage. Sauté for 5 minutes or until tender-crisp. Add remaining ingredients; mix well. Cook for 5 minutes, stirring frequently.

Carol A. Pherigo, Dracut Grange, Massachusetts

CARROT CASSEROLE

Yields: 6 servings	Pan Size: 1½ quart	Preheat: 350°

1½ lb. carrots, peeled,
  chopped
3 eggs, beaten
1 sm. onion, grated

2 tbsp. butter
2 c. grated sharp Cheddar
  cheese
Dill to taste

Cook carrots in water to cover in saucepan until tender. Drain and mash carrots. Add remaining ingredients; mix well. Spoon into greased casserole. Bake for 40 minutes.

Irene R. Moll, Chalfont Grange, Pennsylvania

AUNT MAUDE'S CARROT LOAF

Yields: 8 servings	Pan Size: 4 cup	Preheat: 350°

2 c. grated carrots
1 tbsp. minced onion
2 eggs, beaten
½ c. bread crumbs
3 tbsp. melted butter

½ c. evaporated milk
1 tbsp. sugar
1 tsp. salt
1 pkg. frozen peas, cooked
1 recipe white sauce

Combine carrots, onion, eggs, bread crumbs, butter, evaporated milk, sugar and salt in bowl; mix well. Pack into ring mold. Place in larger pan of water. Bake for 1 hour. Stir peas into hot white sauce. Invert carrot loaf onto serving plate. Spoon creamed peas into center.

Frances Lyke, Stephens Mill's Grange, New York

SCALLOPED CARROTS

Yields: 6 servings	Pan Size: 2 quart	Preheat: 350°

4 c. sliced carrots
6 oz. Cheddar cheese, sliced
1 med. onion, minced
2 tbsp. butter
2 tbsp. flour
¼ tsp. dry mustard

⅛ tsp. celery salt
½ tsp. salt
⅛ tsp. pepper
1 c. milk
Butter
½ c. bread crumbs

Cook carrots in a small amount of water in saucepan until tender-crisp; drain. Layer carrots and cheese ½ at a time in casserole. Sauté onion in 2 tablespoons butter in saucepan for 2 to 3 minutes. Add flour and seasonings; mix well. Stir in milk gradually. Cook until thickened, stirring constantly. Pour over layers. Dot with additional butter. Sprinkle with crumbs. Bake for 30 minutes.

Norma Jean Davis, Hopewell Grange, Illinois

KIRCINTOTT KARFLOL TEFFOLOS MARTASSAL (HUNGARY)
Deep-Fried Cauliflower with Sour Cream Sauce

Yields: 6 servings	Pan Size: deep 2 quart

Flowerets of 1 med. head	¼ tsp. pepper
cauliflower	⅔ c. fine dry bread crumbs
2 egg yolks, lightly beaten	½ tsp. salt
1 c. sour cream	¼ tsp. pepper
2 tsp. lemon juice	2 eggs, lightly beaten
¼ tsp. paprika	¼ c. milk
½ tsp. salt	Oil for deep frying

Soak cauliflower in cold salted water to cover in saucepan for 30 minutes. Drain and rinse. Cook in water to cover for 20 minutes or until tender-crisp; drain. Combine egg yolks, sour cream, lemon juice, paprika, ½ teaspoon salt and ¼ teaspoon pepper in double boiler. Cook over simmering water for 3 to 5 minutes or until thickened and smooth, stirring constantly; keep warm. Mix bread crumbs, ½ teaspoon salt and ¼ teaspoon pepper in bowl. Dip cauliflower into mixture of eggs and milk; coat with bread crumbs. Deep-fry several at a time in 365-degree oil; drain on paper towels. Place in serving dish. Spoon sour cream sauce over top.

Dorothy Peterson, Orwell Grange, Ohio

CELERY PARMIGIANA

Yields: 6 servings	Pan Size: 1½ quart	Preheat: 350°

4 c. sliced celery	4 slices crisp-fried bacon,
¼ c. chopped onion	crumbled
½ clove of garlic, minced	2 tomatoes, peeled, chopped
1 tsp. salt	1 c. Parmesan cheese

Combine celery, onion, garlic, salt and *1 cup water* in saucepan. Simmer, covered, for 20 minutes. Drain. Place in casserole. Layer bacon, tomatoes and cheese over celery. Bake, uncovered, for 15 minutes.

LUCY'S CORN FRITTERS

Yields: 4 to 6 servings	Pan Size: 10 inch

4 med. ears fresh corn	½ tsp. salt
2 tbsp. flour	½ tsp. sugar
½ tsp. baking powder	2 eggs

Cut kernels from ears of corn; scrape cobs well. Combine with remaining ingredients in bowl. Pour by ½ cupfuls onto greased medium-hot griddle. Cook until brown on both sides. Serve hot with butter.
Note: This is my great-great grandmother's recipe.

Lucille A. Grow, North Creek Valley Grange, Washington

CUCUMBERS AND ONIONS AU GRATIN

Yields: 6 servings	Pan Size: 1½ quart	Preheat: 450°

3 lg. cucumbers, peeled	Salt and pepper to taste
1¼ lb. small whole onions	1 c. bread crumbs
3 tbsp. flour	Parmesan cheese
2 tbsp. butter	Paprika
2 c. milk	Chopped parsley

Cut cucumbers lengthwise into halves, discarding seed. Cut into ¼ x 1½-inch strips. Combine with salted water to cover in saucepan. Simmer until tender-crisp; drain. Cook onions in water to cover in saucepan until tender-crisp; drain. Blend flour and butter in small saucepan. Cook until bubbly. Stir in milk, salt and pepper. Cook until thickened, stirring constantly. Pour over cucumbers and onions in buttered casserole. Top with bread crumbs, Parmesan cheese, paprika and parsley. Bake for 20 minutes or until light brown.

Jeanette Schofield, Friend of Middlebury Grange, Vermont

CHINESE SCALLOPED EGGPLANT

Yields: 6 servings	Pan Size: 1 quart	Preheat: 375°

1 med. eggplant, peeled, chopped	1 c. drained bean sprouts
1 sm. onion, finely chopped	1 c. drained canned mushrooms
1 c. chopped celery	⅛ tsp. paprika
2 tbsp. chopped parsley	½ tsp. salt
	½ c. grated cheese

Combine eggplant, onion and celery with *½ cup water* in saucepan. Cook until tender; drain. Add parsley. Layer eggplant mixture, bean sprouts and mushrooms in casserole until all ingredients are used, ending with eggplant. Sprinkle with paprika, salt and cheese. Bake for 30 minutes.

Eldred Dipman, Ash Valley Grange, Kansas

MJEDDRAH (ISRAEL) Lentils and Rice

Yields: 6 servings   Pan Size: 2 quart

1½ c. lentils	¼ c. olive oil
2 tsp. salt	¾ c. rice
2 c. coarsely chopped onions	1½ tbsp. butter

Soak lentils in cold water to cover in saucepan for several hours. Drain. Add *4 cups water* and 1 teaspoon salt. Bring to a boil over medium heat; reduce heat. Simmer for several minutes, stirring occasionally. Cook onions, covered, with 1 teaspoon salt in olive oil in skillet until transparent. Sauté rice lightly in butter in skillet for 2 minutes. Add onions and rice to lentils. Simmer just until rice and lentils are tender, adding hot water if necessary to make of desired consistency; do not overcook.
Note: It is traditionally believed that this is the dish for which Esau sold his birthright to his brother, Jacob.

Irene Cates, Cincinnatus Grange, New York

OKRA FOOGARTH

Yields: 10 servings   Pan Size: 12 inch

2 med. onions, chopped	2 lb. okra, sliced
2 lg. cloves of garlic, minced	6 med. tomatoes, peeled,
½ tsp. ginger	chopped
½ tsp. cayenne pepper	2 tbsp. coconut
½ c. oil	2 tsp. salt

Sauté onions and garlic with ginger and cayenne pepper in oil in skillet for 5 minutes. Stir in remaining ingredients. Bring to a boil; reduce heat. Simmer, covered, for 5 minutes. Simmer, uncovered, until sauce is of desired consistency and coats okra well.
Note: May use Japanese okra or frozen okra.

Rachel H. Mann, Woodpecker Community Grange, Virginia

BAKED ONION RINGS

Yields: 6 servings   Pan Size: 9 x 13 inch   Preheat: 350°

12 med. onions, sliced	Salt and pepper to taste
½ 7-oz. package potato	2 cans cream of mushroom
chips, crushed	soup
8 oz. mild Cheddar	½ c. milk
cheese, grated	Paprika

Alternate layers of onion rings, potato chip crumbs and cheese in greased baking dish until all ingredients are used. Sprinkle with salt and pepper. Pour mixture of soup and milk over top. Sprinkle with paprika.

Glen Chilton, Shive Grange, Texas

CREAMED ONIONS WITH MUSHROOMS AND CARROTS

Yields: 6 to 8 servings	Pan Size: 2 quart

24 sm. white onions	¾ tsp. salt
1½ c. diagonally sliced carrots	¼ tsp. thyme
3 tbsp. butter, melted	⅛ tsp. pepper
2 tbsp. flour	8 oz. mushrooms, thickly sliced
1 c. milk	

Cook onions in lightly salted boiling water to cover in saucepan for 8 to 10 minutes or just until tender. Add carrots. Cook for 3 minutes or just until tender. Drain, reserving ½ cup liquid. Blend butter and flour in saucepan. Cook over medium heat for 2 minutes, stirring constantly. Stir in cooking liquid, milk, salt, thyme and pepper. Bring to a boil, stirring constantly. Simmer for 3 minutes. Add mushrooms. Cook over low heat for 5 minutes. Add onions and carrots. Cook, covered, for 3 minutes.

Photograph for this recipe on page 135.

SWIVELKUCHEN (ALSACE-LORRAINE) Onion Pie

Yields: 6 servings	Pan Size: 9 inch	Preheat: 400°

1 recipe 1 crust pie pastry	Freshly grated nutmeg
¼ c. unsalted butter	and pepper to taste
2 tbsp. olive oil	3 egg yolks
1½ lb. yellow onions, thinly	¾ c. (or less) heavy cream
sliced	5 tbsp. chopped lean bacon
Salt to taste	2 tbsp. olive oil

Line pie plate with thinly-rolled pastry; prick bottom lightly with fork. Chill, covered, in refrigerator. Melt butter with 2 tablespoons olive oil in skillet. Add onions. Cook, covered, for 10 minutes or until tender, stirring frequently. Season to taste. Beat egg yolks and cream in bowl until thick. Add onions, mixing until slightly thickened. Spoon into pie shell. Place on baking sheet. Bake for 30 minutes. Sauté bacon in 2 tablespoons olive oil in skillet until crisp. Sprinkle over pie.

Meta L. Stack, West Stockbridge Grange, Massachusetts

COLCANNON (IRELAND) Potatoes and Cabbage

Yields: 4 to 6 servings	Pan Size: 10 inch

6 potatoes, cooked	1 tbsp. butter
Salt and pepper to taste	1½ c. chopped cabbage, cooked
1 onion, minced	Melted butter

Mash potatoes; season to taste. Sauté onion in 1 tablespoon butter in skillet for 10 minutes; do not brown. Add potatoes and cabbage; beat to mix well. Cook over low heat until heated through. Serve hot with "lashings" of melted butter over the "lot."

Blanche Rice, Hamburg Grange, New York

SCALLOPED POTATOES AND CARROTS

Yields: 6 to 8 servings	Pan Size: 2 quart	Preheat: 350°

4 c. thinly sliced peeled potatoes	¼ c. butter
3 c. thinly sliced peeled carrots	¼ c. flour
½ c. chopped onion	¼ tsp. dillweed
⅓ c. chopped parsley	2 tsp. seasoned salt
	3 c. milk

Combine potatoes and carrots in casserole. Sauté onion and parsley in butter in saucepan. Stir in flour, dillweed and seasoned salt. Stir in milk gradually. Cook until thickened, stirring constantly. Pour over vegetables; mix well. Bake, covered, for 30 minutes. Bake, uncovered, for 1 hour or until vegetables are tender.

Gwendolyn Swenson, Oak Leaf Grange, Minnesota

GOURMET POTATOES

Yields: 8 servings	Pan Size: 2 quart	Preheat: 325°

8 med. potatoes	⅓ c. chopped green onions
2 c. shredded Cheddar cheese	1 tsp. salt
¼ c. butter	½ tsp. pepper
1½ c. sour cream	

Cook unpeeled potatoes in water to cover in saucepan; drain. Cool. Peel and coarsely shred potatoes. Melt cheese with butter in saucepan, stirring constantly. Add sour cream, green onions and seasonings; mix well. Fold in potatoes. Spoon into buttered casserole. Bake for 25 minutes.

Christine Sechler, Kingwood Grange, Pennsylvania

LANTTULAATIKKO (FINLAND) Rutabaga Casserole

Yields: 8 to 10 servings	Pan Size: 2 quart	Preheat: 350°

6 c. chopped peeled rutabaga	½ c. heavy cream
2 eggs, beaten	½ c. packed brown sugar
½ c. cornflake crumbs	¼ c. butter
	½ tsp. salt

Cook rutabaga in salted water to cover in saucepan until tender. Drain and mash. Add remaining ingredients; mix well. Spoon into buttered casserole. Bake for 1 hour or until light brown.
Note: This is traditionally served at Christmas.

Sylvia M. Woerner, Schenevus Valley Grange, New York

SPINACH-CHEESE PIE (GREECE)

Yields: 8 servings　　　　Pan Size: 9 x 13 inch　　　　Preheat: 350°

1 egg	2 pkg. frozen spinach,
1½ tsp. oil	thawed, drained
1 c. (or more) flour	3 eggs
¼ tsp. salt	2 c. milk
1⅔ c. feta cheese	½ c. melted butter

Beat 1 egg with oil and *¼ cup warm water* in bowl. Add mixture of flour and salt; mix well. Knead in enough additional flour to make easily handled dough. Divide into 2 portions. Roll into 2 rectangles on floured surface. Fit 1 rectangle into buttered baking dish. Layer cheese and spinach over pastry. Process 3 eggs and milk in blender until smooth. Pour over spinach. Drizzle butter over top. Top with remaining pastry. Seal edges; cut vents. Brush with additional melted butter. Bake for 40 minutes or until brown.

Eldora Dickens, North Bayside Grange, Oregon

SPINACH SOUFFLÉ WITH SHRIMP SAUCE

Yields: 8 to 10 servings　　　　Pan Size: 2 quart　　　　Preheat: 350°

2 pkg. frozen chopped	3 c. white sauce
spinach	½ tsp. salt
8 eggs, separated	Dash of pepper
1 med. onion, chopped	1 can shrimp, drained
1 lb. cheese, grated	

Cook spinach in salted water in saucepan; drain well. Combine beaten egg yolks, onion, cheese, spinach, 1¼ cups white sauce and seasonings in bowl; mix well. Fold in stiffly beaten egg whites. Spoon into buttered casserole. Bake for 40 to 45 minutes or until set. Mix shrimp with remaining white sauce in saucepan. Heat to serving temperature. Serve over soufflé.

Eleanor Kincaid, Friend of Lookout Mt. Grange, Oregon

APPLE-STUFFED ACORN SQUASH

Yields: 8 servings　　　　Pan Size: 9 x 13 inch　　　　Preheat: 325°

4 med. acorn squash	4 tart red apples, chopped
2 tbsp. margarine	8 slices crisp-fried bacon,
¾ c. Smucker's apple jelly	crumbled

Cut squash into halves lengthwise; scoop out and discard seed. Place cut side up in baking dish. Pour *1 cup boiling water* around squash. Bake, covered with foil, for 1 hour. Heat margarine and jelly in saucepan until melted. Add apples. Spoon into squash cavities. Bake, uncovered, until squash is tender. Sprinkle with bacon.

Photograph for this recipe on page 101.

CRUNCHY SQUASH CASSEROLE

Yields: 8 servings	Pan Size: 2 quart	Preheat: 350°

2   10-oz. packages frozen squash
1 c. chopped onion
1 tbsp. margarine
8 oz. sour cream
1 can cream of chicken soup

1 can sliced water
    chestnuts, drained
6 oz. stuffing mix
6 tbsp. melted margarine

Cook squash according to package directions; drain well. Sauté onion in 1 tablespoon margarine in saucepan. Add squash, onion, sour cream, soup and water chestnuts; mix well. Combine stuffing mix and 6 tablespoons melted margarine in bowl. Stir ¾ of the stuffing mixture into squash mixture; mix well. Spoon into lightly greased casserole. Sprinkle with remaining stuffing mixture. Bake for 20 minutes.

Eunice Massey, Brogden Grange, North Carolina

STEAMED SQUASH CASSEROLE

Yields: 6 to 8 servings	Pan Size: 2 quart	Preheat: 350°

5 or 6 squash, sliced
1 lg. green pepper, sliced
1 lg. onion, sliced
¾ c. mayonnaise
2 eggs, beaten

2 c. grated sharp Cheddar cheese
Salt and pepper to taste
Seasoned salt
1 stack Ritz crackers, crushed
1 stick butter, melted

Combine squash, green pepper and onion in steamer basket in large saucepan. Steam for 15 minutes or until tender. Combine with mayonnaise, eggs, cheese and seasonings in casserole; mix gently. Top with mixture of cracker crumbs and butter. Bake for 25 minutes or until brown and bubbly.
Note: May use yellow squash, zucchini or combination of the two.

William H. Walker III
Commissioner, Tennessee Department of Agriculture

SQUASH CASSEROLE

Yields: 8 to 10 servings	Pan Size: 6 cup	Preheat: 350°

2 or 3 acorn, butternut or
    Hubbard squash
¼ c. butter
2 tbsp. grated onion

½ tsp. rosemary
¼ tsp. coriander
1 tsp. salt
½ to ¾ c. chopped pecans

Cut squash into halves; discard seed. Place cut side down in ¼-inch boiling water in baking dish. Bake for 30 to 35 minutes or until fork tender. Scoop out pulp; measure 4 to 5 cups. Beat until smooth in mixer bowl. Add next 5 ingredients; mix well. Spoon into casserole. Sprinkle with pecans. Bake for 20 minutes.

Katherine E. Langworthy, Fabius Grange, Michigan

JERRY'S SQUASH CASSEROLE

Yields: 6 servings	Pan Size: 1 quart	Preheat: 300°

3 med. crookneck squash,
  sliced
2 med. onions, chopped
1 lg. green pepper, chopped
1 sm. red pepper, chopped
1 can chopped mushrooms,
  drained

6 tbsp. margarine
6 tbsp. flour
1 lg. can evaporated milk
Salt and pepper to taste
1 c. grated cheese
1½ c. herb-flavored croutons

Combine squash, onions, peppers and mushrooms in water in saucepan. Cook until tender; drain. Blend margarine and flour in saucepan. Stir in evaporated milk gradually. Cook until thickened, stirring constantly. Stir in salt, pepper, squash mixture and cheese; mix well. Spoon into baking dish. Sprinkle with croutons. Bake for 45 minutes.

Jerry Mealey, Holley Grange, Oregon

POSH SQUASH

Yields: 6 to 8 servings	Pan Size: 9 x 13 inch	Preheat: 375°

2 lb. crookneck or patty
  pan squash
2 eggs
1 sm. onion, finely chopped
¼ c. chopped green pepper

1 c. mayonnaise
¼ tsp. thyme
Salt and pepper to taste
¾ c. Parmesan cheese
1 tbsp. butter

Cut squash into ½-inch slices. Cook in small amount of boiling salted water in saucepan for 5 minutes or just until tender; drain. Beat eggs in bowl. Add next 6 ingredients and squash; mix well. Spoon into baking dish. Sprinkle with cheese. Dot with butter. Bake for 25 minutes.

Ruth Jacobson, Lorane Grange, Oregon

MAPLE-WALNUT SWEET POTATOES

Yields: 6 to 8 servings	Pan Size: 1½ quart	Preheat: 400°

8 med. sweet potatoes
¼ c. maple syrup
¼ c. butter

½ tsp. salt
Pinch of cloves
½ c. chopped walnuts

Bake sweet potatoes for 50 minutes or until soft. Cut into halves. Cool slightly; peel. Press through sieve into bowl. Add syrup, butter, salt and cloves; mix well. Turn into buttered casserole. Sprinkle with walnuts. Bake at 400 degrees for 20 minutes.

Photograph for this recipe on page 135.

SWEET POTATO FLUFF

Yields: 6 servings   Pan Size: 9 x 9 inch   Preheat: 425°

¼ c. butter, softened	2 c. mashed cooked
½ c. sugar	sweet potatoes
3 tbsp. lemon juice	1 c. milk
1 tbsp. grated lemon rind	½ tsp. cinnamon
3 eggs, separated	

Cream butter and sugar in bowl until fluffy. Blend in lemon juice and rind. Add beaten egg yolks, sweet potatoes, milk and cinnamon; mix well. Fold in stiffly beaten egg whites gently. Spoon into greased baking dish. Bake for 10 minutes; reduce temperature to 350 degrees. Bake for 40 minutes longer.

Isabel M. Burt, Raritan Valley Grange, New Jersey

SWEET POTATO SOUFFLÉ

Yields: 8 servings   Pan Size: 2 quart   Preheat: 350°

3 c. mashed cooked	2 tbsp. vanilla extract
sweet potatoes	1 c. packed brown sugar
1½ c. sugar	½ c. self-rising flour
3 eggs	½ c. butter, softened
1 c. milk	½ c. chopped pecans
1½ c. butter, softened	

Combine sweet potatoes, sugar, eggs, milk, 1½ cups butter and vanilla in bowl; mix well. Spoon into casserole. Mix remaining ingredients by hand in bowl until crumbly. Sprinkle over casserole. Bake for 45 minutes to 1 hour or until brown and set.

Joe Frank Harris
Governor of Georgia

SWEET POTATO CASSEROLE

Yields: 12 servings   Pan Size: 9 x 13 inch   Preheat: 350°

3 c. mashed cooked	1 tsp. vanilla extract
sweet potatoes	1 c. packed brown sugar
½ c. melted margarine	½ c. flour
1 c. sugar	½ c. melted margarine
¼ c. milk	1 c. chopped nuts
1 c. coconut	

Combine sweet potatoes, ½ cup margarine, sugar, milk, coconut and vanilla in bowl; mix well. Spoon into baking dish. Mix remaining ingredients in bowl until crumbly. Sprinkle over casserole. Bake for 20 to 30 minutes or until brown.

Valera Riley, Paulding Grange, Ohio

FRIED GREEN TOMATOES

Yields: 4 servings	Pan Size: 10 inch

1¼ lb. green tomatoes	Salt to taste
⅓ c. cornmeal	½ tsp. pepper
⅓ c. flour	¼ c. oil
1 tsp. onion powder	

Slice tomatoes ¼ inch thick. Combine cornmeal, flour, onion powder, salt and pepper in shallow dish; mix well. Dip tomatoes in cornmeal mixture, coating well. Sauté half the tomatoes in 2 tablespoons oil in skillet for 1½ minutes on each side; drain on paper towels. Sauté remaining tomatoes in remaining oil.

Lillian Deist, Meigsville Grange, Ohio

SCALLOPED TOMATOES

Yields: 4 servings	Pan Size: 1 quart	Preheat: 375°

1 20-oz. can tomatoes	Dash of pepper
1 c. small bread cubes	½ c. bread crumbs
2 tbsp. sugar	2 tbsp. bacon drippings
2 tbsp. butter	Butter
⅛ tsp. salt	

Combine tomatoes, bread cubes, sugar, 2 tablespoons butter, salt and pepper in bowl; mix well. Spoon into buttered baking dish. Sauté bread crumbs in bacon drippings in small skillet. Sprinkle over tomatoes. Dot with additional butter. Bake until bubbly and brown.

Helen B. LaFond, Halestown Grange, New Hampshire

ZUCCHINI CASSEROLE

Yields: 4 to 6 servings	Pan Size: 2 quart	Preheat: 350°

2 lb. zucchini	2 eggs, beaten
1 med. onion	½ c. oil
1 med. green pepper	½ c. Waverly wafer crumbs
⅓ bunch parsley	Salt and pepper to taste

Cut zucchini, onion and green pepper into pieces. Process vegetables and parsley a small amount at a time in food processor until coarsely chopped. Combine with eggs, oil, cracker crumbs and seasonings in bowl; mix well. Spoon into greased casserole. Bake for 1 hour.

Mr. and Mrs. Richard Lyng
Secretary, U.S. Department of Agriculture

LAYERED VEGETABLE CASSEROLE

Yields: 8 servings   Pan Size: 2 quart   Preheat: 350°

1 bunch broccoli
1 c. green beans
4 med. carrots, peeled, sliced
   diagonally
1 c. cauliflowerets
1 med. onion, cut into
   halves, sliced lengthwise

2 cloves of garlic, minced
Butter
Juice of 1 lemon
1 tsp. (or more) savory
Freshly ground pepper
Salt to taste
8 oz. tomato juice

Cut broccoli into spears. Cook in small amount of water in saucepan just until tender-crisp; drain. Arrange spoke-fashion with stems toward center in buttered casserole. Cook beans, carrots and cauliflower in same manner. Layer over broccoli. Sauté onion and garlic lightly in a small amount of butter in skillet until transparent; remove from heat. Stir in remaining ingredients. Pour over vegetables. Bake, covered, for 20 minutes or until heated through.
Note: May substitute snow peas for green beans.

Mario Cuomo
Governor of New York

RATATOUILLE TOPPING

Yields: 4 servings   Pan Size: 12 inch

1 sm. eggplant, cubed
1 red onion, chopped
3 cloves of garlic, minced
1 green pepper, coarsely
   chopped

1 red pepper, coarsely chopped
2 tomatoes, coarsely chopped
1 c. cooked cut green beans
1 zucchini, cut into 1-in. strips
1 c. sliced mushrooms

Sauté eggplant in large skillet over medium heat until tender. Add onion and garlic. Sauté for 1 minute. Add peppers. Cook for 1 minute longer. Add tomatoes and *½ cup water*. Simmer for 3 minutes. Add green beans, zucchini and mushrooms. Cook until heated through. Serve on hot baked potatoes.

Photograph for this recipe on page 102.

CHEESE GRITS SOUFFLÉ

Yields: 6 servings   Pan Size: 1½ quart   Preheat: 350°

1 c. quick-cooking grits
1 tsp. salt
6 tbsp. butter
1 roll garlic cheese
2 eggs, beaten

¼ c. milk
Salt and pepper to taste
1 c. cornflake crumbs
2 tbsp. melted butter

Cook grits with salt and *4½ cups water* in saucepan until water is absorbed. Add 6 tablespoons butter and cheese, stirring until well blended. Cool. Mix eggs and milk in bowl. Season with salt and pepper. Add to grits mixture; mix well. Spoon into buttered casserole. Top with mixture of cornflake crumbs and melted butter. Bake, covered, for 45 minutes or until set.

Willard Scott
The Today Show-NBC, New York

ORANGE BULGUR

Yields: 4 to 6 servings   Pan Size: 10 inch

½ c. chopped onion
½ c. chopped celery
1 clove of garlic, crushed
¼ c. unsalted butter
1 c. bulgur
1 c. Florida orange juice

1   15-oz. can kidney beans, drained
4 oz. fresh mushrooms, sliced
⅓ c. raisins
¼ c. wheat germ
2 oranges, sectioned

Sauté onion, celery and garlic in butter in skillet for 1 minute. Add bulgur. Sauté for 5 minutes. Add orange juice and *1 cup water*. Add beans, mushrooms and raisins. Simmer, covered, for 15 minutes or until bulgur is tender and liquid is absorbed. Spoon into serving dish. Garnish with wheat germ and orange sections.
Note: This is an excellent stuffing for tomatoes, green peppers and acorn squash.

Photograph for this recipe on page 136.

CHILIES RELLENOS

Yields: 6 servings   Pan Size: 8x12 inch   Preheat: 350°

16 canned whole green
   chili peppers
1 lb. Monterey Jack
   cheese
3 eggs

¼ c. flour
1½ c. milk
Pinch of salt
Grated Colby longhorn cheese

Wash and seed peppers; dry on paper towel. Cut Monterey Jack cheese into 16 strips. Place 1 strip in each pepper. Arrange stuffed peppers in buttered baking dish. Beat eggs, flour, milk and salt in bowl until smooth. Pour over peppers. Top with Colby cheese. Bake for 35 minutes or until knife inserted in center comes out clean. Serve with tossed salad.

Flo Carter, David Crockett Grange, Texas

COWBOY QUICHE

Yields: 10 servings	Pan Size: 9 x 13 inch	Preheat: 350°

**5 cans whole green chilies,
  drained, seeded
28 oz. Monterey Jack
  cheese, grated**

**5 eggs, beaten
1 tbsp. flour
1   13-oz. can evaporated milk
Salt and pepper to taste**

Grease bottom of baking dish lightly. Layer chilies and cheese ½ at a time in prepared dish. Beat eggs, flour, evaporated milk and seasonings in bowl until smooth. Pour over layers. Bake for 30 minutes or until set. Let stand for 30 minutes before serving.

*James A. Baker III
Secretary, U.S. Department of the Treasury*

BASIC BREAD STUFFING

Yields: 16 cups	Pan Size: 10 inch

**4 c. chopped celery
1 c. chopped onion
1 c. butter
16 c. soft bread cubes**

**1 tbsp. salt
1½ tsp. poultry seasoning
½ tsp. each sage, pepper
Hot broth**

Sauté celery and onion in butter in skillet. Combine with bread, seasonings and enough broth to moisten in bowl; mix well.
Note: May add chopped cooked giblets, 1 cup sautéed apple, 4 cups chopped boiled chestnuts or 8 ounces sautéed mushrooms. Use milk for broth with chestnuts.

Photograph for this recipe on page 135.

ROASTER FULL OF TURKEY DRESSING

Yields: 50 servings	Pan Size: roaster	Preheat: 350°

**10 loaves bread
1 lg. bunch celery, chopped
1 to 2 lb. onions, chopped
1 lb. margarine
12 eggs, beaten**

**2 to 3 tbsp. poultry seasoning
1 to 2 tbsp. sage
2 tbsp. salt
1 tsp. pepper
Broth**

Dry or toast bread. Break into small pieces; place in large bowl. Cook celery and onions in water to cover in saucepan until tender; remove from heat. Add margarine; stir until melted. Add to bread; mix well. Mix in eggs. Add seasonings and enough broth to make very moist mixture. Adjust seasonings. Pour into roaster. Bake for 1½ to 2 hours or until firm in center.

Home Economics Committee of Williamsport Grange, Ohio

WILD RICE DRESSING

Yields: 5 servings   Pan Size: large saucepan

1½ c. wild rice	¼ c. chopped green pepper
1 tsp. salt	1 c. chopped celery and leaves
½ c. chopped onion	1 can mushrooms, drained
1 stick butter	Salt and pepper to taste

Wash rice thoroughly in warm water. Cook with salt according to package directions for 20 minutes. Rinse under cold water; drain. Sauté onion in butter in saucepan. Add green pepper, celery and mushrooms. Sauté until tender. Stir in rice, salt and pepper. Stuff into chicken or turkey. Roast as directed.

Judge Cornelia G. Kennedy
Michigan, Member of Bicentennial Commission

SPANISH RICE

Yields: 4 servings   Pan Size: 1½ quart   Preheat: 350°

6 tbsp. rice	1 c. chopped tomatoes
½ c. shredded cheese	2 tbsp. butter
1 onion, chopped	1 tsp. salt
1 green pepper, chopped	¼ tsp. pepper

Combine all ingredients and *2 cups boiling water* in bowl; mix well. Spoon into casserole. Bake for 1 hour or until rice is tender, stirring occasionally.

Mrs. James H. Hessler, Capt. John Brady Grange, Pennsylvania

MOTHER'S HICKORY NUT LOAF

Yields: 6 servings   Pan Size: 5x 9 inch   Preheat: 350°

1 c. rice, cooked	½ c. butter
1 c. finely chopped	½ c. cracker crumbs
hickory nuts	1 c. chopped tomatoes
1 egg	1 tbsp. sugar
½ c. sugar	1 tbsp. flour
½ tsp. salt	½ tsp. salt

Combine rice with next 5 ingredients in bowl; mix well. Pack into loaf pan. Sprinkle with cracker crumbs. Bake for 20 minutes. Combine tomatoes, 1 tablespoon sugar, flour and ½ teaspoon salt in saucepan. Cook until thickened, stirring constantly. Invert loaf onto serving plate. Spoon sauce over top. Serve hot or cold.

Clara Mae McCammon, Blendon Grange, Ohio

PRESIDENT REAGAN'S FAVORITE MACARONI AND CHEESE

Yields: 6 servings	Pan Size: 1½ quart	Preheat: 350°

8 oz. macaroni
1 tsp. butter
1 egg, beaten

3 cups grated sharp cheese
1 tsp. each dry mustard, salt
1 c. milk

Cook macaroni according to package directions; drain well. Reserve a small amount of cheese. Add butter, egg and remaining cheese to hot macaroni; mix well. Pour into buttered casserole. Mix dry mustard, salt and *1 tablespoon hot water* in small bowl. Stir in milk. Pour over casserole. Sprinkle with remaining cheese. Bake for 45 minutes or until set and top is crusty.

President Ronald Reagan
The White House

SPAETZLE (GERMANY) Drop Noodles

Yields: 4 servings	Pan Size: 4 quart

1 egg, lightly beaten
2⅓ c. sifted flour

3 tsp. salt
¼ c. butter, melted

Beat egg and *1 cup water* in bowl until smooth. Sift flour and 1 teaspoon salt together. Mix into egg mixture gradually. Batter will be very thick. Bring 8 cups water with 2 teaspoons salt to a boil in saucepan. Press enough batter to form 1 layer of noodles through spaetzle press into boiling water. Cook until noodles rise to surface. Cook for 5 to 8 minutes longer or until noodles test tender when pressed against side of pan. Remove with slotted spoon to warm serving bowl. Repeat process until all noodles are cooked. Add butter to noodles; toss lightly.

Ruth Lampman
Secretary, Texas State Grange

GNOCCHI (ITALY) Potato Dumplings

Yields: 3 servings	Pan Size: 6 quart

1 med. potato, cooked,
** mashed**
1 egg, beaten
2 tsp. garlic salt

3 c. (about) flour
2 tbsp. salt
½ c. melted butter
Salt to taste

Combine potato, egg, garlic salt and enough flour to make soft but easily handled dough. Roll into two ½ inch diameter ropes on floured surface. Cut into 1-inch pieces; roll in additional flour. Bring 4 quarts water and 2 tablespoons salt to a boil in saucepan. Drop gnocchi into water. Cook just until gnocchi float to top. Remove to serving dish with slotted spoon. Add melted butter and salt. Serve with Parmesan cheese and spaghetti sauce.

Tami Phelps, Cedar Hill Grange, New Mexico

Breads

The aroma of baking bread is one of the world's most tantalizing fragrances, and our love of the "staff of life" is not only universal but as ancient as history. Bread was originally flat, unleavened, and sun-baked. The art of baking leavened bread was developed by the Egyptians, improved by the Romans, and given guild status in the Middle Ages. During the Revolutionary War, bread baking was considered so important that the Continental Congress appointed a "Director of Baking in the Grand Army of the United States."

In the Colonies—unlike much of the world—bread making was most often done at home, and even today, the best breads come from our own kitchens. There, the only limitations are ingenuity and imagination. Combinations of favorite flavors, banana with peach, maple with applesauce, or Cheddar cheese with bacon, individualize breads and muffins. The addition of various grains as oats, rye, buckwheat, corn, and soy adds flavor and texture. The batter for quick breads, altered only in the proportion of the ingredients, may be baked into biscuits, muffins, pancakes, or loaves. Yeast breads, shaped by tradition or whimsy, appear as rings, rounds, ovals, twists, "elephant ears," or "snails." *The Glory of Cooking* offers recipes for all of these, all perfect for "breaking bread" with friends and loved ones.

ANGEL BISCUITS AND MAPLE BUTTER

Yields: 1 dozen	Pan Size: 7x11 inch	Preheat: 400°

1 pkg. dry yeast	2 tbsp. sugar
2½ c. flour	½ c. shortening
½ tsp. soda	1 c. buttermilk
1 tsp. baking powder	1 c. maple syrup
1 tsp. salt	¾ c. melted butter

Dissolve yeast in *¼ cup warm water*. Combine dry ingredients in bowl. Cut in shortening until crumbly. Add buttermilk and yeast; mix well. Refrigerate if desired. Knead lightly on floured surface; roll and cut with biscuit cutter. Place in greased pan. Let rise slightly. Bake until brown. Cook maple syrup in saucepan to 238 degrees on candy thermometer, soft-ball stage. Add butter; beat with rotary beater until thick and creamy. Serve warm on biscuits.
Note: Maple butter is also good on gingerbread or waffles.

Sheila Conrad, University Grange, Vermont

SKY-HIGH BISCUITS

Yields: 20 biscuits	Pan Size: 9 x 9 inch	Preheat: 450°

2 c. all-purpose flour	¾ tsp. cream of tartar
1 c. whole wheat flour	¾ c. butter
4½ tsp. baking powder	1 egg, beaten
2 tbsp. sugar	1 c. milk
½ tsp. salt	

Combine dry ingredients in bowl. Cut in butter until crumbly. Add egg and milk; stir just until mixed. Knead lightly on floured surface. Pat 1 inch thick; cut with biscuit cutter. Arrange in greased pan or place 2 inches apart on greased baking sheet for crusty biscuits. Bake for 12 to 15 minutes or until golden.

E. Margaret Lockcuff, Pine Run Grange, Pennsylvania

SWEET POTATO BISCUITS

Yields: 1½ dozen	Pan Size: baking sheet	Preheat: 450°

¾ c. mashed cooked sweet potatoes	1½ c. unbleached flour
½ c. melted butter	1 tbsp. baking powder
½ c. milk	½ tsp. salt

Combine first 3 ingredients in bowl; mix well. Add mixture of flour, baking powder and salt; mix well. Roll ½ inch thick on floured surface; cut with 2-inch biscuit cutter. Place on lightly greased baking sheet. Bake for 15 to 20 minutes or until brown.

Grace Davis Stevenson, Harvest Moon Grange, Maine

BAKED DOUGHNUTS

Yields: 2 dozen	Pan Size: baking sheet	Preheat: 400°

1 c. sugar
5 c. sifted flour
¼ tsp. salt
2 tsp. baking powder
6 eggs, well beaten
½ c. butter, softened
3 tbsp. milk

1 tsp. lemon extract
1 tsp. vanilla extract
½ tsp. lemon rind
2½ c. sifted confectioners' sugar
5 tbsp. heavy cream
¾ tsp. lemon extract

Sift first 4 ingredients into large bowl. Add eggs, butter, milk, 1 teaspoon lemon extract, vanilla and lemon rind; mix until smooth. Roll ½ inch thick on well-floured surface; cut with floured doughnut cutter. Place 1 inch apart on lightly greased and floured baking sheets. Bake for 13 to 16 minutes or until golden. Cool. Blend confectioners' sugar with cream and ¾ teaspoon lemon extract. Dip doughnut tops in icing. Let stand until set.

Bernice I. Best, Mt. Joy Grange, Pennsylvania

PORZELKY (GERMANY) New Year's Doughnuts

Yields: 3 to 4 dozen

2½ c. raisins
1 c. flour
1 pkg. dry yeast
2 tsp. sugar
2½ c. lukewarm milk
3 eggs, beaten

¾ c. sugar
1½ tsp. salt
¼ c. melted shortening
6 c. flour
Oil for deep frying

Soak raisins in hot water to cover for 5 minutes; drain well. Coat with 1 cup flour; set aside. Dissolve yeast and 2 teaspoons sugar in *½ cup warm water*. Let stand until bubbly. Mix with milk in large bowl. Add eggs, ¾ cup sugar, salt and shortening; mix well. Stir in 6 cups flour gradually. Mix in raisins. Dough will be stiff. Do not knead. Let rise in warm place until doubled in bulk. Cut pieces of dough with spoon dipped in hot oil. Deep-fry until golden brown; drain. Roll in confectioners' sugar.

Deborah Shorthill, Indian Creek Grange, Kansas

BUCKWHEAT CAKES

Yields: 3 dozen	Pan Size: electric skillet	Preheat: 375°

4 c. stone-ground
  buckwheat flour
¼ c. wheat germ
4 tsp. dry yeast

4 eggs, separated
¾ tsp. salt
8 tbsp. blackstrap molasses
Safflower oil

Sift buckwheat flour and wheat germ into large pottery bowl. Dissolve yeast in *1 cup warm water*. Add to flour mixture with *3 cups warm water*; stir vigorously until well blended. Let rise, covered, in refrigerator overnight. Beat egg yolks and salt by hand. Add egg yolks and molasses to batter; mix well. Beat egg whites with flat wire whisk until stiff but not dry. Fold gently into batter. Heat 1 tablespoon oil in electric skillet. Drop batter by large spoonfuls into skillet. Cook until brown on both sides. Remove to warm plate. Repeat process until all batter is cooked, adding oil each time. Serve with butter and pure maple syrup.

Phyllis Schlafly
Illinois, Member of Bicentennial Commission

COTTAGE CHEESE PANCAKES (RUSSIA)

Yields: 4 servings	Pan Size: skillet

1 lb. small curd cottage cheese
4 eggs, slightly beaten
1 c. flour
2 tsp. oil

½ tsp. salt
1 tbsp. milk
Butter

Mix cottage cheese and eggs in bowl. Add flour, oil, salt and milk in 1 addition; mix well. Drop by tablespoonfuls into butter in skillet over medium heat. Brown on both sides. Serve with honey or lightly sugared fresh fruit.

Pamela Rapach, Alder Creek Grange, Washington

UNUSUAL PANCAKES

Yields: 5 servings	Pan Size: 10 inch

1 c. flour
½ c. quick-cooking oats
¼ c. yellow cornmeal
1 tsp. salt
2 tsp. baking powder

2 tsp. soda
2 c. buttermilk
2 eggs
2 tbsp. oil

Combine dry ingredients in bowl. Add enough buttermilk to moisten; mix well. Add eggs 1 at a time, mixing well after each addition. Add remaining buttermilk; mix well. Stir in oil. Bake in hot oiled skillet.

Mrs. Creta A. Tennant, Bethlehem Grange, Ohio

APRICOT-NUT BREAD

Yields: 1 loaf   Pan Size: 5 x 9 inch   Preheat: 350°

1 c. finely chopped dried apricots
2½ c. sifted flour
¼ to ½ tsp. salt
¼ tsp. soda
2 eggs

1 c. buttermilk
¼ c. apricot nectar
3 tbsp. melted butter
1 c. chopped nuts

Add *1 tablespoon hot water* to apricots. Let stand for several minutes. Sift dry ingredients into large mixer bowl. Add mixture of eggs, buttermilk, apricot nectar and butter; mix well. Stir in apricots and nuts. Pour into greased loaf pan. Bake for 60 to 70 minutes or until loaf tests done. Cool on wire rack.

Grace M. Moody, Olathe Grange, Kansas

BANANA-PEACH BREAD

Yields: 1 loaf   Pan Size: 5 x 9 inch   Preheat: 325°

1¼ c. all-purpose flour
½ c. whole wheat flour
1 c. sugar
1 tsp. soda
1 tsp. salt
½ c. mashed peaches

1 c. mashed banana
¼ c. corn oil margarine, softened
2 tbsp. orange juice
¼ tsp. lemon juice
¼ c. raisins
1 egg

Grease bottom and corners of loaf pan. Sift dry ingredients into mixer bowl. Add remaining ingredients. Beat at low speed until blended. Beat at medium speed for 3 minutes. Pour into prepared pan. Bake for 70 minutes or until loaf tests done. Cool in pan for 5 minutes. Remove to wire rack to cool completely.

Elsie I. Sumner, Upper St. Clair Grange, Pennsylvania

DATE-CHEESE BREAD

Yields: 1 loaf   Pan Size: 5 x 9 inch   Preheat: 350°

8 oz. dates, finely chopped
1¾ c. flour
½ c. sugar
¼ tsp. salt

1 tsp. soda
1 egg, beaten
1 c. grated cheese
¾ c. chopped nuts

Pour *¾ cup boiling water* over dates. Let stand for 5 minutes. Sift dry ingredients into bowl. Add dates and remaining ingredients; mix well. Pour into greased loaf pan. Bake for 50 minutes. Cool on wire rack.

Mrs. Giles Benedict, Twin Grange, New York

CAPE COD CRANBERRY BREAD

Yields: 1 loaf   Pan Size: 5 x 9 inch   Preheat: 350°

¼ c. shortening
2 c. sifted flour
1 c. sugar
1½ tsp. each baking powder, soda
1 tsp. salt

1 tsp. grated orange rind
¾ c. orange juice
1 egg, well beaten
1 c. coarsely chopped cranberries
½ c. chopped nuts

Cut shortening into sifted dry ingredients in bowl until crumbly. Combine orange rind, orange juice and egg in small bowl; mix well. Add to dry ingredients; mix just until moistened. Stir in cranberries and nuts. Spoon into greased and floured pan. Bake for 1 hour. Cool on wire rack. Let stand, wrapped in plastic wrap, overnight.

Professor Thomas H. O'Connor,
Boston College, Member of Bicentennial Commission

WALNUT-DATE LOAF

Yields: 1 loaf   Pan Size: 5 x 9 inch   Preheat: 350°

2 eggs
½ c. Hellmann's mayonnaise
1½ tsp. vanilla extract
2½ c. flour
¾ c. sugar

1 tbsp. baking powder
¼ tsp. salt
1¼ c. chopped dates
1 c. coarsely chopped walnuts

Beat eggs, *¾ cup water*, mayonnaise and vanilla until smooth. Add to mixture of remaining ingredients; stir just until moistened. Pour into greased and floured pan. Bake for 50 minutes or until loaf tests done. Cool on wire rack.

Photograph for this recipe on page 169.

ORANGE MARMALADE BREAD

Yields: 1 loaf   Pan Size: 5 x 9 inch   Preheat: 350°

2 c. flour
1 tbsp. baking powder
½ tsp. salt
½ c. sugar
1 c. broken walnuts

1 tbsp. grated orange rind
1 c. orange marmalade
2 eggs
1 c. orange juice
2 tbsp. melted butter

Sift dry ingredients into bowl. Mix in walnuts and orange rind. Combine marmalade, eggs, orange juice and butter in bowl; beat until blended. Add to dry ingredients; mix well. Pour into greased loaf pan. Bake for 1 hour or until loaf tests done. Cool in pan for 10 minutes. Remove to wire rack to cool completely. Slice thinly. Serve with butter whipped with additional marmalade.

Gloria Hovik, Fidelity Grange, Washington

ORANGE-NUT BREAD

Yields: 1 loaf   Pan Size: 5 x 9 inch   Preheat: 350°

1 orange	**2 c. sifted flour**
¾ c. raisins	**1 tsp. baking powder**
1 egg, beaten	**1 tsp. soda**
1 c. sugar	**¼ tsp. salt**
2 tbsp. melted butter	**½ c. chopped nuts**

Squeeze juice from orange; discard pulp and grind rind. Add enough boiling water to orange juice to measure 1 cup; set aside. Combine rind, raisins, orange juice, egg, sugar and butter in bowl; mix well. Sift in mixture of flour, baking powder, soda and salt; mix well. Stir in nuts. Pour ingo greased loaf pan. Bake for 50 minutes or until bread tests done. Cool in pan on wire rack.

D. Vincent Andrews
Master, Florida State Grange

OLIVE'S HOBO BREAD

Yields: 3 loaves   Pan Size: three 1 pound   Preheat: 350°

4 tsp. soda	**2 c. sugar**
2 c. raisins	**½ tsp. salt**
4 c. flour	**¼ c. oil**

Pour mixture of soda and *2 cups boiling water* over raisins in bowl. Let stand overnight; do not stir. Sift flour, sugar and salt together. Stir into raisins with spoon. Add oil; mix well. Batter will be thick. Pour into greased and floured cans. Bake at 350 degrees for 30 minutes. Reduce temperature to 325 degrees. Bake for 30 minutes longer or until bread tests done, covering with foil if necessary to prevent overbrowning. Roll each can on side to loosen bread. Remove to wire rack to cool.

Mary L. Knudson
Rhode Island Director of Women's Activities

BROWN BREAD

Yields: 10 servings   Pan Size: 22 ounce

1 cup All-Bran	**½ tsp. salt**
½ c. sugar	**1 c. sour milk**
1 c. flour	**1 tbsp. molasses**
1 tsp. soda	**½ c. raisins**

Combine All-Bran, sugar, flour, soda and salt in bowl. Add sour milk and molasses; mix well. Stir in raisins. Pour into can; cover tightly. Place in saucepan with water to half the depth of can. Steam, covered, for 3 hours. Remove to wire rack to cool.

Mrs. Joseph Bell, Southington Grange, Connecticut

GRAMMY UPTON'S BROWN BREAD

Yields: 12 servings	Pan Size: 3 pound

1 c. each oats, cornmeal, flour	**¾ c. molasses**
2 tsp. soda	**1 c. raisins**
1 tsp. salt	

Combine first 5 ingredients in bowl. Add *2 cups hot water* and molasses; mix well. Stir in raisins. Pour into greased shortening can. Cover with foil; secure with string. Place in large saucepan with water to depth of half the can. Steam for 3 hours. Invert onto wire rack to cool. Slice by drawing a piece of string through bread.
Note: This was a favorite recipe of Grandmother, who was married in 1860.

Frances E. Towne
New Hampshire Director of Women's Activities

ZUCCHINI BREAD

Yields: 2 loaves	Pan Size: 5 x 9 inch	Preheat: 325°

3 eggs	**3 c. flour**
1 c. oil	**1 tsp. baking powder**
2 c. sugar	**1 tsp. soda**
2 c. grated peeled zucchini	**2 tsp. cinnamon**
2 tsp. vanilla extract	**1 tsp. salt**

Beat eggs in bowl until frothy. Add oil and sugar; beat until thick. Stir in zucchini, vanilla and dry ingredients. Pour into 2 greased and floured loaf pans. Bake for 1 hour or until bread tests done. Remove to wire rack to cool.

Joseph Gerace
Commissioner, New York Department of Agriculture and Markets

ZUCCHINI-NUT BREAD

Yields: 2 loaves	Pan Size: 5 x 9 inch	Preheat: 325°

3 eggs	**¼ tsp. soda**
1 c. oil	**2 tsp. cinnamon**
2 c. sugar	**½ tsp. each ginger, nutmeg**
2 c. grated peeled zucchini	**1 tsp. salt**
3 c. flour	**1 tsp. vanilla extract**
1 tsp. baking powder	**½ c. chopped nuts**

Beat eggs in bowl until smooth. Add oil, sugar and zucchini; mix well. Add sifted dry ingredients, vanilla and nuts; mix just until moistened. Pour into 2 greased loaf pans. Bake for 1 hour or until loaves test done. Cool on wire rack.

Samuel Pierce
Secretary, U.S. Department of Housing and Urban Development

Recipes for this photograph on pages 166, 176, 178.

BROCCOLI SPOON BREAD

Yields: 4 to 6 servings   Pan Size: 2 quart   Preheat: 375°

1½ c. broccoli flowerets	¼ c. chopped onion
¾ c. yellow cornmeal	2 tbsp. butter
2 tbsp. flour	4 eggs, separated
1 tsp. salt	1 c. milk
2 tbsp. butter	1 c. shredded Cheddar cheese
1 c. sliced celery	¼ tsp. hot sauce

Cook broccoli in 1-inch boiling salted water in covered saucepan for 10 to 12 minutes or until tender-crisp; drain. Mix *2 cups water* with mixture of cornmeal, flour and salt in medium saucepan. Cook until thick, stirring constantly. Stir in 2 tablespoons butter. Sauté celery and onion in 2 tablespoons butter in skillet. Add to cornmeal mixture; mix well. Blend in beaten egg yolks. Add milk, cheese, hot sauce and broccoli flowerets; mix well. Fold in stiffly beaten egg whites. Pour into buttered casserole Bake for 55 to 60 minutes or until golden.

Photograph for this recipe on page 67.

MAPLE-APPLESAUCE MUFFINS

Yields: 1½ dozen   Pan Size: muffin   Preheat: 375°

¼ c. sugar	2 c. flour
½ c. shortening	1 tbsp. baking powder
¾ c. maple syrup	1 tsp. salt
2 eggs	½ tsp. cinnamon
¾ c. applesauce	

Cream sugar and shortening in bowl until light and fluffy. Add syrup, eggs and applesauce; mix well. Mixture may appear curdled. Sift in dry ingredients; stir just until moistened. Fill greased muffin cups ⅔ full. Bake for 20 minutes.

Gloria Miller, Riverside Grange, Vermont

CORN MUFFINS

Yields: 6 servings   Pan Size: muffin   Preheat: 450°

¾ c. flour	¾ c. cornmeal
⅓ c. sugar	1 egg
2 tsp. baking powder	2 tbsp. oil
½ tsp. salt	¾ c. milk

Sift flour, sugar, baking powder and salt into bowl. Mix in cornmeal. Beat egg, oil and milk in bowl until smooth. Stir in cornmeal mixture with spoon; do not beat. Fill greased muffin cups ⅔ full. Bake for 15 minutes.

Recipe for this photograph on page 177.

Michael S. Dukakis
Governor of Massachusetts

CHEDDAR-BACON MUFFINS

Yields: 1 dozen	Pan Size: muffin	Preheat: 400°

1¾ c. flour
2 tbsp. sugar
1 tsp. baking powder
1 tsp. salt
1½ c. shredded Cheddar cheese
1 egg, beaten

1 c. milk
3 tbsp. melted butter
10 slices crisp-fried bacon, crumbled
2 tbsp. bacon drippings

Sift dry ingredients into bowl. Stir in cheese. Add egg, milk and butter; stir just until moistened. Stir in bacon. Spoon into muffin cups greased with bacon drippings. Bake for 20 to 25 minutes or until brown.
Note: May substitute ham and Swiss cheese for bacon and Cheddar and increase butter to ⅓ cup.

Noela Irene Birt, Phoenix Grange, Oregon

OLD-FASHIONED GRAHAM GEMS

Yields: 1 dozen	Pan Size: muffin	Preheat: 425°

1 c. sifted all-purpose flour
1 tbsp. baking powder
1 tsp. salt
1 c. graham flour

¼ c. packed brown sugar
1 egg, well beaten
1 c. milk
⅓ c. shortening, melted

Sift all-purpose flour, baking powder and salt into bowl. Add graham flour and brown sugar; mix well. Combine egg, milk and shortening in small bowl. Stir into dry ingredients until moistened; batter will be lumpy. Spoon into greased muffin cups. Bake for 20 minutes or until muffins test done.

Beulah Winter, Michigan State Grange

WHOLE WHEAT MUFFINS

Yields: 1½ dozen	Pan Size: muffin	Preheat: 425°

1 c. flour
½ tsp. salt
4 tsp. baking powder
½ c. packed brown sugar
1 c. whole wheat flour

1 c. milk
2 eggs, beaten
⅓ c. melted shortening
½ c. chopped walnuts

Sift flour, salt and baking powder into bowl. Stir in mixture of brown sugar and whole wheat flour. Add mixture of milk and eggs. Add shortening; mix just until moistened. Add nuts. Spoon into greased muffin cups. Bake for 15 minutes.

Lourene W. Cooke, Eureka Grange, Pennsylvania

CHEDDAR PULLMAN LOAF

Yields: 1 loaf	Pan Size: 3 x 12 inch	Preheat: 400°

2 pkg. dry yeast	4 tsp. salt
1 tsp. sugar	5½ c. flour
1¾ c. milk	1½ c. shredded Cheddar cheese
¼ c. unsalted butter	

Dissolve yeast and sugar in *¼ cup water*. Let stand until doubled in bulk. Heat milk, butter and salt in saucepan until butter melts. Stir into 4 cups flour in mixer bowl. Add yeast. Beat with dough hook, adding 1½ cups flour gradually. Knead on floured surface for 10 minutes or until smooth and elastic. Place in greased bowl, turning to grease surface. Let rise, covered with plastic wrap, until tripled in bulk. Flatten on floured surface. Knead in cheese gradually. Place in bowl. Let rise until doubled in bulk. Roll into 8 x 12-inch rectangle. Roll as for jelly roll; seal seam. Place seam side down in greased pan; cover with buttered foil. Let rise until pan is ⅘ full. Bake for 40 minutes. Reduce temperature to 325 degrees; remove foil. Bake for 15 minutes longer. Rub crust with butter. Cool on wire rack.

Helen J. Jacobson, Mahoning Valley Grange, Pennsylvania

CHRISTMAS FRUIT BREAD (ITALY)

Yields: 8 loaves	Pan Size: 5 x 9 inch	Preheat: 350°

1½ c. sugar	4 tsp. soda
3½ c. honey	2¼ lb. glazed red cherries
¾ c. aniseed	1½ lb. walnuts
20 c. flour	24 oz. semisweet chocolate chips

Mix sugar, honey and aniseed in large bowl. Stir in *8 cups boiling water* gradually. Add mixture of flour and soda gradually; mix well. Stir in cherries, walnuts and chocolate chips. Pour into greased and floured loaf pans; smooth tops with moistened metal spatula. Garnish with additional cherries. Bake for 50 minutes or until loaves test done. Remove to wire racks to cool.

Photograph for this recipe on page 238.

DILL-ONION BREAD

Yields: 3 loaves	Pan Size: 4 x 8 inch	Preheat: 350°

2 pkg. dry yeast
1 tsp. honey
2 c. large curd cottage cheese
2 tbsp. grated onion
¼ c. butter
4 tsp. dillseed

1 tbsp. baking powder
1 tsp. salt
2 eggs
4 to 4½ c. whole wheat flour
½ tsp. soda
1 tbsp. coarse salt

Dissolve yeast in *½ cup warm water*. Stir in honey. Combine cottage cheese, onion, butter, dillseed, baking powder, soda and 1 teaspoon salt in bowl; mix well. Mix in yeast and eggs. Add enough flour gradually to make a stiff dough, mixing well after each addition. Knead on floured surface for 10 minutes or until smooth and elastic, kneading in additional flour if necessary. Place in greased bowl, turning to grease surface. Let rise, covered, in warm place for 1 hour or until doubled in bulk. Knead gently for 2 minutes. Shape into 3 loaves; place each in buttered pan. Let rise, covered, for 45 minutes or until doubled in bulk. Sprinkle with coarse salt. Bake for 40 minutes or until loaves test done. Remove to wire rack to cool.

Timothy W. Schultz
Commissioner, Colorado Department of Agriculture

CREOLE CASSEROLE BREAD

Yields: 12 servings

1 c. milk
3 tbsp. dark
  brown sugar
1 tbsp. salt
2 tbsp.
  Fleischmann's
  margarine

2 pkg.
  Fleischmann's
  dry yeast
4 c. flour
1 tsp.
  cinnamon
½ tsp. nutmeg

Scald milk in saucepan. Stir in brown sugar, salt and margarine; cool to lukewarm. Dissolve yeast in 1 cup 105 to 115-degree water in bowl. Add milk mixture, flour and spices; mix for 2 minutes. Let rise, covered, in warm place, for 1 hour or until more than doubled in bulk. Stir batter down; beat vigorously for 30 seconds. Spoon into greased casserole. Bake for 1 hour or until bread tests done.

SALT-FREE OATMEAL BREAD

Yields: 2 loaves	Pan Size: 4½ x 8½ inch	Preheat: 375°

1 c. quick-cooking oats	⅔ c. packed brown sugar
3 tbsp. unsalted butter	1 tbsp. sugar
2 pkg. dry yeast	1 c. whole wheat flour
1 tsp. sugar	5 c. (about) all-purpose flour

Bring *2 cups water* to a boil in saucepan. Stir in oats and butter. Cook for 1 minute, stirring constantly; remove from heat and cover. Cool to lukewarm. Dissolve yeast and 1 teaspoon sugar in *⅓ cup warm water*. Combine oats, yeast, brown sugar and 1 tablespoon sugar in mixer bowl; mix well. Add whole wheat flour. Beat for 3 minutes. Add enough all-purpose flour to make medium stiff dough. Knead on floured surface for 10 minutes or until smooth and elastic. Place in greased bowl, turning to grease surface. Let rise until doubled in bulk. Shape into 2 loaves; place in greased loaf pans. Let rise until doubled in bulk. Bake for 30 minutes or until loaves test done.

Ida Dustrude, Mohawk Grange, Oregon

POPPY SEED LOAF (HUNGARY)

Yields: 1 loaf	Pan Size: 14 inch	Preheat: 350°

1 pkg. dry yeast	¾ c. raisins
½ c. lukewarm milk	2 tbsp. honey
2½ to 3 c. flour	2 tsp. cinnamon
¼ c. melted butter	2 tbsp. butter
¼ c. sugar	1 tbsp. sugar
½ tsp. salt	1 egg, beaten
1 egg	1 c. confectioners' sugar
¾ c. milk	2 tbsp. milk
¾ c. poppy seed	

Mix yeast and lukewarm milk in large bowl. Let stand for 5 minutes. Add about 2½ cups flour, melted butter, sugar, salt and 1 egg; mix well. Turn onto floured surface; knead in remaining ½ cup flour. Knead for 10 minutes or until smooth and elastic. Place in greased bowl, turning to grease surface. Chill, covered, overnight. Combine ¾ cup milk and next 6 ingredients in saucepan. Bring to a boil; reduce heat. Simmer for 10 minutes, stirring frequently. Cool. Roll dough into 10x14-inch rectangle. Spread with poppy seed mixture; roll as for jelly roll. Place on greased baking sheet. Slice 1 inch thick to but not through bottom. Pull slices alternately to sides. Let rise, covered, for 45 minutes or until doubled in bulk. Brush with mixture of beaten egg and *1 tablespoon water*. Bake for 30 minutes or until golden. Cool on wire rack. Drizzle with mixture of confectioners' sugar and 2 tablespoons milk.

Photograph for this recipe on page 237.

ENGLISH MUFFIN BREAD

Yields: 2 loaves   Pan Size: 5 x 9 inch   Preheat: 400°

2 c. milk
2 pkg. yeast
1 tbsp. sugar
2 tsp. salt

¼ tsp. soda
5½ to 6 c. flour
Cornmeal

Heat milk and *½ cup water* in saucepan until very warm. Add to mixture of yeast, sugar, salt, soda and 3 cups flour in mixer bowl. Beat until well mixed. Stir in enough remaining flour to make stiff batter. Pour into 2 greased loaf pans sprinkled with cornmeal. Sprinkle batter with cornmeal. Let rise, covered, for 45 minutes. Bake for 25 minutes. Remove to wire rack. Cool completely. Slice and toast.

Rebecca L. Meyer, Union Grange, Illinois

BRAIDED SESAME RING

Yields: 1 loaf   Pan Size: baking sheet   Preheat: 375°

2 c. flour
2 pkg. dry yeast
¼ c. sugar
1 tsp. salt
3 eggs

½ c. mayonnaise
4½ c. (about) flour
1 egg, beaten
2 tbsp. sesame seed

Combine first 4 ingredients in mixer bowl. Beat in *1½ cups warm water* gradually. Beat at medium speed for 2 minutes. Beat in 3 eggs, mayonnaise and 2 cups flour. Beat for 2 minutes. Add enough remaining flour to make medium dough. Knead on floured surface until smooth and elastic. Place in greased bowl, turning to grease surface. Let rise, covered, until doubled in bulk. Divide into 3 portions. Let rest for 10 minutes. Shape each portion in 24-inch rope. Place side by side on greased baking sheet; braid loosely and shape into circle, sealing ends. Let rise, covered with towel, for 1½ hours or until doubled in bulk. Brush with beaten egg; sprinkle with sesame seed. Bake for 40 minutes. Cool on wire rack.

Photograph for this recipe on page 169.

DARK RYE BREAD (GERMANY)

Yields: 2 loaves   Pan Size: two 8 inch   Preheat: 400°

⅓ c. molasses
2 tbsp. butter
1 tbsp. sugar
1 tbsp. salt
3 c. sifted all-purpose flour

2 pkg. dry yeast
¼ c. cocoa
1 tbsp. caraway seed
2½ to 3½ c. rye flour

Combine first 4 ingredients and *2 cups water* in saucepan. Heat until warm, stirring occasionally. Combine all-purpose flour, yeast, cocoa and caraway seed in mixer bowl. Add warm molasses mixture. Beat at low speed for 30 seconds, scraping bowl constantly. Beat at high speed for 3 minutes. Stir in enough rye flour to make soft dough. Knead on floured surface for 5 minutes or until smooth. Let rest, covered, for 20 minutes. Divide into 2 portions. Shape into loaves. Place in pie plates. Brush with oil. Cut 3 deep slashes in top of each loaf. Let rise for 45 to 60 minutes or until doubled in bulk. Bake for 25 to 30 minutes or until loaves test done.

Lucille Pierson, Leonidas Grange, Michigan

FINN RYE BREAD (FINLAND)

Yields: 4 loaves	Pan Size: Four 5x9 inch	Preheat: 350°

2 c. rye	2 pkg. dry yeast
4 c. buttermilk	1 tsp. sugar
1 tsp. caraway seed	½ c. cornmeal
1 c. dark molasses	10 c. flour
¼ c. melted butter	2 tsp. salt

Combine rye flour, buttermilk and caraway seed in large mixer bowl. Let stand overnight. Add molasses and butter. Dissolve yeast and sugar in *½ cup warm water*. Stir into buttermilk mixture. Add cornmeal and *½ cup water*. Add flour and salt; beat well. Let rise for 1 hour or until doubled in bulk. Knead on floured surface until smooth and elastic. Shape into 4 loaves. Place in greased loaf pans. Let rise until doubled in bulk. Bake for 1 hour or until loaves test done.

June E. Kyllonen, Eagle Cliff Grange, Washington

BASIC WHEAT BREAD

Yields: 2 loaves	Pan Size: 5x9 inch	Preheat: 400°

2 c. all-purpose flour	¼ c. honey
2 pkg. dry yeast	1 tbsp. salt
1 c. milk	1 egg
¼ c. oil	4 to 4½ c. whole wheat flour

Combine all-purpose flour and yeast in large mixer bowl. Combine milk, *1 cup water*, oil, honey and salt in saucepan. Heat to lukewarm. Add milk mixture to flour mixture. Beat at medium speed for 3 minutes or until smooth. Add egg; mix well. Stir in enough whole wheat flour to make moderately stiff dough. Turn onto lightly floured surface. Let rest, covered, for 10 minutes. Knead for 5 to 10 minutes or until smooth and elastic. Let rest, covered, for 20 minutes. Shape into 2 loaves; place in greased loaf pans. Brush with additional oil. Let rise in warm place for 1 hour or until doubled in bulk. Bake for 35 to 40 minutes.

Photograph for this recipe on page 170.

"FROM THE LAND OF KANSAS" WHEAT BREAD

Yields: 2 loaves   Pan Size: 5 x 9 inch   Preheat: 350°

1 c. rolled wheat	2 pkg. dry yeast
2 tsp. salt	2½ to 3 c. all-purpose flour
½ c. honey	1½ to 2 c. whole wheat flour
2 tbsp. butter	

Pour *2 cups boiling water* over rolled wheat in bowl. Let stand until softened. Stir in salt, honey and butter. Cool. Dissolve yeast in *⅓ cup 105 to 115-degree water*. Blend into wheat mixture. Add flours gradually, mixing well after each addition. Knead on floured surface for 10 minutes or until smooth and elastic. Place in lightly oiled bowl, turning to oil surface. Let rise, covered, in warm place for 1 hour or until doubled in bulk. Divide into 2 portions. Knead briefly. Shape into 2 loaves; place in 2 greased loaf pans. Let rise, covered, until doubled in bulk. Bake for 35 to 40 minutes or until bread tests done. Remove to wire rack to cool.

Don Jacka
Acting Secretary, Kansas State Board of Agriculture

WHOLESOME WHEAT BREAD

Yields: 2 loaves   Pan Size: baking sheet   Preheat: 350°

1 c. dark corn syrup	1 tsp. salt
½ c. Hellmann's mayonnaise	1 tsp. cinnamon
2 c. whole wheat bread	2 eggs
2 pkg. dry yeast	3½ to 4 c. whole wheat flour

Combine corn syrup, mayonnaise and *1 cup water* in saucepan. Heat to 120 degrees, stirring occasionally. Combine with mixture of 2 cups flour, yeast, salt and cinnamon in large mixer bowl. Beat at medium speed for 2 minutes. Beat in eggs and 2 cups flour at low speed. Beat at medium speed for 2 minutes. Stir in enough remaining flour with wooden spoon to make medium dough. Knead on floured surface for 10 minutes or until smooth and elastic. Place in greased bowl, turning to grease surface. Let rise, covered, for 1 minute or until doubled in bulk. Divide into 2 portions. Let rest for 10 minutes. Shape each into 4x8-inch oval; make three ¼-inch deep slashes in top of each. Place on greased and floured baking sheet. Let rise for 1½ hours or until doubled in bulk. Bake for 30 to 40 minutes or until loaves sound hollow when tapped on bottom. Cool on wire rack.

Photograph for this recipe on page 169.

CARAMEL PECAN ROLLS

Yields: 8 servings	Pan Size: 9 x 13 inch	Preheat: 350°

1 pkg. dry yeast	½ c. packed brown sugar
¼ c. sugar	1 tbsp. light corn syrup
1 tsp. salt	⅔ c. chopped pecans
2 tbsp. butter, softened	Butter, softened
1 egg	½ c. sugar
3¼ to 3½ c. flour	2 tsp. cinnamon
⅓ c. melted butter	

Dissolve yeast in *1 cup warm water* in bowl. Add sugar, salt, 2 tablespoons butter and egg; mix well. Add 2 cups flour; mix well. Add remaining flour; mix well. Place in greased bowl. Refrigerate, covered, for overnight to 5 days. Mix melted butter, brown sugar, corn syrup and pecans in bowl; pour into greased baking pan. Roll dough into 9 x 15-inch rectangle. Spread with softened butter; sprinkle with mixture of ½ cup sugar and cinnamon. Roll as for jelly roll. Cut into 1-inch slices; place in prepared pan. Let rise, covered, for 1½ hours. Bake for 25 to 30 minutes. Invert onto serving tray.

Joan Wiggins, Bath Grange, Ohio

CORNMEAL ROLLS

Yields: 5 dozen	Pan Size: 9 x 13 inch	Preheat: 425°

2 pkg. yeast	1 tsp. salt
½ c. yellow cornmeal	2 eggs
2 c. cold milk	5½ to 6 c. flour
⅔ c. butter	Shortening
⅔ c. sugar	

Dissolve yeast in *½ cup warm water*. Stir cornmeal into milk in saucepan. Cook over low heat until bubbly, stirring constantly. Pour into large bowl. Add butter, sugar and salt; stir until butter melts. Stir in yeast. Add eggs 1 at a time, mixing well after each addition. Add flour; mix well. Knead on floured surface until smooth and elastic. Place in greased bowl, turning to grease surface. Let rise until doubled in bulk. Melt shortening in baking pans. Shape dough into rolls; roll in melted shortening and arrange in pans. Bake for 10 minutes.

Helen A. Odell, Frances Grange, Washington

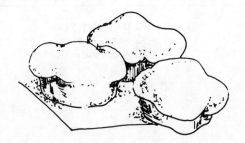

CREAM CHEESE ROLLS

Yields: 40 rolls   Pan Size: two 9 x 9 inch   Preheat: 325°

3½ c. flour	1 c. milk
2 tbsp. sugar	2 tbsp. margarine
1 tsp. salt	4 oz. cream cheese, softened
1 pkg. fast-rising yeast	2½ c. flour

Mix first 4 ingredients in mixer bowl. Heat milk, margarine and *1 cup water* to 130 degrees in saucepan. Add cream cheese and milk mixture to flour mixture. Beat at medium speed for 3 minutes. Add 1½ cups flour; mix well. Spread 1 cup flour on floured surface; add dough. Knead for 5 minutes. Place in well-oiled bowl, turning to oil surface. Let rise, covered with waxed paper, for 30 minutes or until doubled in bulk. Shape into walnut-sized balls; place in well-oiled pans. Let rise until doubled in bulk. Bake for 30 minutes. Brush tops with additional margarine.

Madeline McCain, Ash Valley Pomona Grange, Kansas

REFRIGERATOR ROLLS

Yields: 4 to 5 dozen   Preheat: 400°

2 pkg. dry yeast	¾ c. sugar
1 tsp. sugar	2 eggs, beaten
2 c. milk, scalded, cooled	4 tsp. salt
to lukewarm	10 to 11 c. flour
⅔ c. oil	

Dissolve yeast and 1 teaspoon sugar in *1 cup lukewarm water* in bowl. Add lukewarm milk and next 4 ingredients; beat until well mixed. Add enough flour to make a soft dough. Let rest for 10 minutes. Knead on floured surface until smooth and elastic. Place in greased bowl, turning to grease surface. Store, covered, in refrigerator. Pinch off desired amount of dough; punch down unused dough and return to refrigerator. Shape into rolls. Place in greased baking pan. Let rise until doubled in bulk. Bake for 15 to 20 minutes or until brown.

Jane Reed, Millbrook Grange, Illinois

REFRIGERATOR ALL-BRAN ROLLS

Yields: 3 dozen   Pan Size: three   9 inch   Preheat: 425°

1 c. All-Bran	2 pkg. dry yeast
¾ c. sugar	2 eggs, beaten
2 tsp. salt	6½ c. flour
1 c. lard	

Pour *1 cup boiling water* over All-Bran, sugar, salt and lard in bowl; mix well. Cool. Dissolve yeast in *1 cup lukewarm water*. Add yeast, eggs and flour to bran mixture; mix well. Do not knead. Chill, covered, in refrigerator overnight. Shape into rolls. Place in greased baking pans. Let rise until doubled in bulk. Bake for 15 to 20 minutes or until golden brown.

Mrs. Herbert Birkenholz, Sugar Grove Grange, Iowa

FOOLPROOF BUTTERHORNS

Yields: 3 dozen	Pan Size: 10 x 15 inch	Preheat: 375°

1½ pkg. dry yeast	1 stick margarine
1 tbsp. sugar	4 c. flour
3 eggs, lightly beaten	¼ c. sugar
1 c. milk, scalded, cooled	½ tsp. salt
to lukewarm	

Dissolve yeast and 1 tablespoon sugar in *¼ cup warm water* in bowl. Beat eggs with milk in small bowl. Add to yeast; mix well. Cut margarine into mixture of remaining ingredients in bowl. Add yeast mixture; stir until mixture forms ball. Place in greased bowl, turning to grease surface. Chill, covered, in refrigerator overnight. Roll into 2 circles on floured surface. Cut into wedges. Roll wedges up from wide end. Place on greased baking sheet. Let rise until doubled in bulk. Bake for 12 to 15 minutes or until golden brown.

Helen E. Rinker, Klondike-Piney Grange, Wyoming

QUICK AND EASY YEAST ROLLS

Yields: 1¼ dozen	Pan Size: 9 x 9 inch	Preheat: 350°

1 pkg. dry yeast	1 egg
2 tbsp. oil	2½ to 2¾ c. flour
2 tbsp. sugar	Butter, softened
½ tsp. salt	

Dissolve yeast in *¾ cup warm water* in bowl. Add oil, sugar, salt and egg; mix well. Add 1 cup flour; mix until smooth. Cover with cloth. Place on rack over bowl of hot water. Let rise for 25 minutes. Add enough flour to make stiff dough. Knead on floured surface for 3 minutes. Shape into 16 balls. Place in greased baking pan. Let rise, covered, over hot water for 25 minutes or until doubled in bulk. Bake for 12 to 15 minutes or until golden brown. Brush with butter.

Marion Halter, Friesburg Grange, New Jersey

SIXTY-MINUTE ROLLS

Yields: 2 to 3 dozen	Pan Size: 10 x 14 inch	Preheat: 425°

1½ c. flour
3 tbsp. sugar
1 tsp. salt
2 pkg. dry yeast

1 c. milk
¼ c. margarine
2 to 3 c. flour

Mix first 4 ingredients in mixer bowl. Combine milk, margarine and ½ *cup water* in saucepan. Heat to 120 to 130 degrees; margarine need not melt. Stir into flour mixture gradually. Beat at medium speed for 2 minutes. Add ½ cup flour. Beat at high speed for 2 minutes. Stir in enough remaining flour to make soft dough. Knead on lightly floured surface until smooth and elastic. Place in greased bowl, turning to grease surface. Place bowl in pan of 98-degree water. Let rise for 15 minutes. Shape into rolls; place on greased baking sheet. Let rise in warm place for 15 minutes. Bake for 12 minutes. Cool on wire rack.

Karen Ray, Cedar Hill Grange, New Mexico

SNAILS

Yields: 1½ dozen	Pan Size: baking sheet	Preheat: 350°

1 pkg. dry yeast
1½ c. milk, scalded
½ c. butter
½ c. mashed potatoes
⅔ c. sugar
2 tsp. salt
2 eggs, beaten

7 to 8 c. unbleached flour
Butter, melted
2 c. confectioners' sugar
2 tbsp. melted butter
Pinch of salt
½ tsp. vanilla extract

Dissolve yeast in ½ *cup warm water.* Combine milk, ½ cup butter, potatoes, sugar and 2 teaspoons salt in large bowl. Cool to lukewarm. Add yeast, eggs and 1½ cups flour; beat until smooth. Add enough remaining flour to make medium dough. Knead on floured surface until smooth and elastic. Place in greased bowl, turning to grease surface. Let rise, covered, until doubled in bulk. Roll ¼ inch thick. Brush generously with melted butter. Cut into ¾ x 12-inch strips. Coil into circle resembling snail on greased baking sheet. Let rise until doubled in bulk. Bake for 15 to 20 minutes or until golden. Frost with mixture of confectioners' sugar, 2 tablespoons melted butter, pinch of salt, vanilla and *3 tablespoons boiling water.* Sprinkle with nuts.

Eileen Walker, Winona Grange, Washington

SOUR CREAM TWISTS

Yields: 2 dozen	Pan Size: baking sheet	Preheat: 375°

1 pkg. dry yeast	2 tbsp. shortening
¾ c. lukewarm sour cream	3 c. flour
3 tbsp. sugar	Butter, softened
⅛ tsp. soda	Brown sugar
1 tsp. salt	Cinnamon to taste
1 egg	

Dissolve yeast in ¼ *cup warm water* in large bowl. Add sour cream, sugar, soda, salt, egg, shortening and flour; mix well. Knead on floured surface until smooth. Roll into 6x24-inch rectangle. Brush with butter; sprinkle with brown sugar and cinnamon. Fold over lengthwise. Cut into 1-inch strips. Twist each; place on greased baking sheet, pressing ends to sheet. Let rise, covered, for 1 hour. Bake for 12 to 15 minutes. Frost warm twists with confectioners' sugar glaze.

Shirley J. Cerny, German Grange, Pennsylvania

ELEPHANT EARS

Yields: 1½ dozen	Pan Size: baking sheet	Preheat: 400°

2 c. sugar	½ c. margarine, softened
4 tsp. cinnamon	1 egg yolk
1 pkg. yeast	½ c. milk, scalded
2 c. flour	2 tbsp. margarine, softened
2 tbsp. sugar	⅓ c. melted margarine
½ tsp. salt	

Mix 2 cups sugar with cinnamon; set aside. Dissolve yeast in ¼ *cup warm water*. Mix flour, 2 tablespoons sugar and salt in bowl. Cut in ½ cup margarine until crumbly. Add egg yolk, cooled milk and yeast; mix well. Chill for 2 hours. Turn onto floured cloth. Let rest, covered with towel, for 10 minutes. Roll into 10x18-inch rectangle. Spread with 2 tablespoons margarine. Sprinkle with a portion of cinnamon-sugar. Roll as for jelly roll, sealing edge. Cut into 1-inch slices. Press each slice into 5-inch circle on waxed paper sprinkled with cinnamon-sugar. Brush with melted margarine. Sprinkle with cinnamon-sugar and nuts. Place on ungreased baking sheet. Bake for 10 minutes. Cool on wire rack.

Mrs. Jim Willoughby, Newark Grange, Ohio

FELLESDOGSBULLAR SEMLOR (SWEDEN) Fat Tuesday Buns

Yields: 12 to 16 buns	Pan Size: baking sheet	Preheat: 450°

1 oz. yeast
¼ tsp. salt
⅓ c. sugar
½ tsp. ground cardamom
6 tbsp. butter, melted
½ c. milk
3 c. flour

1 egg, beaten
Sugar
7 oz. almond paste
¾ c. chopped hazel nuts
1 c. whipping cream, whipped
3 tbsp. confectioners' sugar

Mix first 6 ingredients in bowl. Add flour; mix until smooth and satiny. Let stand, covered, for 10 minutes. Knead on lightly floured surface. Shape into buns; place on baking sheet. Let rise until doubled in bulk. Brush with beaten egg; sprinkle with sugar. Bake for 5 to 10 minutes or until golden brown. Cool. Cut off tops. Spoon in mixture of almond paste and hazel nuts. Top with whipped cream. Replace tops; garnish with sprinkle of confectioners' sugar.

Nikolos Hultgren, White Oak Grange, Maine

POVITICA (SERBIA) Walnut Bread

Yields: 5 loaves	Pan Size: 5 x 9 inch	Preheat: 350°

2 c. milk, scalded
½ c. sugar
2 tsp. salt
2 pkg. dry yeast
1 tsp. sugar
3 eggs, beaten
½ c. melted shortening

8 to 10 c. flour
2 sticks butter
3 to 4 c. sugar
2 c. (or more) flour
8 to 10 c. ground English walnuts
2 to 3 tsp. cinnamon
1 egg yolk

Combine scalded milk, ½ cup sugar and salt in bowl; mix well. Cool to lukewarm. Dissolve yeast and 1 teaspoon sugar in *1 cup warm water*; let stand for 15 minutes. Beat eggs with shortening in small bowl. Add *1 cup warm water*, egg mixture and yeast to cooled milk; mix well. Beat in 4 to 6 cups flour. Knead in enough remaining flour to form an easily handled dough. Knead on floured surface until smooth and elastic. Place in large greased bowl, turning to grease surface. Let rise, covered, for 1 hour or until doubled in bulk. Melt butter in saucepan. Add next 4 ingredients. Cook until sugar is dissolved. Knead dough lightly. Divide into 5 portions. Place in greased bowls, turning to grease surfaces. Let rise, covered, for 1 hour or until doubled in bulk. Roll and stretch each portion into 18 x 24-inch rectangle on floured cloth. Spread with walnut filling. Roll as for jelly roll. Fold in half. Place in greased pans. Let rise for 1 hour or until doubled in bulk. Beat egg yolk with *2 teaspoons water*. Brush on bread. Bake for 1 hour and 15 minutes. Cool on wire rack.

Rachel Shorthill Vukas, Indian Creek Grange, Kansas

Desserts

Desserts are the final, and for many the best, course of the meal, an important part of any complete menu. As elaborate as Viennese pastry or as simple as fresh fruit, the dessert spans the globe, and every country has variations on the same theme: baked goods including cakes, pies, pastries, and cookies; puddings, from simple custards to elegant steamed mixtures and soufflés; frozen ices, ice cream, and sherbet; lucious fruits in cobblers, creams, and shortcake. In the United States, we have always been a nation of sweet lovers. Colonial cookbooks included many elaborate desserts. George Washington consumed a small fortune in ice cream, and his wife, Martha, made the dessert party with its table full of confections a stylish way to entertain.

The choice of dessert should be appropriate to the menu, and *The Glory of Cooking* offers a wealth of recipes from which to choose. Boost the nutritional value of menus by adding additional fruit, milk, eggs, or cereal to desserts. Create variety by following a rich dinner with something light and tart or a simple supper with something rich. Complement the flavors, colors and textures of the preceding courses with a final, well-chosen touch. And above all, keep the old traditions of your—or any—heritage alive, or create new ones with the many desserts included here, from special treats to a grand finale.

Miscellaneous

ANGEL REFRIGERATOR DESSERT

Yields: 12 servings

¾ c. sugar
9 tbsp. flour
3 c. milk
3 eggs
¾ tsp. salt

1 tbsp. vanilla extract
1 angel food cake
1 c. whipping cream
Coconut

Combine sugar, flour, milk, eggs, salt and vanilla in heavy saucepan; beat until smooth. Cook over medium heat until thickened, stirring constantly. Place in pan of ice water to cool completely. Remove brown crumbs from cake; cut into 1-inch cubes. Fold cake and stiffly whipped cream into custard. Spoon into serving dish. Sprinkle with coconut. Chill for 6 to 8 hours.

Lowilda W. Benskin, Mariposa Grange, Iowa

APPLE DUMPLINGS

Yields: 8 servings	Pan Size: 9 x 13 inch	Preheat: 375°

2 c. sugar
¼ tsp. cinnamon
¼ tsp. nutmeg
2 c. flour
2 tsp. baking powder

1 tsp. salt
¾ c. shortening
½ c. milk
6 apples, peeled, sliced
¼ c. butter

Combine sugar, cinnamon, nutmeg and *2 cups water* in saucepan. Cook for 5 minutes. Mix remaining dry ingredients in bowl. Cut in shortening until crumbly. Stir in milk to form dough. Divide into 8 portions. Roll each into 10-inch circle on floured surface. Place apples in center of each circle. Dot with butter. Pull up dough to enclose apples; press to seal. Place in greased baking dish. Pour syrup over top. Bake for 35 minutes.

Leoan Swisher, Oxford Community Grange, West Virginia

APPLE PAN DOWDY

Yields: 12 servings	Pan Size: 10 x 10 inch	Preheat: 425°

8 apples
¼ c. sugar
¼ tsp. each salt, cinnamon
⅛ tsp. nutmeg
⅓ c. molasses

2 tbsp. melted butter
½ c. shortening
1½ c. flour
¼ tsp. salt
2 tbsp. milk

Peel apples and cut into ½-inch wedges. Place in buttered baking dish. Sprinkle with mixture of sugar, ¼ teaspoon salt, cinnamon and nutmeg. Pour mixture of molasses, butter and *¼ cup water* over apples. Cut shortening into mixture of flour and ¼ teaspoon salt in bowl. Stir in *¼ cup water*. Roll into 10-inch square on floured surface. Place over apples. Brush with milk. Bake for 10 minutes; reduce temperature to 325 degrees. Break crust into apples with spoon. Bake for 1 hour longer.

Evelyn Bierly, Charity, Oregon

APPLE DESSERT (YUGOSLAVIA)

Yields: 8 servings	Pan Size: 9 x 13 inch	Preheat: 425°

2 c. flour
1 c. packed brown sugar
2 c. quick-cooking oats
1 tsp. each soda, salt
1 c. margarine, softened

6 c. shredded golden
  Delicious apples
1½ c. sugar
Butter
Cinnamon

Combine first 6 ingredients in bowl, mixing until crumbly. Place slightly more than half the crumbs in baking dish. Layer apples and sugar over crumbs; dot with butter. Sprinkle with cinnamon and remaining crumbs. Bake for 30 minutes; reduce temperature to 350 degrees. Bake until bottom is brown. Serve hot or cold with whipped cream, ice cream or lemon sauce.

Kathryn R. McDonald, Riverside Valley Grange, Washington

APPLE ROLLS

Yields: 8 servings	Pan Size: 9 x 13 inch	Preheat: 350°

2 c. sugar
2 c. flour
¼ tsp. salt
2 tbsp. sugar
2 tsp. baking powder

½ c. lard
1 c. milk
Finely chopped apples
Cinnamon
Cinnamon-sugar

Cook 2 cups sugar and *2 cups water* in saucepan until syrupy. Mix flour, salt, 2 tablespoons sugar and baking powder in bowl. Cut in lard until crumbly. Stir in milk. Roll ½ inch thick on floured surface. Spread with apples. Sprinkle with cinnamon. Roll as for jelly roll to enclose apples. Cut into 1½-inch slices. Place in baking dish. Add syrup to dish. Sprinkle with cinnamon-sugar. Bake for 45 minutes to 1 hour or until golden brown and apples are tender.

Ginny Mangel, Eureka Grange, Pennsylvania

STEAMED APPLE PUDDING

Yields: 8 to 12 servings

1½ c. fine dry bread crumbs
½ c. flour
1 tsp. baking powder
½ tsp. each soda, salt
1 tsp. cinnamon
½ c. sugar

2 eggs
½ c. molasses
2 tbsp. melted butter
2 c. chopped tart apples
1 c. whole fresh cranberries

Combine dry ingredients in bowl. Stir in mixture of eggs, molasses and butter. Fold in apples and cranberries. Pour into greased and sugared pudding mold. Cover tightly with greased foil; secure with string. Place mold on rack in deep saucepan. Add enough simmering water to cover half the mold. Cover saucepan. Steam for 2 to 2½ hours or until pudding tests done. Cool in mold for 10 minutes. Unmold onto serving plate. Serve with whipped cream or ice cream.

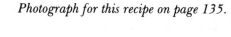

Photograph for this recipe on page 135.

BANANAS IN SAUCE

Yields: 4 to 6 servings   Pan Size: double boiler

2 eggs	¼ c. vinegar
1 tbsp. flour	6 bananas
1 c. sugar	¼ c. chopped peanuts

Beat eggs with ½ cup water in double boiler. Add mixture of flour and sugar; mix well. Add vinegar gradually. Cook until thickened, stirring constantly. Cool. Slice bananas into glass serving dish. Spoon sauce over bananas. Sprinkle with peanuts.

Cleo Moody, Pleasant Grove Grange, Ohio

OREGON BLACKBERRY PUFF PUDDING

Yields: 12 servings   Pan Size: 9 x 13 inch   Preheat: 375°

6 c. (heaping) blackberries	2 eggs
4 tsp. tapioca	1 c. sifted flour
1½ c. sugar	2 tsp. baking powder
¼ c. margarine, softened	¼ tsp. salt
1 c. sugar	½ c. milk

Place blackberries in baking dish. Sprinkle with mixture of tapioca and 1½ cups sugar. Cream margarine and 1 cup sugar in mixer bowl until light and fluffy. Blend in eggs. Add mixture of sifted flour, baking powder and salt alternately with milk; mix well. Spoon evenly over blackberries. Bake until topping is light brown.

Dottie D. George, Rogue River Valley Grange, Oregon

BLACKBERRY SLUMP

Yields: 4 to 6 servings   Pan Size: 2 quart

2½ c. blackberries	2 tbsp. sugar
½ tsp. lemon juice	2 tsp. baking powder
⅓ c. sugar	¼ tsp. salt
Salt to taste	1 tbsp. butter
1 c. flour	½ c. milk

Combine blackberries, lemon juice, ⅓ cup sugar, salt to taste and 1 cup water in saucepan. Cook for 5 minutes. Combine remaining ingredients in bowl; mix well. Drop by spoonfuls into simmering blackberries. Cook, covered, for 10 minutes; do not remove lid during cooking time.

J. A. Kruise, Harmony Grange, Pennsylvania

BLUEBERRY AND SPICE BREAD PUDDING

Yields: 8 to 10 servings   Pan Size: 9 x 9 inch   Preheat: 350°

2 c. blueberries	**1 can sweetened**
6 c. bread cubes	**condensed milk**
2 eggs	**1 tsp. vanilla extract**
¼ c. melted butter	**½ tsp. each cinnamon, nutmeg**

Toss blueberries and bread cubes in greased baking dish. Beat eggs in mixer bowl. Add remaining ingredients and *1½ cups warm water*; mix well. Pour over bread and blueberries; moistening well. Bake for 40 to 45 minutes or until knife inserted in center comes out clean. Serve warm or cold.

Mrs. J. Leroy Feusier, Smithville Grange, Ohio

BUTTERSCOTCH PUDDING

Yields: 4 servings   Pan Size: 2 quart   Preheat: 350°

1½ c. flour	**½ c. milk**
1 tsp. baking powder	**½ c. raisins**
½ c. packed brown sugar	**½ c. packed brown sugar**
1 tbsp. margarine	**1 tbsp. margarine**

Combine flour, baking powder and ½ cup brown sugar in bowl. Add 1 tablespoon margarine and milk; mix well. Stir in raisins. Stir *2 cups hot water* into ½ cup brown sugar and 1 tablespoon margarine in baking dish; dissolve completely. Spoon batter carefully into syrup in dish; do not stir. Bake for 30 to 40 minutes or until light brown.

Mary Forsythe, Shiloh Community Grange, Ohio

CARAMEL DUMPLINGS

Yields: 12 servings   Pan Size: 9 x 13 inch   Preheat: 375°

1 c. packed brown sugar	**½ c. sugar**
½ c. sugar	**½ c. milk**
1 tbsp. butter	**1¼ c. flour**
1 tsp. vanilla extract	**2 tsp. baking powder**
1 tbsp. butter, softened	**½ c. chopped nuts**

Bring first 4 ingredients and *2½ cups boiling water* to a boil in saucepan. Cook for 5 minutes. Pour into baking dish. Cream 1 tablespoon butter and ½ cup sugar in mixer bowl until light and fluffy. Add milk, flour, baking powder and nuts; mix well. Drop by spoonfuls into hot syrup in baking dish. Bake for 20 minutes or until brown.

Jeannine Burke, Steptoe Grange, Washington

BAKED CHEESECAKE

Yields: 9 to 10 servings	Pan Size: 9 inch springform	Preheat: 350°

19 oz. cream cheese, softened, cut into 1-in. cubes	**3 eggs, lightly beaten**
Grated rind of 1 lemon	**2 c. sour cream**
1 tsp. vanilla extract	**½ c. sugar**
½ c. sugar	**1 tsp. vanilla extract**

Beat cream cheese at medium speed in mixer bowl until light. Blend in lemon rind and 1 teaspoon vanilla. Add ½ cup sugar gradually, beating until fluffy. Add eggs ¼ cup at a time, beating well after each addition. Pour into buttered springform pan. Shake pan gently to settle batter. Bake on center rack for 25 minutes or until center is set. Spread mixture of remaining ingredients over cheesecake. Rotate pan gently to settle. Bake for 10 minutes. Turn off oven. Let stand in oven with door ajar for 30 minutes. Cool completely on wire rack. Place on serving plate; remove side of pan. Chill for 2 hours. Cover loosely with plastic wrap. Chill for 6 hours or longer. Garnish with red and green grapes.

Beth A. Cullen, Round Butte Grange, Montana

ORANGE CHEESECAKE

Yields: 12 to 18 servings	Pan Size: 9 inch	Preheat: 400°

1 c. sifted flour	**3 tbsp. flour**
¼ c. sugar	**1 tbsp. grated orange rind**
1 tbsp. grated orange rind	**¼ tsp. salt**
½ c. butter	**¼ tsp. vanilla extract**
1 egg yolk	**5 eggs**
½ tsp. vanilla extract	**2 egg yolks**
40 oz. cream cheese, softened	**¼ c. frozen Florida orange juice concentrate, thawed**
1¾ c. sugar	

Mix first 4 ingredients in bowl. Cut in butter until crumbly. Add 1 egg yolk and ½ teaspoon vanilla; mix well. Pat ⅓ of the dough over bottom of springform pan. Bake for 5 minutes. Cool. Pat remaining dough over side of pan to ½ inch from top, sealing to bottom. Combine cream cheese, 1¾ cup sugar, 3 tablespoons flour, 1 tablespoon orange rind, salt and ¼ teaspoon vanilla in mixer bowl. Beat at low speed until smooth. Add whole eggs and 2 egg yolks 1 at a time, beating well after each addition. Stir in orange juice. Pour into prepared pan. Place on foil on oven rack. Bake for 8 to 10 minutes. Reduce temperature to 225 degrees. Bake for 1 hour and 20 minutes longer. Let stand at room temperature until completely cool. Chill in refrigerator until serving time. Place on serving plate; remove side of pan. Garnish with orange sections and mint sprigs.

Photograph for this recipe on page 203.

EASY CHEESECAKE

Yields: 20 servings	Pan Size: 10 inch	Preheat: 350°

16 oz. ricotta cheese	3 jumbo eggs
16 oz. sour cream	3 tbsp. flour
16 oz. cream cheese, softened	3 tbsp. cornstarch
1½ c. sugar	4½ tsp. vanilla extract
1 stick butter, softened	4½ tsp. lemon juice

Place ingredients in order listed in large mixer bowl. Beat at low speed until moistened. Beat at medium speed until mixed. Beat at high speed for 10 minutes. Spoon into greased and floured springform pan. Bake for 1 hour. Turn off oven. Let cheesecake stand in closed oven for 1 hour. Cool on wire rack. Store in refrigerator.

Julieann Smith, West Bridgewater Grange, Massachusetts

PINEAPPLE CHEESECAKE

Yields: 12 servings	Pan Size: 9 x 13 inch	Preheat: 350°

1 c. butter	16 oz. cottage cheese
1¼ c. flour	8 oz. cream cheese, softened
¼ c. sugar	2 eggs
¾ tsp. baking powder	½ c. sugar
1 egg	3 tbsp. flour
1 29-oz. can crushed pineapple, drained	1½ c. milk
½ c. sugar	1 tsp. lemon juice
1 tbsp. cornstarch	1 tsp. vanilla extract
	Cinnamon to taste

Combine butter, 1¼ cups flour, ¼ cup sugar, baking powder and egg in bowl; mix well. Press into greased baking dish. Combine pineapple, ½ cup sugar and cornstarch in saucepan. Cook until thickened, stirring constantly. Cool. Spread in prepared dish. Combine next 8 ingredients in mixer bowl; beat until smooth. Pour over pineapple. Sprinkle with cinnamon. Bake for 1 hour and 15 minutes. Cool in pan.

Monica Szerlag, Anthony Grange, Rhode Island

CHERRY PUDDING

Yields: 20 servings	Pan Size: 12 x 15 inch	Preheat: 350°

1 qt. cherries	2 tsp. baking powder
2 c. flour	2 tbsp. butter
1 c. milk	3 c. sugar

Drain cherries, reserving juice. Mix next 4 ingredients and 1 cup sugar in bowl. Pour into baking dish. Top with mixture of cherries and remaining sugar. Bring reserved cherry juice to a boil in saucepan. Pour over cherries; do not stir. Bake for 40 minutes.

Barbara Foreman, Friend of Charity Grange, Oregon

POTS DE CRÈME AU CHOCOLAT (FRANCE) Chocolate Custard

Yields: 6 servings

4 eggs, separated	½ c. confectioners' sugar
2 sq. baking chocolate, melted	½ tsp. vanilla extract
	½ c. whipping cream

Beat egg yolks in mixer bowl until thick. Blend in chocolate, confectioners' sugar and flavoring. Fold in stiffly beaten egg whites gently. Spoon into 6 demitasse cups. Chill for several hours to overnight. Top with stiffly whipped cream at serving time.

Professor Charles A. Wright
University of Texas, Member of Bicentennial Commission

CHOCOLATE SUNDAY PUDDING

Yields: 6 servings   Pan Size: 2 quart   Preheat: 350°

1 c. flour	1 c. chopped nuts
⅔ c. sugar	½ c. packed brown sugar
2 tbsp. cocoa	¼ c. sugar
2 tbsp. baking powder	3 tbsp. cocoa
½ tsp. salt	¼ tsp. salt
½ c. milk	1 tsp. vanilla extract
2 tbsp. melted butter	

Combine flour, ⅔ cup sugar, 2 tablespoons cocoa, baking powder, ½ teaspoon salt, milk, butter and nuts in bowl; mix well. Spoon into greased baking dish. Mix remaining dry ingredients in bowl. Sprinkle over batter. Pour mixture of vanilla and *1 cup boiling water* over top; do not stir. Bake for 1 hour. Serve warm or cold with whipped cream.

Erna Cheldelin, Buena Vista Grange, Washington

COFFEE SOUFFLÉ

Yields: 6 servings   Pan Size: double boiler

1 tbsp. unflavored gelatin	¼ tsp. salt
½ c. milk	3 eggs, beaten
1½ c. hot coffee	½ tsp. vanilla extract
⅔ c. sugar	

Soften gelatin in milk in double boiler. Add coffee and half the sugar. Heat until gelatin and sugar dissolve. Add remaining sugar, salt and beaten egg yolks. Cook until thickened, beating constantly. Cool. Fold in stiffly beaten egg whites and vanilla. Spoon into serving dish. Chill until serving time.

Mary Carter, Holden Grange, Maine

QUICK CHERRY CRISP

Yields: 6 servings	Pan Size: 8 x 8 inch	Preheat: 350°

¾ c. sugar	¾ c. flour
¼ c. flour	¾ c. sugar
4 c. fresh or frozen cherries	½ c. chopped nuts
1 stick margarine	Cinnamon to taste

Combine ¾ cup sugar, ¼ cup flour and cherries in bowl; mix lightly. Spread in baking dish. Cut margarine into remaining flour and sugar in bowl until crumbly. Mix in nuts. Sprinkle over cherries. Sprinkle with cinnamon. Bake for 20 minutes.

Kathie Joseph, Enterprise Junior Grange, Illinois

COOKIE PUDDING

Yields: 6 to 8 servings	Pan Size: 1½ quart	Preheat: 325°

¼ c. raisins	1 tsp. vanilla extract
2 c. milk	½ tsp. cinnamon
4 eggs	¼ tsp. nutmeg
½ c. sugar	2 c. cookie crumbs

Soak raisins in water to cover for 3 to 5 minutes; drain. Combine next 4 ingredients in blender container. Process for 1 minute. Combine with cookie crumbs and raisins in baking dish; mix well. Sprinkle with cinnamon and nutmeg. Bake for 30 to 40 minutes or until knife inserted in center comes out clean.

Phillis I. Ellyson, Danville Grange, New Hampshire

CRANBERRY-APPLE BAKE

Yields: 8 servings	Pan Size: 8 x 8 inch	Preheat: 350°

3 c. sliced apples	½ c. flour
2 c. cranberries	¾ c. packed brown sugar
¾ c. plus 2 tbsp. sugar	½ c. chopped pecans
1 c. quick-cooking oats	1 stick margarine

Layer apples, cranberries and sugar in baking pan. Mix remaining ingredients in bowl until crumbly. Sprinkle over fruit. Bake for 35 to 40 minutes or until brown.

Josephine Greeley, Iron Bridge Grange, Virginia

CRANBERRY CHIFFON MOLD

Yields: 6 to 8 servings	Pan Size: 1½ quart

8 c. cranberries	**3 eggs, separated**
1 pkg. orange gelatin	**¾ c. sugar**
¼ tsp. salt	

Cook cranberries in *1 cup water* in saucepan until cranberries pop. Force through strainer. Dissolve gelatin in *¾ cup boiling water*. Beat egg yolks until light. Beat in ¼ cup sugar. Add hot gelatin gradually, beating constantly. Stir in salt and cranberries. Chill until partially set, stirring occasionally. Beat egg whites until foamy. Add ½ cup sugar gradually, beating constantly until soft peaks form. Fold into gelatin mixture, leaving 2-tone effect. Spoon into mold. Chill until firm. Unmold on serving plate.

Neva Montgomery, St. John's Grange, Ohio

CRANBERRY PUDDING

Yields: 8 servings	Pan Size: 1-pound can

½ c. molasses	**1 c. sugar**
2 tsp. soda	**1 c. cream**
1⅓ c. flour	**2 tbsp. brown sugar**
1 c. cranberries	**⅓ c. butter**
1 tsp. baking powder	

Blend molasses, soda and *½ cup boiling water* in bowl. Toss cranberries with a small amount of flour in bowl. Sift remaining flour and baking powder together. Add to molasses mixture; mix well. Stir in cranberries. Pour into greased can with tight-fitting lid. Place, covered, in saucepan with water to half the depth of can. Steam, covered, for 1½ hours. Invert onto serving plate. Combine remaining ingredients in saucepan. Cook until well blended and heated through. Serve over pudding.

Kent Jones
Commissioner, North Dakota Department of Agriculture

CREAM PUFFS

Yields: 6 puffs	Pan Size: baking sheet	Preheat: 450°

¼ c. shortening	**2 eggs**
½ c. flour	**Whipped cream**
¼ tsp. salt	

Bring *½ cup water* and shortening to a boil in heavy saucepan. Add flour and salt all at once. Cook until mixture forms ball, stirring constantly. Remove from heat. Add eggs 1 at a time, beating well after each addition. Drop by tablespoons 2 inches apart onto greased baking sheet. Bake for 10 minutes. Reduce temperature to 350 degrees. Bake for 25 minutes. Cool. Split and scoop out centers. Fill with whipped cream.

Mary G. McCollam, Middlebury Grange, Vermont

DEPRESSION FIGS

Yields: 1 jar

Green tomatoes, 1 to 1½-in. in diameter   **Brown or unrefined sugar**

Pierce tomatoes 3 or 4 times with fork. Place in boiling water in saucepan for 1 minute. Remove with slotted spoon; drain. Cool. Cut tomatoes into halves. Place cut side up in shallow pans. Sprinkle generously with brown sugar. Place in dehydrator or warm dry place. Let stand until edges begin to curl. Sprinkle again with brown sugar; flatten with bottom of glass. Repeat process for 3 to 4 days or until completely dried. Store in airtight jar in cool place. Use as snack or in fig cakes, breads and cookies.
Note: This recipe is from my grandmother who grew up in Minnesota in the 1860's and 1870's and had many resourceful recipes for making something out of very little.

Joanne O. Passmore, Delaware State Grange

MEXICAN FLAN

Yields: 12 to 14 servings   Pan Size: 5 x 9 inch   Preheat: 350°

½ c. packed brown sugar   **¼ tsp. salt**
8 eggs   **3½ c. evaporated milk**
⅔ c. sugar   **2 tsp. vanilla extract**

Spray baking pan with nonstick cooking spray. Sprinkle brown sugar in baking pan. Beat eggs in bowl. Add sugar, salt, evaporated milk and vanilla; mix well. Pour gently into prepared pan. Place in larger pan of hot water. Bake for 1 hour or until knife inserted in center comes out clean. Chill for 24 hours. Invert onto serving platter.

Dona Gallaher, Sequin Prairie Grange, Washington

FRESH FRUIT COBBLER

Yields: 9 servings   Pan Size: 9-inch baking pan   Preheat: 350°

3 c. fresh fruit   **2 tbsp. sugar**
⅔ c. sugar   **1½ tsp. baking powder**
2 tbsp. flour   **½ tsp. salt**
½ tsp. cinnamon   **⅓ c. oil**
2 tbsp. butter   **3 tbsp. milk**
1 c. sifted flour   **1 egg**

Place fruit in baking pan. Sprinkle with mixture of ⅔ cup sugar, 2 tablespoons flour and cinnamon. Dot with butter. Sift dry ingredients into bowl. Add oil, milk and egg; mix well. Spread evenly over fruit. Bake for 25 to 30 minutes or until brown. Serve warm with cream.

Catherine Hoffman, Capital Grange, Delaware

FRUIT DESSERT

Yields: 8 servings	Pan Size: 9 x 13 inch	Preheat: 350°

2⅓ c. fruit	1 c. sugar
⅓ c. fruit juice	3 eggs
½ c. sugar	1 tsp. vanilla extract
1¼ tbsp. cornstarch	2⅓ c. flour
1 tbsp. butter	3½ tsp. baking powder
½ c. shortening	1 tsp. salt

Combine fruit, juice, ½ cup sugar and cornstarch in saucepan. Cook over medium heat until thickened, stirring constantly; remove from heat. Stir in butter; cool. Cream shortening and 1 cup sugar in mixer bowl until light and fluffy. Add remaining ingredients and fruit mixture; mix well. Pour into greased and floured baking dish. Bake for 35 to 40 minutes or until golden brown.

Virginia Moore, Lykens Township Grange, Pennsylvania

GHURAYBA (LEBANON)

Yields: 4 dozen	Pan Size: cookie sheet	Preheat: 300°

1 c. butter, softened	2 c. flour
1 c. sugar	4 oz. blanched split almonds

Cream butter in mixer bowl until light. Add sugar gradually, mixing until fluffy. Add flour; mix well. Roll on floured surface. Cut with doughnut cutter. Place 3 almond halves on each. Place on cookie sheet. Bake for 25 minutes or until light brown.

May Hourani, Friend of the National Grange, Arlington, Virginia

GOOSEBERRY COBBLER

Yields: 8 servings	Pan Size: 9 x 13 inch	Preheat: 350°

4 c. gooseberries	1 tsp. baking powder
1 tsp. cornstarch	1 tbsp. sugar
¼ c. tapioca	½ tsp. salt
¾ c. sugar	1 stick margarine
Cinnamon to taste	1 egg, beaten
1 c. flour	¼ c. milk

Bring gooseberries and water to cover to a boil in saucepan. Dissolve cornstarch in a small amount of water. Add to gooseberries with tapioca, ¾ cup sugar and cinnamon. Cook until thickened, stirring constantly. Pour into baking dish. Sift remaining dry ingredients together in bowl. Cut in margarine until crumbly. Add mixture of egg and milk. Mix until moistened. Drop by spoonfuls in gooseberry mixture. Bake for 30 to 35 minutes or until brown.

Jan Wade, Greenwich Grange, Ohio

HICKORY NUT PUDDING

Yields: 6 servings	Pan Size: 9 x 9 inch	Preheat: 300°

2 c. packed brown sugar
1 c. flour
1 tsp. baking powder

1 c. sugar
1 c. milk
½ c. chopped hickory nuts

Dissolve brown sugar in *1 cup hot water* in small bowl. Combine remaining ingredients in bowl; mix well. Pour into greased baking dish. Pour brown sugar mixture over top. Bake for 40 minutes. Serve with whipped cream.

Carol Leak, David Crockett Grange, Texas

HOMEMADE ICE CREAM

Yields: 15 to 20 servings	Pan Size: 1 gallon freezer

7 eggs, separated
1 tbsp. vanilla extract
½ tsp. salt
1½ to 2 c. sugar

2 to 3 c. whipping
cream, whipped
Milk

Beat egg whites until stiff peaks form. Beat egg yolks until frothy. Fold gently into egg whites. Add vanilla, salt and sugar. Fold in stiffly whipped cream. Pour into freezer container. Put dasher in place. Fill container with milk. Freeze according to manufacturer's instructions.

Marvis T. Hogen
Secretary, South Dakota Department of Agriculture

KIWIFRUIT PAVLOVA

Yields: 6 servings	

1 c. whipping
cream
1 tbsp. sugar

6 meringue
shells
2 or 3 kiwifruit

Whip cream in mixer bowl until stiff peaks form. Fold in sugar. Mound in meringue shells. Peel and slice kiwifruit; cut slices into halves. Arrange over whipped cream. Serve immediately.

LEMON OMELET (GERMANY)

Yields: 2 servings	Pan Size: 8 inch

3 eggs, separated	**Juice of ½ lemon**
2 tbsp. sugar	**Butter**
2 tsp. flour	**Confectioners' sugar**

Combine egg yolks, sugar, flour and lemon juice in bowl; beat until smooth. Fold in stiffly beaten egg whites. Heat butter in heavy skillet. Pour in egg mixture. Reduce heat to very low. Cook until top of omelet is dry; fold over. Remove to serving plate. Sprinkle with confectioners' sugar.

Magdalen Capaldo, Genesee Grange, Colorado

MINCE DELIGHT

Yields: 8 servings	Pan Size: 6x10 inch	Preheat: 350°

1 cup oats	**¼ tsp. salt**
1 cup flour	**½ c. melted margarine**
¾ c. packed brown sugar	**2 c. apple or green tomato**
½ tsp. soda	**mincemeat**

Combine first 6 ingredients in bowl; mix with fork until crumbly. Press ⅔ of the mixture in baking dish. Spread with mincemeat. Sprinkle with remaining crumbs. Bake for 30 to 35 minutes or until golden brown. Serve hot or cold with cream.

Thelma L. Call, Stafford Grange, New York

QUICK PEACH COBBLER

Yields: 8 servings	Pan Size: 9x12 inch	Preheat: 375°

1 stick margarine	**1 c. sugar**
1 c. milk	**4 c. sliced peaches, sweetened**
1 c. self-rising flour	**to taste**

Melt margarine in baking dish. Combine milk, flour and sugar in bowl; mix well. Spoon into prepared dish; do not stir. Top with peaches; do not stir. Bake for 40 minutes or until light brown. Serve warm with whipped cream or vanilla ice cream.

Tommy Irwin
Commissioner, Georgia Department of Agriculture

PEACH-A-BERRY COBBLER

Yields: 6 servings   Pan Size: 8 inch round   Preheat: 350°

2 c. sliced fresh peaches	**½ c. sugar**
Sugar to taste	**1½ tsp. baking powder**
1 tbsp. cornstarch	**½ tsp. salt**
¼ c. packed brown sugar	**½ c. milk**
1 c. fresh blueberries	**¼ c. butter, softened**
1 tbsp. butter	**2 tbsp. sugar**
1 tbsp. lemon juice	**¼ tsp. nutmeg**
1 c. sifted flour	

Mix peaches with sugar to taste in bowl. Combine cornstarch, brown sugar and *½ cup cold water* in saucepan. Stir in peaches and blueberries. Cook until thickened. Add 1 tablespoon butter and lemon juice. Pour into baking dish. Sift flour, ½ cup sugar, baking powder and salt together into bowl. Add milk and softened butter; beat until smooth. Pour over fruit. Sprinkle with mixture of 2 tablespoons sugar and nutmeg. Bake for 30 minutes or until brown. Serve warm with cream.
Note: May use fresh or frozen fruit, substituting ½ cup drained juice for water.

Ethel L. Wheelock, Susquehanna Valley Grange, New York

PEACH SHERBET

Yields: 4 servings

⅓ c. sweetened condensed	**1 tbsp. melted butter**
milk	**½ c. chopped fresh peaches**
1 tbsp. lemon juice	**1 egg white, stiffly beaten**

Blend condensed milk, lemon juice and *¼ cup water* in bowl. Stir in peaches. Chill in refrigerator. Fold egg white into chilled mixture. Pour into freezer tray. Freeze until partially frozen. Place in mixer bowl. Beat until smooth but not melted. Place in freezer tray. Freeze until firm.

Brenda E. Miller, Virginville Grange, Pennsylvania

SCALLOPED PINEAPPLE

Yields: 6 servings   Pan Size: 7x11 inch   Preheat: 350°

6 slices dry bread	**⅓ c. melted butter**
1 20-oz. crushed pineapple	**2 eggs, beaten**
1 c. sugar	**½ c. packed brown sugar**
⅓ c. half and half	

Toast bread and cut into cubes. Mix with undrained pineapple. Combine sugar, half and half, butter and eggs in bowl; beat until smooth. Stir in pineapple mixture gently. Spoon into buttered baking dish. Sprinkle with brown sugar. Bake for 45 minutes.

Ruby Holderness, Milbrook Grange, Illinois

ENGLISH PLUM PUDDING

Yields: 12 servings   Pan Size: 3 quart mold

3 eggs	1 tsp. soda
1 c. Brandy	1 tsp. each cinnamon, cloves
2 c. finely chopped suet	and allspice
1 c. sugar	3 lb. raisins
1 c. molasses	½ c. butter, softened
1 c. bread crumbs	2 c. sifted confectioners' sugar
1 c. flour	1 tsp. Brandy

Beat eggs lightly in bowl. Add 1 cup Brandy, suet, sugar, molasses and bread crumbs; mix well. Sift flour, soda and spices together. Add to molasses mixture; mix well. Stir in raisins. Spoon into greased mold. Place in saucepan filled with water to half the depth of mold. Steam for 3 hours. Invert onto serving plate. Cream butter and confectioners' sugar in mixer bowl until light and fluffy. Mix in 1 teaspoon Brandy. Serve with pudding.

Joy Beatie
California Director of Women's Activities

DAD'S HOLIDAY PUDDING (ENGLAND)

Yields: 12 to 16 servings   Pan Size: pudding steamer

1 lb. raisins	1 tsp. salt
1 lb. dried currants	1 lb. brown sugar
2 c. flour	Juice of 2 lemons
8 oz. bread, crumbled	Grated rind of 2 lemons
1 tsp. cinnamon	8 oz. each candied orange rind,
½ tsp. each cloves, ginger	lemon rind and citron
and allspice	1 lb. finely ground suet
1 tsp. soda	½ c. molasses

Pour *1 cup boiling water* over raisins and currants in bowl. Let stand for 30 minutes. Combine first 8 ingredients in bowl. Add mixture of brown sugar and lemon juice, lemon rind, candied fruit, suet, molasses and raisin mixture; mix well. Fill greased molds ½ to ⅔ full. Cover molds with waxed paper; secure with string. Place in steamer with water to half the depth of molds. Steam for 3 hours. Invert onto heated serving plates. Serve with favorite sauce.

Mrs. Charles Vargason, Ovid Grange, New York

RHUBARB CRUMBLE

Yields: 4 to 6 servings	Pan Size: 8 x 8 inch	Preheat: 375°

3 c. chopped rhubarb	⅔ c. flour
3 tbsp. orange juice	½ c. packed brown sugar
¾ c. sugar	¼ tsp. soda
¼ tsp. cinnamon	⅔ c. quick-cooking oats
1 tbsp. butter, softened	¼ c. butter, softened

Spread rhubarb in baking pan. Sprinkle with orange juice, sugar and cinnamon. Dot with 1 tablespoon butter. Mix remaining dry ingredients in bowl. Cut in ¼ cup butter until crumbly. Sprinkle over rhubarb. Bake for 40 minutes.

Minnie Pike, Kendrew Grange, New York

RHUBARB SHORTCAKE

Yields: 9 servings	Pan Size: 8 x 8 inch	Preheat: 350°

2 c. cut rhubarb	1 egg
3 tbsp. margarine, softened	Dash of salt
¾ c. sugar	1 c. sugar
½ c. milk	¾ tsp. cinnamon
1 c. flour	1 tbsp. cornstarch
1 tsp. baking powder	

Place rhubarb in greased baking dish. Cream margarine and ¾ cup sugar in mixer bowl until light and fluffy. Add milk, flour, baking powder, egg and salt; mix well. Pour over rhubarb. Mix 1 cup sugar, cinnamon and cornstarch in bowl. Sprinkle over top. Pour *1 cup boiling water* over all. Bake for 45 minutes.

Grace Duesterbeck, Fairfield Grange, Wisconsin

RICE PUDDING (DENMARK)

Yields: 100 servings	Pan Size: stockpot

2 gal. milk	⅓ c. vanilla extract
3 tbsp. cinnamon	3½ c. sliced almonds
5¼ c. rice	4 c. whipping cream,
1¾ c. sugar	whipped

Mix milk and cinnamon in stockpot with wire whisk. Bring to a boil. Stir in rice and sugar; reduce heat. Simmer, uncovered, for 25 minutes or until rice is soft but not mushy. Pour into shallow pan; stir in vanilla. Chill, covered, in refrigerator. Stir in almonds; fold in whipped cream gently. Spoon ½ cup pudding into each dessert dish. Garnish with additional whipped cream and almonds.

Photograph for this recipe on page 238.

Recipe for this photograph on page 191.

MERINGUE RICE PUDDING (SWEDEN)

Yields: 6 to 8 servings	Pan Size: 1½ quart	Preheat: 350°

½ c. rice	¼ c. butter
½ tsp. salt	2½ c. milk
3 eggs, separated	1 tsp. vanilla extract
¼ tsp. salt	¼ tsp. almond extract
½ c. sugar	2 tbsp. sugar
1 tbsp. cornstarch	

Stir rice and ½ teaspoon salt into *1⅓ cups boiling water* in saucepan. Bring to a boil; reduce heat. Simmer, covered, for 15 to 20 minutes or until rice is tender and liquid is absorbed. Beat egg yolks with ¼ teaspoon salt, ½ cup sugar and cornstarch in bowl. Stir in butter, milk, flavorings and rice. Spoon into baking dish. Bake for 1 hour, stirring occasionally. Beat egg whites until stiff peaks form. Add 2 tablespoons sugar, 1 teaspoon at a time, beating constantly until stiff peaks form. Spoon over pudding, sealing to edge. Bake for 10 to 15 minutes longer or until golden brown. Cool for 2 hours before serving.

Isabelle Eckberg, Kylertown Grange, Pennsylvania

OLD FAVORITE STRAWBERRY SHORTCAKE

Yields: 8 servings	Pan Size: baking sheet	Preheat: 450°

2 c. sifted flour	½ c. light cream
2 tbsp. sugar	3 tbsp. butter, softened
1 tbsp. baking powder	4 c. sweetened sliced
½ tsp. salt	strawberries
½ c. butter	1 c. whipping cream
1 egg, beaten	

Sift dry ingredients together into bowl. Cut in butter until crumbly. Add mixture of egg and light cream. Mix just until dough clings together. Knead several times on floured surface. Pat ¾ inch thick. Cut into 2½-inch circles. Place on ungreased baking sheet. Bake for 8 to 10 minutes or until brown. Split shortcakes. Spread with 3 tablespoons butter. Spoon strawberries between and over tops of shortcake halves. Serve warm with stiffly whipped cream.

Merle Campbell, Tecumseh Grange, Kansas

Recipe for this photograph on page 218.

STRAWBERRY YUM-YUM

Yields: 8 to 10 servings	Pan Size: 9 x 9 inch	Preheat: 350°

1 c. flour	1 c. sugar
½ c. butter	2 tsp. lemon juice
¼ c. packed brown sugar	1 10-oz. package frozen
½ c. chopped nuts	strawberries, thawed
2 egg whites	1 c. whipping cream, whipped

Mix first 4 ingredients in bowl until crumbly. Press into 8 x 8-inch pan. Bake for 20 to 25 minutes. Cool. Stir until crumbly. Sprinkle half the mixture into greased 9 x 9-inch pan. Combine egg whites, sugar, lemon juice and strawberries in mixer bowl. Beat at medium speed for 15 to 20 minutes or until mixture triples in bulk. Fold into whipped cream gently. Spread in prepared pan. Top with remaining crumbs. Freeze until firm.

Eleanor Gunser, Middletown Grange, Pennsylvania

DEVONSHIRE STRAWBERRIES

Yields: 8 servings	Pan Size: 1 quart

1 env. unflavored gelatin	½ c. sugar
1 c. sour cream	1 tsp. vanilla extract
1 c. whipping cream	4 c. fresh sliced strawberries

Soften gelatin in ¾ *cup cold water* in small saucepan. Heat over low heat until gelatin dissolves. Stir into sour cream in bowl; set aside. Whip cream in mixer bowl until thickened. Add sugar gradually, beating until soft peaks form. Fold in vanilla and sour cream gently. Rinse 1-quart mold with cold water. Spoon sour cream mixture into mold. Chill until firm. Unmold onto serving plate. Arrange strawberries around mold.

Grace Welch, Emerald Mound Grange, Illinois

WHITE HOUSE SHERBET

Yields: 12 servings	Pan Size: 9 x 13 inch

Grated rind of 2 lemons	2½ c. sugar
½ c. lemon juice	4 c. cold milk

Combine lemon rind with ½ *cup cold water* in small bowl. Let stand for 20 minutes. Pour lemon juice over sugar in bowl. Add lemon rind mixture and milk; mix well. Pour into dish. Freeze until partially set. Remove to bowl. Beat until smooth. Repeat process several times. Freeze until firm.
Note: This recipe came from Great-aunt Achsah who was born in 1845.

Irene Sommers, Turtle Grange, Wisconsin

THREE JELL-O DESSERT SALAD

Yields: 12 to 14 servings   Pan Size: 9 x 13 inch

3 sm. packages Jell-O, **assorted colors** **2 c. graham cracker crumbs** **¼ c. butter, melted** **¼ c. sugar**	**1 tbsp. unflavored gelatin** **1 c. pineapple juice, heated** **1 pt. whipping cream** **½ c. sugar** **1 tsp. vanilla extract**

Dissolve each package Jell-O in *1½ cups boiling water*. Pour each into shallow pan. Chill until set. Combine next 3 ingredients in bowl; mix well. Press half the crumb mixture into dish. Soften unflavored gelatin in *¼ cup cold water*. Combine with hot pineapple juice in bowl, stirring until gelatin dissolves; cool. Whip cream with ½ cup sugar and vanilla in bowl until stiff peaks form. Stir in juice mixture. Cut congealed Jell-O into cubes. Fold into whipped cream. Spoon into prepared dish. Sprinkle with remaining crumbs. Chill for 4 hours or longer. Cut into squares.

Dorothy Hutchins
Maine Director of Women's Activities

CHOCOLATE SAUCE

Yields: 4 cups   Pan Size: double boiler

4 sq. unsweetened chocolate **2 tbsp. butter** **3 c. sugar**	**6 tbsp. light corn syrup** **Pinch of salt** **1 tsp. vanilla extract**

Melt chocolate and butter in double boiler over boiling water; blend well. Add *1 cup boiling water* gradually. Stir in sugar and corn syrup gradually. Add salt. Simmer for 12 to 15 minutes or to desired consistency. Cool slightly. Stir in vanilla.

Malcolm Baldrige
Secretary, U.S. Department of Commerce

HOT FUDGE SAUCE

Yields: 4 cups   Pan Size: 2 quart

½ c. butter **4 sq. unsweetened** **chocolate**	**3 c. sugar** **1 13-oz. can evaporated milk** **1 tsp. vanilla extract**

Melt butter with chocolate in double boiler; mix well. Add sugar ¼ cup at a time, stirring constantly. Stir in salt. Add evaporated milk gradually, mixing well after each addition. Stir in vanilla. Store in covered container in refrigerator. Reheat to serve.

Linda S. Pilc, Curriers Grange, New York

MAPLE GRAVY SAUCE

Yields: 4 cups	Pan Size: 1½ quart

1 c. flour	**1 qt. maple syrup**
½ c. butter, melted	**1½ tsp. vanilla extract**

Blend flour into melted butter in saucepan or glass bowl. Add syrup gradually; mix well. Cook or microwave on High until thickened, stirring frequently. Stir in vanilla. Serve over spice cake.

Mrs. James Company, Beaver Falls Grange, New York

PRALINE SAUCE

Yields: 2 cups	Pan Size: 2 quart

1 c. light corn syrup	**1 egg, beaten**
½ c. sugar	**1 tbsp. vanilla extract**
⅓ c. margarine	**1 c. coarsely chopped pecans**

Combine syrup, sugar, margarine and egg in heavy saucepan; mix well. Bring to a boil over medium heat, stirring constantly. Boil for 2 minutes; do not stir. Remove from heat. Stir in vanilla and pecans. Serve warm or at room temperature over ice cream.

Ruth Caven Johnston, Wilmington Grange, Pennsylvania

RHUBARB SAUCE

Yields: 5 cups	Pan Size: 2 quart

4 c. chopped rhubarb	**¼ tsp. soda**
1 c. sugar	**1 pkg. frozen strawberries**

Combine rhubarb, sugar, baking powder and a small amount of water in saucepan. Cook until rhubarb is tender. Stir in strawberries.

Phyllis Pratt, Albion Grange, Maine

CREAMY FROZEN YOGURT

Yields: 6 quarts	Pan Size: ice cream freezer

4 c. light cream	**4 to 6 c. favorite fruit**
4 c. yogurt	**1 tbsp. vanilla extract**
4 to 6 eggs	

Combine all ingredients in bowl; mix well. Pour into ice cream freezer container. Freeze according to manufacturer's instructions.

Spurlin Soya, Eagle Cliff Grange, Washington

Cakes

MRS. COOKE'S ANGEL CAKE

Yields: 10 servings	Pan Size: 10-inch tube	Preheat: 300°

½ c. sugar
1 c. confectioners' sugar
1¾ tsp. cream of tartar
1½ c. egg whites, at room
   temperature

¼ tsp. salt
1 tsp. vanilla extract
½ tsp. almond extract
1 c. sifted cake flour

Sift sugars and 1 teaspoon cream of tartar together. Beat egg whites and salt in mixer bowl until foamy. Add ¾ teaspoon cream of tartar; beat until stiff peaks form. Add sifted sugar 2 tablespoons at a time, folding 10 times after each addition. Add flavoring; fold 6 times. Add flour 2 tablespoons at a time, folding 20 times after each addition. Add *4 teaspoons water* 1 at a time, folding 15 times after each addition. Bake for 60 minutes. Invert on funnel to cool. Loosen from side of pan with knife. Remove to serving plate.

Pearl Buell, Klondike-Piney Grange, Wyoming

ANGEL SUNSHINE CAKE

Yields: 20 servings	Pan Size: tube	Preheat: 325°

5 eggs, separated	**Pinch of salt**
½ c. sugar	**¼ tsp. cream of tartar**
½ c. cake flour	**½ c. sugar**
1 tbsp. cornstarch	**½ c. cake flour**
1 tsp. baking powder	**½ tsp. vanilla extract**
½ tsp. orange extract	

Beat egg yolks until thick and lemon-colored. Add ½ cup sugar and *3 tablespoons cold water*; beat until smooth. Add sifted mixture of next 3 dry ingredients and orange flavoring; mix well. Spoon into ungreased tube pan. Beat egg whites and salt until soft peaks form. Add cream of tartar; beat until stiff peaks form. Fold in remaining ingredients. Spoon over layer in pan. Bake for 50 minutes or until cake tests done. Cool in pan. Invert onto cake plate.

Arlene Waltz, Lycova Grange, Pennsylvania

CAROLINA APPLE CAKE

Yields: 15 servings	Pan Size: tube	Preheat: 350°

4 eggs, beaten	**3 c. chopped peeled apples**
1½ c. oil	**1 c. chopped nuts**
2 c. sugar	**¼ c. milk**
3 c. flour	**1 tbsp. butter**
1 tsp. each soda, salt	**1 c. packed brown sugar**
2 tsp. vanilla extract	**Vanilla extract to taste**

Beat eggs, oil and sugar in mixer bowl until smooth. Sift in flour, soda and salt; mix well. Stir in 2 teaspoons vanilla, apples and nuts. Pour into greased and floured tube pan. Bake for 1 hour or until cake tests done. Remove to wire rack to cool. Bring remaining ingredients to a boil in saucepan. Simmer for 10 minutes. Cool. Drizzle evenly over cake.

James G. Martin
Governor of North Carolina

CHEESY APPLE CAKE

Yields: 16 servings	Pan Size: 9 x 13 inch	Preheat: 350°

8 to 10 c. sliced apples	**1¾ c. flour**
1¾ tsp. cinnamon	**1 c. milk**
½ tsp. nutmeg	**3 eggs**
1 tbsp. lemon juice	**1 tsp. baking powder**
2 c. sugar	**2 tsp. vanilla extract**
Butter, softened	**1 to 2 c. grated Cheddar cheese**

Mix apples with 1½ teaspoons cinnamon, nutmeg and lemon juice in bowl. Spread evenly in cake pan. Combine 1½ cups sugar, ⅓ cup butter, ¾ cup flour, milk, eggs, baking powder and vanilla in mixer bowl; beat until smooth. Pour over apples. Cream ½ cup butter and ½ cup sugar in mixer bowl until light. Add 1 cup flour, ¼ teaspoon cinnamon and cheese; mix until crumbly. Sprinkle over cake. Bake for 1 hour or until cake tests done.

Erva Marie Flint, Lake Francis Grange, California

FRESH APPLE CAKE

Yields: 12 to 15 servings	Pan Size: 9 x 13 inch	Preheat: 350°

4 c. coarsely chopped apples	2 c. sifted flour
2 c. sugar	2 tsp. soda
2 eggs	2 tsp. cinnamon
½ c. oil	1 tsp. salt
2 tsp. vanilla extract	1 c. chopped walnuts

Mix apples and sugar in bowl; set aside. Beat eggs lightly in large bowl. Blend in oil and vanilla. Sift flour, soda, cinnamon and salt together. Add to egg mixture alternately with apples, mixing well after each addition. Stir in walnuts. Pour into greased and floured baking pan. Bake for 1 hour or until cake tests done. Let cool in pan for 15 minutes. Remove to wire rack to cool completely. Serve with vanilla ice cream or whipped cream.

Gus R. Douglass
Commissioner, West Virginia Department of Agriculture

OLD-FASHIONED STACK CAKE

Yields: 25 servings	Pan Size: 8 inch	Preheat: 370°

1 c. sugar	3 eggs, beaten
½ c. butter, softened	¾ c. buttermilk
3 c. flour	1 lb. dried apples
1 tsp. each soda, baking powder	1 c. sugar
¼ tsp. salt	1 tsp. allspice
1 tsp. nutmeg	

Cream 1 cup sugar and butter in bowl until light and fluffy. Sift flour, soda, baking powder, salt and nutmeg into bowl. Add creamed mixture, eggs and buttermilk; mix well. Divide into 8 portions. Roll into 8-inch circles. Fit into greased and floured cake pans. Bake until light brown. Cool on wire rack. Combine apples and enough water to cover in saucepan. Cook until tender. Add 1 cup sugar and allspice. Cook for 20 minutes. Mash and cool. Spread fruit mixture between cake layers on serving plate. Chill in refrigerator. Serve with whipped cream.
Note: May substitute dried peaches for apples.

Lena Brown, Volunteer Grange, Tennessee

SUGARLESS CHOPPED APPLE CAKE

Yields: 8 servings Pan Size: 8 x 12 inch Preheat: 325°

1 c. shortening	1 tsp. soda
3 eggs	1 tsp. cinnamon
1 tsp. instant coffee powder	½ tsp. each cloves, allspice
½ c. sour cream	1 c. frozen apple juice
1 tsp. vanilla extract	concentrate
1 c. whole wheat flour	1 c. raisins
1 c. all-purpose flour	½ c. chopped nuts
1½ tsp. baking powder	1½ c. chopped apples

Cream shortening in mixer bowl until light. Beat in eggs until smooth. Dissolve coffee in a small amount of hot water. Add to egg mixture with sour cream and vanilla; mix well. Add sifted dry ingredients alternately with apple juice concentrate, mixing well after each addition. Stir in raisins, nuts and apples. Spoon into greased and floured cake pan. Bake until cake tests done. Cool in pan.

Meryl Hayes, Buena Vista Grange, Washington

HONEY-APPLESAUCE CAKE

Yields: 12 to 15 servings Pan Size: 9 x 13 inch Preheat: 325°

½ c. butter, softened	½ tsp. salt
1 c. honey	1 tsp. cinnamon
1½ c. sweetened applesauce	½ tsp. each cloves, nutmeg
3 c. flour	1 c. chopped nuts
2 tsp. soda	1 c. raisins

Grease cake pan and line bottom with waxed paper. Cream butter in mixer bowl until light and fluffy. Blend in honey and applesauce. Add mixture of sifted dry ingredients. Beat for 2 minutes. Stir in nuts and raisins. Pour into prepared pan. Bake for 1 hour and 20 minutes or until cake tests done. Invert onto wire rack to cool; remove waxed paper. Dust with confectioners' sugar if desired.

Nellie E. Pedersen, North Creek Valley Grange, Washington

OUR FAVORITE BANANA-NUT CAKE

Yields: 16 servings Pan Size: 9 x 13 inch Preheat: 350°

⅔ c. butter-flavored	⅔ c. buttermilk
shortening	1½ c. lightly mashed bananas
1⅔ c. sugar	⅔ c. chopped nuts
3 eggs	6 tbsp. margarine
2¼ c. sifted flour	1 c. packed brown sugar
1¼ tsp. baking powder	¼ c. milk
1¼ tsp. soda	2 c. (about) confectioners' sugar
1 tsp. salt	1 tsp. vanilla extract

Cream shortening and sugar in mixer bowl until light and fluffy. Blend in eggs. Add next 4 dry ingredients and buttermilk; mix well. Stir in bananas and nuts. Pour into greased and floured cake pan. Bake for 45 to 50 minutes or until cake tests done. Cover with waxed paper; cool. Melt margarine in saucepan. Add brown sugar; bring to a boil. Cook for 1 to 2 minutes. Stir in milk. Bring to a boil again; remove from heat. Add confectioners' sugar gradually, mixing until of desired consistency. Stir in vanilla. Remove waxed paper from cake. Spread frosting over top.

Ruth Baker, Williamsport Grange, Ohio

BLUEBERRY PICNIC CAKE

Yields: 12 servings	Pan Size: 9 x 13 inch	Preheat: 350°

3 c. flour	1 tbsp. baking powder
2 c. sugar	1 tsp. salt
1 c. butter	3 eggs, separated
Grated rind of 1 lemon	1½ c. milk
½ tsp. allspice	2 c. fresh blueberries

Mix flour and sugar in bowl; cut in butter until crumbly. Reserve 1 cup mixture for topping. Add lemon rind, allspice, baking powder and salt to remaining mixture. Add mixture of egg yolks and milk; beat until smooth. Fold in stiffly beaten egg whites gently. Pour into greased and floured pan. Layer blueberries and reserved crumb mixture over top. Bake for 40 minutes or until golden brown.

BLUEBERRY BRUNCH CAKE

Yields: 12 servings   Pan Size: 9 x 13 inch   Preheat: 350°

2 c. blueberries	3 eggs
½ c. sugar	½ c. milk
1 tbsp. cornstarch	1 tsp. vanilla extract
½ c. butter, softened	1 tbsp. lemon rind
3 oz. cream cheese, softened	½ c. confectioners' sugar
2¼ c. cake flour	1 tbsp. butter
1 c. sugar	2 tsp. milk
2 tsp. baking powder	¼ tsp. lemon extract
1 tsp. salt	

Combine first 3 ingredients and *½ cup water* in saucepan. Cook until thickened, stirring frequently. Cool. Cut butter and cream cheese into mixture of cake flour, sugar, baking powder and salt in bowl until crumbly. Reserve 1 cup crumbs for topping. Add eggs, milk, vanilla and lemon rind to remaining crumbs, beat well. Pour into greased cake pan. Spoon blueberries over batter. Sprinkle with reserved crumbs. Bake for 35 to 45 minutes or until golden. Cool for 30 minutes. Combine remaining ingredients in small bowl; mix well. Drizzle over warm cake. Cut into squares.

Alice Emery, Auburn Grange, New York

GRANDMA SHAVER'S BURNT SUGAR CAKE

Yields: 12 servings   Pan Size: three 8 inch   Preheat: 350°

1 c. sugar	1 c. warm milk
½ c. butter, softened	2½ c. flour
1½ c. sugar	2 tsp. baking powder
3 eggs, separated	1 tsp. vanilla extract

Melt 1 cup sugar in heavy skillet over medium heat, stirring frequently. Add *½ cup boiling water*; mix well. Cream butter in mixer bowl. Add 1½ cups sugar gradually, beating until light and fluffy. Add egg yolks, milk, and 2 cups flour, beating well after each addition. Beat for 5 minutes. Add enough burnt sugar syrup to make of desired color. Add ½ cup flour, baking powder and vanilla; mix well. Fold in stiffly beaten egg whites gently. Pour into greased and floured cake pans. Bake for 25 minutes or until cake tests done. Cool in pans for 10 minutes. Cool on wire rack. Frost as desired.

Millie E. Patterson, Crystal Grange, Washington

RICH BUTTER CAKE

Yields: 8 to 10 servings   Pan Size: two 9 inch round   Preheat: 350°

⅔ c. butter, softened	2½ c. cake flour
1½ c. sugar	2¾ tsp. baking powder
3 eggs	1 tsp. salt
1 tsp. vanilla extract	¾ c. milk

Cream butter, sugar, eggs and vanilla in mixer bowl until light and fluffy. Add sifted dry ingredients alternately with milk, mixing well after each addition. Spoon into greased and floured cake pans. Bake for 30 minutes or until cake tests done. Remove to wire rack to cool. Frost with favorite frosting.

Georgia H. Taylor, Potomac Grange, Washington D.C.

BUTTERMILK CAKE

Yields: 12 servings	Pan Size: 9 x 13 inch	Preheat: 350°

1 c. packed brown sugar	2½ c. flour
½ c. sugar	3 tbsp. cocoa
½ c. butter, softened	1 tsp. baking powder
2 eggs, well beaten	¼ tsp. salt
2 tsp. soda	Flavoring to taste
1¼ c. buttermilk	

Cream sugars and butter in bowl until light and fluffy. Add eggs; mix well. Dissolve soda in buttermilk. Sift flour, cocoa, baking powder and salt. Add to creamed mixture alternately with buttermilk, mixing well after each addition. Blend in flavoring. Pour into greased cake pan. Bake until cake tests done. Cool in pan. Frost as desired.

Edith E. Becker, Elk Grove Grange, California

BLUE RIBBON CARROT CAKE

Yields: 12 servings	Pan Size: 9 x 12 inch	Preheat: 350°

2 c. flour	1½ c. oil
1 c. sugar	3 c. grated carrots
1 c. packed brown sugar	1 c. chopped walnuts
2 tsp. each baking powder, soda	½ c. butter, softened
1 tsp. salt	8 oz. cream cheese, softened
2 tsp. cinnamon	2 tsp. vanilla extract
½ tsp. nutmeg	1 lb. confectioners' sugar
4 eggs	1 c. chopped walnuts

Frosting (handwritten annotation)

Combine first 8 ingredients in mixer bowl. Beat eggs and oil until light. Add to dry ingredients. Beat at low speed until blended. Fold in carrots and 1 cup walnuts. Pour into greased and floured cake pan. Bake for 45 minutes or until cake tests done. Cool in pan on wire rack for 10 minutes. Invert onto wire rack to cool completely. Cream butter and cream cheese in bowl until fluffy. Blend in vanilla. Add confectioners' sugar gradually; beat until smooth. Fold in 1 cup walnuts. Frost cooled cake.

Dona Mankin, Rickreall Grange, Oregon

CARROT CAKE

Yields: 8 servings	Pan Size: 8 x 8 inch	Preheat: 350°

1½ c. sifted flour	2 eggs
1 c. sugar	1½ c. grated carrots
1 tsp. each baking powder, soda	½ c. crushed pineapple
½ tsp. salt	1 tsp. vanilla extract
1½ tsp. cinnamon	½ c. chopped nuts
⅔ c. oil	¼ c. chopped raisins

Sift first 6 ingredients into bowl. Add oil and eggs; beat well. Stir in carrots, undrained pineapple and vanilla. Add nuts and raisins; mix well. Pour into greased and floured cake pan. Bake at 350 degrees for 35 minutes.

Mary R. Green, Hemlock Grange, New York

BOSTON CREAM PIE

Yields: 6 servings	Pan Size: 8 inch	Preheat: 350°

2 eggs, separated	Vanilla extract
1 c. flour	⅓ c. flour
1½ tsp. baking powder	⅛ tsp. salt
¾ c. sugar	14 tbsp. sugar
⅛ tsp. salt	2 eggs, beaten
½ c. milk, scalded	2 c. milk, scalded

Fold beaten egg yolks gently into stiffly beaten egg whites. Sift 1 cup flour, baking powder, ¾ cup sugar and ⅛ teaspoon salt together 3 times. Fold gently into egg whites. Add ½ cup hot milk and ½ teaspoon vanilla gradually, blending well after each addition. Pour into greased and floured deep cake pan. Bake for 35 minutes. Cool in pan for 10 minutes. Remove to wire rack to cool completely. Split into 2 layers. Sift ⅓ cup flour, ⅛ teaspoon salt and 14 tablespoons sugar into double boiler. Add 2 eggs and 2 cups hot milk, mixing well after each addition. Cook over hot water until thickened, stirring constantly. Stir in vanilla to taste. Cool in refrigerator. Spread between cake layers. Garnish with dusting of confectioners' sugar.

Cynthia Martin, Bellview Grange, Oregon

CHIFFON CAKE

Yields: 16 servings	Pan Size: 10-inch tube	Preheat: 325°

1 c. egg whites	7 egg yolks
½ tsp. cream of tartar	2 tsp. grated lemon rind
2 c. sifted flour	1 tsp. vanilla extract
1½ c. sugar	1 c. milk
1 tbsp. baking powder	¼ c. flour
1 tsp. salt	1 c. sugar
½ c. oil	1 c. shortening

Beat egg whites and cream of tartar in mixer bowl until very stiff peaks form. Sift next 4 dry ingredients into bowl; make well in center. Add oil, egg yolks, lemon rind, vanilla and *¾ cup water*. Beat with wooden spoon until smooth. Fold gently into egg whites. Spoon into ungreased pan. Bake for 55 minutes. Increase temperature to 350 degrees. Bake for 15 minutes longer or until cake tests done. Cool in inverted pan. Loosen cake from side of pan. Invert onto cake plate. Blend milk and ¼ cup flour in saucepan. Cook for 5 minutes, stirring constantly. Cool. Beat in 1 cup sugar and shortening until light and fluffy. Spread on cake.

Marion Martin, Harwill Grange

CHOCOLATE CHIFFON CAKE

Yields: 12 to 15 servings	Pan Size: tube	Preheat: 325°

½ c. cocoa	½ c. oil
1¾ c. cake flour	7 egg yolks
1¾ c. sugar	2 tsp. vanilla extract
1½ tsp. soda	1 c. egg whites
1 tsp. salt	½ tsp. cream of tartar

Combine cocoa and *¾ cup boiling water* in saucepan. Cook until thickened, stirring constantly. Cool. Combine cake flour, sugar, soda and salt in mixer bowl; make well in center. Add oil, egg yolks and vanilla. Beat at medium speed for 1 minute. Beat egg whites and cream of tartar at high speed for 3 to 5 minutes or until very stiff peaks form. Fold in cocoa mixture gently. Pour into ungreased tube pan. Bake for 55 minutes. Increase temperature to 350 degrees. Bake for 15 minutes longer. Invert on funnel to cool completely. Loosen cake from side of pan. Invert onto cake plate.

Geraldine Jensen, Riverview Grange, Nebraska

MEXICAN CHOCOLATE CHIFFON CAKE

Yields: 12 servings	Pan Size: 10-inch tube	Preheat: 325°

¾ c. hot coffee	½ tsp. salt
⅓ c. cocoa	½ c. oil
1¾ c. sifted cake flour	7 eggs, separated
1⅔ c. sugar	2 tsp. vanilla extract
1½ tsp. soda	½ tsp. cream of tartar

Blend hot coffee and cocoa. Cool. Sift flour, sugar, soda and salt into bowl; make well in center. Add oil, egg yolks, vanilla and cocoa mixture to well in order listed; beat until smooth. Beat egg whites and cream of tartar until very stiff peaks form. Pour chocolate mixture gradually over egg whites, folding gently until well blended. Pour into greased pan. Bake at 325 degrees for 55 minutes. Increase temperature to 350 degrees. Bake for 10 to 15 minutes longer or until cake tests done. Cool completely in inverted pan. Remove to serving plate.

Louisa B. Hott
Maryland Director of Women's Activities

LEMON CHIFFON CAKE

Yields: 14 to 16 servings	Pan Size: 10 inch	Preheat: 325°

2¼ c. sifted cake flour
1½ c. sugar
1 tbsp. baking powder
½ tsp. salt
6 egg yolks
½ c. Mazola corn oil
1 tbsp. grated lemon rind

¼ c. lemon juice
6 egg whites
½ tsp. cream of tartar
1 c. confectioners' sugar
½ tsp. grated lemon rind
1 to 2 tbsp. lemon juice

Sift flour, sugar, baking powder and salt into large mixer bowl. Make well in center. Add egg yolks, corn oil, 1 tablespoon lemon rind and ¼ cup lemon juice and *½ cup water*. Beat at medium speed until smooth. Beat egg whites with cream of tartar until very stiff peaks form. Fold in batter gently. Pour into ungreased tube pan. Bake for 65 to 70 minutes or until cake springs back when touched lightly. Cool in inverted pan. Loosen cake from sides of pan. Invert onto cake plate. Blend confectioners' sugar with ½ teaspoon lemon rind and enough lemon juice to make of desired consistency. Drizzle over cake.

Photograph for this recipe on page 204.

WALNUT CHIFFON CAKE

Yields: 12 servings	Pan Size: tube	Preheat: 350°

2 c. flour
1½ c. sugar
1 tbsp. baking powder
½ tsp. salt
9 egg yolks

½ c. oil
1 tsp. vanilla extract
1 c. chopped black walnuts
1 c. egg whites
½ tsp. cream of tartar

Sift first 4 ingredients into mixer bowl; make well in center. Add egg yolks, oil, *¾ cup cold water* and vanilla. Beat well. Add walnuts. Beat egg whites and cream of tartar until stiff peaks form. Fold in walnut mixture gently. Pour into ungreased tube pan. Bake for 1 hour. Invert on funnel to cool completely. Loosen cake from sides of pan. Invert onto cake plate.

Susan Uhler, Lykens Township Grange, Pennsylvania

BROWN SUGAR FUDGE CAKE

Yields: 16 servings	Pan Size: two 9 inch	Preheat: 350°

2¼ c. sifted cake flour
1 tsp. soda
¾ tsp. salt
2 c. packed brown sugar
½ c. shortening

1 tsp. vanilla extract
1 c. buttermilk
3 eggs
2 sq. unsweetened chocolate,
  melted

Sift flour, soda and salt into mixer bowl. Add brown sugar, shortening, vanilla and ⅔ cup buttermilk. Beat at medium speed for 2 minutes. Add remaining buttermilk, eggs and chocolate; mix well. Spoon into greased and floured cake pans. Bake for 30 to 35 minutes or until cake tests done. Cool in pans for 10 minutes. Remove to wire rack to cool completely. Frost as desired.

Charlotte Sherman, Vashon Maury Grange, Washington

CHOCOLATE MERINGUE CAKE

Yields: 12 servings	Pan Size: three 8 inch	Preheat: 350°

½ c. butter, softened	2½ c. sifted cake flour
1 c. sugar	1⅓ tsp. soda
1 tsp. vanilla extract	3 egg whites
½ tsp. salt	¾ c. sugar
½ c. cocoa	

Cream butter and 1 cup sugar in bowl until light and fluffy. Beat in vanilla and salt. Dissolve cocoa in *⅓ cup warm water*. Add to creamed mixture; mix well. Add flour alternately with *1 cup cold water*, beating well after each addition. Fold in soda dissolved in *1 teaspoon boiling water*. Beat egg whites until soft peaks form. Add ¾ cup sugar gradually, beating until stiff peaks form. Fold gently into batter. Pour into greased and floured cake pans. Bake for 30 to 35 minutes or until cake tests done. Cool in pans for 10 minutes. Invert onto wire rack to cool completely. Frost as desired.

Tamara Fryman, Riverview Grange, Nebraska

CHOCOLATE UPSIDE-DOWN FUDGE CAKE

Yields: 6 servings	Pan Size: 9 x 9 inch	Preheat: 350°

¾ c. sugar	1 tsp. vanilla extract
1½ tbsp. cocoa	2 tbsp. butter, melted
¼ tsp. salt	½ c. chopped nuts
1 c. flour	½ c. sugar
1 tsp. baking powder	½ c. packed brown sugar
½ c. milk	3 tbsp. cocoa

Combine first 9 ingredients in bowl; mix well. Pour into buttered cake pan. Mix ½ cup sugar, brown sugar and cocoa with *1 cup boiling water*. Pour over batter. Bake for 40 minutes. Serve warm with whipped cream or ice cream.

Lorraine E. Jones, North and South Palouse Grange, Washington

CHOCOLATE OATMEAL CAKE

Yields: 8 to 12 servings	Pan Size: 8 x 12 inch	Preheat: 350°

1 c. oats	1 c. flour
½ c. shortening	½ c. cocoa
1½ c. sugar	1 tsp. soda
2 eggs	½ tsp. salt
1 tsp. vanilla extract	

Combine oats and *1½ cups boiling water* in bowl; cool. Cream shortening and sugar in bowl until light and fluffy. Add eggs and vanilla; mix well. Add oatmeal and remaining ingredients; mix well. Pour into greased cake pan. Bake for 35 minutes. Cool. Cut into squares.

Roma Schmidt, White Pigeon Grange, Michigan

CRAZY CHOCOLATE CAKE

Yields: 10 servings	Pan Size: two 9 inch	Preheat: 325°

2 c. sugar	Pinch of salt
2 eggs	3 c. sifted flour
1 c. sour milk	1 c. boiling coffee
½ c. cocoa	1 lb. brown sugar
1 c. butter, softened	½ c. milk
2 tsp. soda	½ c. butter
2 tsp. vanilla extract	1 tsp. vanilla extract

Place sugar in mixer bowl. Add next 8 ingredients. Do not stir. Add coffee; beat for 3 minutes. Pour into greased and floured cake pans. Bake until cake tests done. Combine brown sugar and milk in saucepan. Cook over medium heat to 234 to 240 degrees on candy thermometer, soft-ball stage. Remove from heat. Stir in ½ cup butter and vanilla; cool. Beat until of spreading consistency. Spread between layers and over top and side of cake.

Bonnie Whitby, Bellbrook Grange, Ohio

GERMAN CHOCOLATE CAKE

Yields: 10 to 12 servings	Pan Size: two 9 inch	Preheat: 325°

½ c. shortening	2 eggs
1 c. sugar	1 tsp. vanilla extract
1 c. packed brown sugar	2¾ c. flour
1 bar German's sweet	1 tsp. (rounded) soda
chocolate, melted	1 c. buttermilk

Cream shortening in bowl. Add sugar and brown sugar, beating well after each addition. Add chocolate, eggs, ½ cup boiling water and vanilla. Sift flour and soda. Add to creamed mixture alternately with buttermilk, mixing well after each addition. Pour into greased and floured cake pans. Bake for 25 to 35 minutes or until cake tests done. Cool in pans for 10 minutes. Invert onto wire rack to cool completely. Frost as desired.

Kathryn M. Carbon, New London Grange, Pennsylvania

MISSISSIPPI MUD CAKE

Yields: 12 servings	Pan Size: 9 x 12 inch	Preheat: 350°

1 c. margarine, softened	½ c. chopped nuts
2 c. sugar	7 oz. marshmallow creme
4 eggs	¼ c. margarine, melted
1½ c. flour	3 tbsp. milk
½ c. cocoa	2 tbsp. cocoa
1 c. flaked coconut	2 c. confectioners' sugar

Cream 1 cup margarine and sugar in mixer bowl until light and fluffy. Blend in eggs. Add flour and ½ cup cocoa; mix well. Stir in coconut and nuts. Batter will be thick. Spoon into greased and floured pan. Bake until cake tests done. Spread marshmallow creme over hot cake. Cool. Bring mixture of melted margarine, milk and 2 tablespoons cocoa to a boil in saucepan; remove from heat. Mix in confectioners' sugar. Spread over marshmallow layer.

Judge Charles E. Wiggins
California, Member of Bicentennial Commission

PERFECT CHOCOLATE CAKE

Yields: 10 to 12 servings	Pan Size: 9 x 13 inch	Preheat: 350°

1 c. cocoa	½ tsp. baking powder
1 c. butter, softened	½ tsp. salt
2½ c. sugar	6 oz. chocolate chips
4 eggs	1 c. butter
1½ tsp. vanilla extract	½ c. light cream
2¾ c. sifted flour	2½ c. confectioners' sugar
2 tsp. soda	

Whisk cocoa into *2 cups boiling water* in bowl. Cool. Cream 1 cup butter, sugar, eggs and vanilla at high speed in mixer bowl for 5 minutes, scraping bowl occasionally. Add sifted dry ingredients alternately with cocoa mixture, mixing just until moistened after each addition; do not overbeat. Pour into greased and floured pan. Bake for 25 to 30 minutes or until cake tests done. Cool on wire rack. Heat chocolate chips, 1 cup butter and cream in saucepan until chocolate and butter melt; blend well. Whisk in confectioners' sugar. Spread over cake.
Note: May bake in three 9-inch layers and fill with mixture of 2 cups whipped cream, ¼ cup confectioners' sugar and 1 teaspoon vanilla extract.

Ethel Peters, Arkansas State Grange

POTATO CAKE

Yields: 16 servings	Pan Size: two 8 inch	Preheat: 375°

½ c. shortening	2 c. flour
2 c. sugar	1 tsp. soda
¾ c. melted chocolate	1¼ c. sugar
1 c. mashed potatoes	¼ tsp. cream of tartar
2 eggs	2 egg whites, stiffly beaten
2 egg yolks	1 tsp. vanilla extract
1 c. sour milk	1½ c. coconut

Cream shortening and 2 cups sugar in mixer bowl until light and fluffy. Blend in chocolate, potatoes, eggs, egg yolks and sour milk. Add flour and soda; mix well. Pour into greased and floured cake pans. Bake for 20 to 30 minutes or until cake tests done. Cool in pans for 10 minutes. Remove to wire rack to cool completely. Combine 1¼ cups sugar, cream of tartar and *½ cup boiling water* in saucepan. Cook to 234 to 240 degrees on candy thermometer, soft-ball stage. Add to stiffly beaten egg whites gradually, beating constantly until of desired consistency. Beat in vanilla. Fold in coconut. Spread between layers and over top and side of cake.

Beverly Hager, Melrose Grange, Montana

SOUR CREAM CHOCOLATE CAKE

Yields: 12 servings	Pan Size: 9 x 13 inch	Preheat: 350°

2 c. flour	2 eggs
2 c. sugar	1 c. sour cream
½ c. cocoa	1 tsp. vanilla extract
1 tsp. salt	1 tsp. soda

Combine flour, sugar, cocoa and salt in mixer bowl; mix well. Add eggs, sour cream, vanilla and soda dissolved in *1 cup hot water*; beat for 2 minutes. Pour into greased cake pan. Bake for 30 to 40 minutes or until cake tests done. Cool in pan. Frost cooled cake with buttercream pecan icing.

Betty D. Barnes, Stotesbury Grange, Missouri

TEXAS CAKE

Yields: 15 servings	Pan Size: 10 x 16 inch	Preheat: 350°

2 c. flour	½ c. sour cream
2 c. sugar	½ c. margarine
1 tsp. soda	¼ c. cocoa
½ tsp. salt	6 tbsp. milk
2 sticks margarine	1 lb. confectioners' sugar
¼ c. cocoa	1 c. nuts
2 eggs	1 tsp. vanilla extract

Sift first 4 ingredients together into bowl. Combine margarine, cocoa and *1 cup water* in saucepan. Bring to a boil. Add to dry ingredients; mix well. Combine eggs and sour cream in bowl; mix well. Blend into batter. Pour into greased and floured cake pan. Bake for 25 minutes. Combine margarine, ¼ cup cocoa and milk in saucepan. Bring to a boil. Add confectioners' sugar, nuts and vanilla; mix well. Spread over hot cake.

Mary Buscher, Buell Grange, Oregon

TOASTED COCONUT CAKE

Yields: 12 servings	Pan Size: 9 x 9 inch	Preheat: 350°

1 c. cake flour
1 c. sugar
1 tsp. baking powder
Pinch of salt
2 eggs
½ c. hot milk

1 tbsp. butter
8 oz. brown sugar
1 c. coconut
5 tbsp. milk
4 tsp. butter, melted

Sift first 4 ingredients together 3 times. Beat eggs until lemon-colored. Add to flour mixture; mix well. Combine milk and 1 tablespoon butter; mix well. Stir into batter. Pour into greased cake pan. Bake for 35 minutes. Combine remaining ingredients in saucepan; mix well. Heat until warmed through. Spread over warm cake. Broil until light brown and bubbly.

Dorothy Toniazzo, Wintersburg Grange, California

FIVE-FLAVOR CAKE

Yields: 16 servings	Pan Size: 10-inch bundt	Preheat: 325°

2 sticks butter, softened
½ c. shortening
3 c. sugar
5 eggs
3 c. flour
½ tsp. baking powder

1 c. milk
2 tsp. each coconut, rum, butter, vanilla and lemon extracts
1 tsp. almond extract
1 c. sugar

Cream butter, shortening and 3 cups sugar in mixer bowl until light and fluffy. Beat eggs in small mixer bowl until thick and lemon colored. Blend into creamed mixture. Add flour and baking powder alternately with milk, mixing well after each addition. Stir in 1 teaspoon coconut, rum, butter, vanilla and lemon flavorings. Spoon into greased and floured bundt pan. Bake for 1½ hours or until cake tests done. Bring remaining flavorings, 1 cup sugar and *½ cup water* to a boil in saucepan; stir until sugar is dissolved. Pour half the mixture over cake in pan. Cool for several minutes. Invert cake onto cake plate. Pour remaining glaze over top.

Rozella Deife, McIntosh Grange, Washington
Dorothy Jennings, Statesville Grange, Tennessee

FEATHER CAKE

Yields: 6 servings	Pan Size: 9 inch	Preheat: 350°

3 eggs, separated	1 teaspoon vanilla extract
1½ c. flour	1 teaspoon baking powder
1 teaspoon salt	

Beat egg yolks lightly in bowl. Add *¾ cup water*; beat until smooth. Mix in flour, salt and vanilla. Beat egg whites until soft peaks form. Add baking powder, beating until stiff peaks form. Fold into egg yolks mixture. Spoon into greased and floured cake pan. Bake for 45 minutes. Cool on wire rack.

Marion B. Roberts
Massachusetts Director of Women's Activities

APPLESAUCE FRUITCAKE

Yields: 16 servings	Pan Size: 9 x 9 inch	Preheat: 325°

1 c. sifted flour	1 c. sugar
½ c. sliced dates	1½ c. applesauce
½ c. raisins	1 c. sifted flour
½ c. maraschino cherries	1 tsp. cinnamon
½ c. candied fruit mix	2 tsp. soda
½ c. nuts	1 tsp. salt
2 eggs	1 tsp. baking powder
1 stick butter, softened	

Combine 1 cup flour with fruit and nuts in bowl; mix well. Cream eggs, butter and sugar in bowl until light and fluffy. Add applesauce; mix well. Add floured fruit. Sift in remaining dry ingredients; mix well. Spoon into greased cake pan. Bake for 50 minutes or until brown.

Virginia Grenville, King County Pamona Grange, Washington

EASY FRUITCAKE

Yields: 12 servings	Pan Size: 4x8 inch	Preheat: 350°

1½ c. seedless raisins	½ c. maraschino cherries
1 c. sugar	½ c. chopped walnuts
¼ c. oil	½ tsp. lemon extract
½ tsp. salt	2 c. flour
1 tsp. each cloves, cinnamon	1 tsp. soda

Combine first 6 ingredients and *1 cup water* in saucepan. Bring to a boil. Cook for 5 minutes. Cool. Stir in cherries, walnuts and flavoring. Sift in flour and soda; mix well. Spoon into greased loaf pan. Bake for 50 to 60 minutes or until cake tests done. Cool completely on wire rack.

U. Martha Patten, Bartlett Grange, New Hampshire

HICKORY NUT CAKE

Yields: 12 servings	Pan Size: two 9 inch	Preheat: 350°

1 c. (scant) shortening	½ tsp. salt
2 c. sugar	1 c. chopped hickory nuts
4 eggs, separated	1 tsp. flour
3 c. flour	1 tsp. vanilla extract
1 tbsp. baking powder	

Cream shortening and sugar in mixer bowl until light and fluffy. Blend in egg yolks. Sift 3 cups flour, baking powder and salt together. Add to creamed mixture alternately with *1 cup water*, mixing well after each addition. Mix hickory nuts with 1 teaspoon flour. Stir nuts and vanilla into batter. Fold in stiffly beaten egg whites gently. Spoon into greased and floured pans. Bake for 35 minutes. Remove to wire rack to cool. Spread a filling of hickory nuts and sour cream between layers. Frost top and sides with favorite seven-minute frosting.
Note: This recipe from Grandmother Hoyt is nearly 100 years old.

Beulah Winter
Past Chairman, National Grange Deaf Activities

HICKORY NUT CAKE WITH BROWN SUGAR FROSTING

Yields: 10 servings	Pan Size: two 9 inch	Preheat: 350°

3¾ c. sifted cake flour	1½ c. finely ground hickory nuts
4 tsp. baking powder	⅓ c. oil
½ tsp. salt	2 c. sugar
2¼ c. sugar	½ c. packed brown sugar
¾ c. butter, softened	1 c. buttermilk
2 tsp. vanilla extract	1 stick margarine
3 eggs, separated	1 tsp. soda
¾ c. milk	1 tsp. vanilla extract

Grease cake pans; line with waxed paper. Sift first 3 ingredients together 3 times. Cream 2¼ cups sugar, butter and 2 teaspoons vanilla in mixer bowl at high speed until light and fluffy. Add egg yolks; beat well. Add sifted ingredients and milk alternately, beating at medium speed after each addition. Fold in hickory nuts and stiffly beaten egg whites gently. Blend in oil. Pour into prepared cake pans. Bake for 35 minutes or just until cake pulls from side of pan. Cool in pans for 5 minutes. Remove to wire rack to cool. Combine 2 cups sugar, brown sugar, buttermilk, margarine and soda in saucepan. Cook over low heat to firm soft-ball stage, stirring occasionally. Cool to lukewarm. Add 1 teaspoon vanilla. Beat until mixture thickens and loses its gloss. Spread between layers and over top and side of cake.
Note: Mrs. Roush made this cake for her 97th birthday in October, 1986.

Martha E. Roush, Smithville Grange, Ohio

GINGERBREAD

Yields: 12 servings	Pan Size: 9 x 13 inch	Preheat: 350°

½ c. butter, softened
½ c. lard
½ c. sugar
1 egg
1 c. sorghum molasses

2½ c. flour
1 tsp. soda
1 tbsp. ginger
1 tsp. each cinnamon,
  cloves

Cream butter, lard and sugar in mixer bowl until light and fluffy. Blend in egg and molasses. Add sifted dry ingredients; mix well. Blend in *1 cup very hot water*. Pour into greased and floured pan. Bake for 35 minutes. Cut into squares.

Clara Garr
Missouri Director of Women's Activities

ICE CREAM CAKE

Yields: 24 servings	Pan Size: 9 x 13 inch	Preheat: 350°

½ c. melted butter
1 pt. ice cream, softened
2 eggs
2¼ c. flour
1 c. sugar
1 tbsp. baking powder

½ tsp. salt
½ c. milk
½ c. chopped pecans
½ c. caramel ice cream
  topping
¼ c. sour cream

Grease bottom of 9 x 13-inch cake pan. Combine first 8 ingredients in bowl; beat until smooth. Pour into prepared pan. Bake at 350 degrees for 30 to 40 minutes or until cake tests done. Combine pecans, ice cream topping and sour cream in bowl; mix well. Pour over warm cake.

Mildred Mitchell, Ramona Grange, California

ITALIAN CREAM CAKE

Yields: 10 servings	Pan Size: three 9 inch	Preheat: 350°

1 stick butter, softened
½ c. shortening
2 c. sugar
5 eggs, separated
2 c. flour
1 tsp. soda
1 c. buttermilk
1 tsp. vanilla extract

1 sm. can coconut
1 c. chopped nuts
8 oz. cream cheese, softened
½ stick butter, softened
1   16-oz. package confectioners'
  sugar, sifted
1 tsp. vanilla extract

Cream first 3 ingredients in bowl until light and fluffy. Add egg yolks 1 at a time, beating well after each addition. Sift flour and soda together. Add to creamed mixture alternately with buttermilk, beating well after each addition. Add vanilla, coconut and nuts; mix well. Fold in stiffly beaten egg whites. Pour into greased and floured cake pans. Bake for 25 minutes. Cool in pans for 10 minutes. Invert onto wire rack to cool completely. Combine remaining ingredients in mixer bowl. Beat until smooth. Spread between layers and over top and side of cake. Store in refrigerator.

Verlene R. Reeves, Leicester Grange, North Carolina

CHRISTMAS NUT LOAVES

Yields: 3 loaves	Pan Size: three 4x8 inch	Preheat: 325°

1½ c. sifted flour	2 lb. dates, pitted
1½ c. sugar	2 lb. walnuts
1 tsp. baking powder	1 lb. Brazil nuts
1 tsp. salt	5 eggs, beaten
8 oz. maraschino cherries, drained	1 tsp. vanilla extract

Sift first 4 ingredients into bowl. Add fruit and nuts; mix well. Add mixture of eggs and vanilla; mix well. Spoon into greased loaf pans. Bake for 1 hour or until brown. Cool on wire rack.

Mrs. William W. Campbell, Middletown Grange, Pennsylvania

ORANGE-DATE CAKE

Yields: 12 servings	Pan Size: 10-inch tube	Preheat: 325°

1 c. butter, softened	¼ tsp. salt
2 c. sugar	1½ c. buttermilk
4 eggs	2 tbsp. grated orange rind
1⅓ c. chopped dates	1 c. sugar
1 c. chopped pecans	¾ c. orange juice
4 c. flour	2 tbsp. lemon juice
1 tsp. soda	2 tsp. grated orange rind

Cream butter and 2 cups sugar in mixer bowl until light and fluffy. Add eggs 1 at a time, mixing well after each addition. Combine dates and pecans with ¼ cup flour in bowl, tossing to coat well. Add mixture of remaining flour, soda and salt to creamed mixture alternately with buttermilk, mixing well after each addition. Stir in date mixture. Spoon into greased and floured pan. Sprinkle with 2 tablespoons orange rind. Bake for 1 hour and 20 minutes or until cake tests done. Combine remaining ingredients in saucepan. Heat just until sugar dissolves, stirring constantly. Pierce cake with fork. Pour hot orange sauce over cake. Cook cake in pan. Remove to serving plate. Serve with whipped cream.

Mildred M. Hodge
Montana Director of Women's Activities

PEANUT BUTTER CAKE

Yields: 12 servings	Pan Size: two 9 inch	Preheat: 350°

2 sticks margarine	1 c. peanut butter
¼ c. cocoa	6 tbsp. margarine
½ c. buttermilk	¾ c. cocoa
2 eggs, beaten	2⅔ c. confectioners'
1 tsp. vanilla extract	sugar
2 c. sugar	½ c. milk
2 c. flour	1 tsp. vanilla extract
1 tsp. soda	1 c. chopped nuts

Combine first 5 ingredients *1 cup water* in saucepan; mix well. Bring to a boil. Stir in sugar, flour and soda. Pour into greased cake pans. Bake for 25 minutes. Cool in pans for 10 minutes. Invert onto wire rack to cool completely. Spread peanut butter on layers. Cream 6 tablespoons margarine, cocoa, confectioners' sugar, milk and vanilla in bowl until light and fluffy. Stir in nuts. Spread frosting between layers and over top and side of cake.

Jerry Gibson, Eagle Cliff Grange, Washington

OLD-TIME PEPPERMINT CAKE

Yields: 12 servings	Pan Size: two 9 inch	Preheat: 375°

Cocoa	1¼ tsp. soda
⅔ c. butter, softened	¼ tsp. baking powder
1⅔ c. sugar	1 tsp. salt
3 eggs	½ c. crushed peppermint
½ tsp. vanilla extract	candy
2 c. flour	

Grease cake pans and dust with cocoa. Combine butter, sugar, eggs and vanilla in bowl. Beat for 3 minutes. Add mixture of flour, ⅔ cup cocoa, soda, baking powder and salt alternately with *1⅓ cups water*, beating just until blended. Fold in candy. Pour into prepared cake pans. Reduce temperature to 350 degrees. Bake for 30 to 35 minutes or until cake tests done. Cool in pans for 10 minutes. Remove to wire rack to cool completely. Frost as desired.

Amy Lowden, Ohiopyle Grange, Pennsylvania

POUND CAKE (ENGLAND)

Yields: 12 servings	Pan Size: tube	Preheat: 375°

1 lb. butter, softened	½ oz. blanched almonds, finely
1¼ lb. flour	chopped
1 lb. currants, finely chopped	1 lb. sugar
2 oz. candied orange peel,	9 eggs, separated
chopped	Mace to taste
½ oz. citron, finely chopped	

Line tube pan with buttered parchment. Cream butter in bowl until light and fluffy. Add a small amount of flour to fruit and almonds; toss to coat. Dredge remaining flour into butter; mix well. Add sugar and floured fruit and almonds; mix well. Add well beaten egg yolks. Beat for 20 minutes. Fold in stiffly beaten egg whites and mace gently. Pour into prepared pan. Bake for 15 minutes. Reduce temperature to 350 degrees. Bake for 1¼ to 1¾ hours longer or until cake tests done. Cool in pan on wire rack. Remove to cake plate; peel off paper. Glaze as desired.
Note: Ingredients are weighed and mixed by hand in this old recipe.

Marguerite Walker, Selah Heights Grange, Washington

HOLIDAY POUND CAKE (ITALY)

Yields: 10 to 12 servings	Pan Size: tube	Preheat: 350°

1 lb. butter, softened	½ sm. bottle of almond extract
2 c. sugar	3½ c. flour
6 eggs	1 c. pine nuts
1 tbsp. vanilla extract	

Cream butter and sugar in bowl until light and fluffy. Add eggs 1 at a time, beating well after each addition. Add flavorings; mix well. Stir in flour. Reserve a small amount of pine nuts for topping. Fold remaining pine nuts into batter. Pour batter into greased and floured tube pan. Sprinkle with reserved pine nuts. Bake for 1 hour. Place shallow pan of water on lower oven rack. Bake for 30 minutes longer. Cool in pan for 10 minutes. Remove to wire rack to cool completely.

Charlene Stone, Montgomery Grange, California

MOIST PINEAPPLE POUND CAKE

Yields: 12 servings	Pan Size: 10-inch tube

1 c. butter, softened	1 tsp. vanilla extract
½ c. shortening	¾ c. undrained crushed
2¾ c. sugar	pineapple
6 eggs	¼ c. butter, melted
3 c. flour	1½ c. confectioners' sugar
1 tsp. baking powder	1 c. drained crushed pineapple
¼ c. milk	

Cream 1 cup butter, shortening and sugar in mixer bowl until light and fluffy. Add eggs 1 at a time, mixing well after each addition. Add sifted flour and baking powder alternately with milk, mixing well after each addition. Stir in vanilla and ¾ cup pineapple. Spoon into greased and floured pan. Place in cold oven; set temperature to 325 degrees. Bake for 1¼ hours or until cake tests done. Cool in pan for 10 minutes. Mix remaining ingredients in bowl. Invert cake onto serving plate. Spread glaze over warm cake.

Vinnie G. Kiser
North Carolina Director of Women's Activities

PRUNE AND NUT CAKE

Yields: 8 servings	Pan Size: two 9 inch	Preheat: 350°

2¼ c. sifted flour
1 tsp. soda
¼ tsp. salt
½ tsp. cloves
1 tsp. cinnamon
1 tsp. allspice
½ c. butter, softened
1½ c. sugar
2 eggs, well beaten

1 c. cooked chopped prunes
1 c. sour milk
¾ c. chopped nuts
6 tbsp. flour
1½ c. milk
¾ c. butter, softened
¾ c. shortening
1½ c. sugar
2 tsp. vanilla extract

Sift 2¼ cups flour; measure again. Sift with soda, salt, cloves, cinnamon and allspice. Cream ½ cup butter in mixer bowl until light. Add 1½ cups sugar gradually, creaming until fluffy. Blend in eggs. Stir in prunes. Add sifted dry ingredients alternately with sour milk, mixing well after each addition. Stir in nuts. Pour into greased and floured cake pans. Bake for 40 minutes or until cake tests done. Cool on wire rack. Whisk 6 tablespoons flour into milk in saucepan. Cook until thickened, stirring constantly. Cool. Cream ¾ cup butter and shortening in mixer bowl until light. Add 1½ cups sugar gradually, beating constantly. Beat for 4 minutes. Add cooked mixture gradually, beating constantly. Beat for 4 minutes. Blend in vanilla. Spread between layers and over top and side of cake.

Nelle Strecker
Friend of the National Grange

MADZOONOV GARGANTAG (ARMENIA) Yogurt Spice Cake

Yields: 8 to 10 servings	Pan Size: 10-inch tube	Preheat: 325°

½ c. butter, softened
1½ c. sugar
3 eggs
2 c. flour
1 tsp. each baking powder,
   soda and cinnamon
½ tsp. nutmeg
¼ tsp. salt

1 c. plain yogurt
½ c. packed brown sugar
1 tbsp. melted butter
½ c. chopped almonds
¼ c. coconut
½ c. milk
¼ tsp. vanilla extract

Cream softened butter and sugar in mixer bowl until light and fluffy. Add eggs; beat until smooth. Add mixture of flour and next 5 ingredients alternately with yogurt, mixing well after each addition. Pour into greased and floured tube pan. Bake for 1 hour or until cake tests done. Cool in pan for 5 minutes. Invert onto baking sheet. Cool completely. Mix brown sugar and remaining ingredients in bowl. Spoon over cake. Broil 3 inches from preheated broiler for 2 minutes or until light brown.

Photograph for this recipe on page 237.

ROCKY MOUNTAIN CAKE

Yields: 10 to 12 servings   Pan Size: three 9 inch   Preheat: 325°

1 c. margarine, softened	1 can coconut
2 c. sugar	¼ c. chopped citron
3 c. flour	1 egg, well beaten
½ tsp. soda	⅓ tsp. baking powder
1 tsp. cream of tartar	¼ tsp. salt
¾ to 1 c. milk	2 egg whites
4 egg whites	1½ c. sugar
1½ c. raisins	¼ tsp. cream of tartar
8 oz. dates, chopped	1½ tsp. light corn syrup
1 c. chopped almonds	1 tsp. vanilla extract
1 c. chopped walnuts	½ c. grated coconut

Cream margarine and 2 cups sugar in mixer bowl until light and fluffy. Add sifted flour, soda and 1 teaspoon cream of tartar alternately with milk, mixing well after each addition. Beat in 4 egg whites. Pour into greased and floured cake pans. Bake for 25 minutes. Cool in pans for 5 minutes. Remove to wire rack to cool completely. Combine next 9 ingredients in bowl; mix well. Spread between cake layers. Combine 2 egg whites, 1½ cups sugar, ¼ teaspoon cream of tartar, corn syrup and *5 tablespoons cold water* in double boiler; mix well. Cook over boiling water for 7 minutes, beating constantly at high speed. Remove from heat. Add vanilla. Beat until of spreading consistency. Fold in coconut. Spread between layers and over top and side of cake.

Dale Caldwell, North Carolina State Grange

BERRY ROLL

Yields: 10 servings   Pan Size: 10 x 15 inch   Preheat: 375°

4 eggs, separated	1 tsp. baking powder
¼ c. sugar	¼ tsp. salt
½ tsp. vanilla extract	Confectioners' sugar
½ c. sugar	Whipped cream
¾ c. flour	1½ c. fresh berries

Beat egg yolks in bowl until thick and lemon-colored. Add ¼ cup sugar and vanilla gradually, beating constantly. Beat egg whites in bowl until soft peaks form. Add ½ cup sugar gradually, beating until stiff peaks form. Fold in egg yolks and sifted flour, baking powder and salt gently. Spread in waxed paper-lined baking pan. Bake for 12 minutes. Loosen edge with knife; invert onto towel sprinkled with confectioners' sugar. Remove waxed paper. Place clean sheet of waxed paper on cake. Roll cake and waxed paper quickly as for jelly roll. Wrap in towel; cool. Mix 1 cup whipped cream and berries in bowl. Unroll cake; discard waxed paper. Spread with berry mixture; roll. Place seam side down on serving plate. Top with remaining berries and additional whipped cream.

Betty-Jane Gardiner
Connecticut Director of Women's Activities

KARETHOPETA (GREECE) Sour Cream Cake

Yields: 10 to 12 servings	Pan Size: 9 x 13 inch	Preheat: 350°

1 c. melted butter	2 c. flour
2 c. sugar	1 tsp. each cinnamon, cloves
6 eggs, well beaten	1 c. sour cream
1 c. finely chopped pecans	3 c. sugar
2½ tsp. soda	Juice of ½ lemon
¼ c. Bourbon	

Pour slightly cooled butter into mixer bowl. Add 2 cups sugar gradually, beating well after each addition. Add eggs; beat well. Add pecans, mixture of soda and Bourbon, flour and spices; mix well. Fold in sour cream. Pour into buttered cake pan. Bake for 1 hour or until cake tests done. Cool. Combine 3 cups sugar, lemon juice and *2 cups water* in saucepan. Bring to a boil. Pour over cooled cake. Let stand until all syrup is absorbed. Cut into squares or diamonds.

Helen Neos, Friend of Potomac Grange, Washington D.C.

THREE-COLORED LAYER CAKE

Yields: 16 servings	Pan Size: three 9 inch	Preheat: 350°

¾ c. shortening	1¼ c. milk
1¾ c. sugar	¼ tsp. cinnamon
3 eggs	⅛ tsp. each cloves, allspice
1 tsp. vanilla extract	1 sq. baking chocolate, melted
3 c. flour	1 tbsp. sugar
4 tsp. baking powder	¼ tsp. soda
1 tsp. salt	

Cream shortening and sugar in bowl until light and fluffy. Add eggs and vanilla; mix well. Sift flour, baking powder and salt together 2 times. Add to creamed mixture with milk; mix well. Divide into 3 portions. Blend spice into 1 portion. Add chocolate, 1 tablespoon sugar and soda dissolved in *1 tablespoon hot water* to 1 portion; mix well. Pour each portion into greased and floured cake pan. Bake for 20 minutes. Cool in pans for 10 minutes. Remove to wire rack to cool completely.

Mary Doane, Stony Fork Grange, Pennsylvania

★ ★

Cookies

ANNA'S ALMOND TARTS (HOLLAND)

Yields: 2 dozen	Pan Size: cookie sheet	Preheat: 350°

¾ c. butter, softened
½ c. sugar
½ c. packed brown sugar
1 egg
1¾ c. sifted cake flour

¼ tsp. soda
¼ tsp. salt
½ tsp. vanilla extract
1 can almond paste

Cream butter, sugar and brown sugar in mixer bowl until light and fluffy. Blend in egg. Add flour, soda, salt and vanilla; mix well. Roll very thin on floured surface. Cut with round cookie cutter. Spread almond paste on half the cookies. Top with remaining cookies; seal edges. Place on cookie sheet. Bake for 12 minutes or until golden brown.

Florence Harper, Issaquah Valley Grange, Washington

AMISH COOKIES

Yields: 6 dozen	Pan Size: cookie sheet	Preheat: 350°

1 c. shortening	2 eggs
1 c. oil	4¼ c. flour
1 c. sugar	1 tsp. cream of tartar
1 c. confectioners' sugar	1 tsp. soda
1 tsp. vanilla extract	

Cream shortening, oil, sugar and confectioners' sugar in bowl until light and fluffy. Beat in vanilla and eggs. Add dry ingredients; mix well. Shape into small balls. Place on greased cookie sheet. Flatten with glass dipped in sugar. Bake for 10 minutes.

Ina Smith, Friend of Capital City Grange, Nebraska

SPRINGERLE (GERMANY) Aniseed Cookies

Yields: 5 dozen	Pan Size: cookie sheet	Preheat: 300°

4 eggs, beaten	Butter the size of a walnut,
16 oz. confectioners' sugar	(2½ tbsp.)
¼ tsp. baking powder	Flour
Several drops of anise oil	Aniseed

Combine eggs, confectioners' sugar, baking powder, anise oil and butter in mixer bowl. Beat for 30 minutes. Add enough flour to make a stiff dough; mix well. Roll ½ inch thick on floured surface. Roll rectangular designs on dough with springerle rolling pin or press with springerle mold. Cut rectangles apart. Place on cookie sheet sprinkled with aniseed. Let stand overnight. Bake for 20 minutes or until very light brown. Store in covered container.
Note: Flavor improves if allowed to ripen for several weeks.

Mary G. McMullin, Klondike-Piney Grange, Wyoming

APPLESAUCE COOKIES

Yields: 3 dozen	Pan Size: cookie sheet	Preheat: 375°

½ c. shortening	1 tsp. soda
1 c. sugar	1 tsp. cinnamon
1 egg	1 tsp. nutmeg
1¼ c. flour	1 c. applesauce
1½ tsp. salt	½ c. finely chopped nuts

Cream shortening, sugar and egg in bowl until light and fluffy. Add mixture of flour, salt, soda, cinnamon and nutmeg; mix well. Add applesauce and nuts alternately, mixing well after each addition. Drop by spoonfuls onto greased cookie sheet. Bake for 10 minutes or until golden brown.

Juanita H. Doherty, Missouri Flat Grange, Oregon

APPLESAUCE-SPICE BARS

Yields: 32 bars   Pan Size: 10x15 inch   Preheat: 350°

¼ c. shortening	1 c. applesauce
⅔ c. packed brown sugar	⅔ c. raisins
1 egg	3 tbsp. butter
1 c. flour	1½ c. confectioners' sugar
1 tsp. soda	1 tbsp. milk
½ tsp. salt	1 tsp. vanilla extract
½ tsp. pumpkin pie spice	Chopped nuts

Cream shortening and brown sugar in mixer bowl until light and fluffy. Blend in egg. Add next 4 dry ingredients and applesauce; mix well. Stir in raisins. Spread in greased baking pan. Bake for 15 minutes. Cool. Melt butter in saucepan. Cook until lightly browned. Add confectioners' sugar, milk and vanilla; mix well. Spread on baked layer. Sprinkle with nuts. Cut into bars.

Eula B. Reed, Waterford Grange, Ohio

APRICOT-OATMEAL BARS

Yields: 3 dozen   Pan Size: 9 x 13 inch   Preheat: 350°

1¼ c. flour	¼ tsp. salt
1¼ c. quick-cooking oats	2 tsp. vanilla extract
½ c. sugar	1 10-oz. jar apricot preserves
¾ c. melted butter	½ c. coconut
½ tsp. soda	

Combine first 7 ingredients in mixer bowl. Beat at low speed for 1 to 2 minutes or until crumbly. Reserve 1 cup crumb mixture. Press remaining crumbs into greased baking pan. Spread with preserves to within ½ inch of edge. Sprinkle with reserved crumbs and coconut. Bake for 22 to 27 minutes or until edges are light brown. Cool. Cut into bars.

Esther Lehman, Eureka Grange, Pennsylvania

BANANA-NUT BARS

Yields: 3 dozen	Pan Size: 10x15 inch	Preheat: 350°

⅔ c. margarine, softened	1 tsp. soda
1½ c. sugar	¼ tsp. salt
2 eggs, separated	¼ c. sour cream
1 c. mashed banana	½ tsp. vanilla extract
1½ c. flour	½ c. chopped nuts

Cream margarine and sugar in mixer bowl until light and fluffy. Blend in egg yolks and banana. Add sifted dry ingredients alternately with sour cream, mixing well after each addition. Fold in vanilla, stiffly beaten egg whites and nuts. Pour into greased and floured baking pan. Bake for 30 minutes. Cool. Frost or dust with confectioners' sugar if desired.

Doris Kent, Washington Grange, Oklahoma

DELUXE BROWNIES

Yields: 1½ dozen	Pan Size: 9x9 inch	Preheat: 325°

⅓ c. butter, softened	1 c. sifted flour
1 c. sugar	½ tsp. baking powder
2 eggs	½ tsp. salt
½ tsp. vanilla extract	6 tbsp. cocoa
½ c. mashed peaches	1 c. chopped nuts

Cream butter and sugar in mixer bowl until light and fluffy. Blend in eggs and vanilla. Add remaining ingredients; mix well. Spoon into buttered baking pan. Bake for 30 to 40 minutes or until brownies test done. Cool. Cut into squares.

Ruth Duggan, Fairview Grange, Idaho

MINT BROWNIES

Yields: 2 dozen	Pan Size: 9x13 inch	Preheat: 350°

1 c. sugar	1 c. butter, softened
4 eggs, beaten	2 c. confectioners' sugar
½ tsp. salt	2 to 3 tbsp. Creme de Menthe
1 c. flour	1 c. chocolate chips
16 oz. chocolate syrup	6 tbsp. butter

Combine first 5 ingredients and ½ cup butter in mixer bowl; mix well. Pour into greased and floured baking pan. Bake for 30 minutes; cool. Cream ½ cup butter, confectioners' sugar and Creme de Menthe in bowl until light and fluffy. Spread over cool brownies. Melt chocolate chips and 6 tablespoons butter in small saucepan. Cool. Spread over creamed layer.

Andrea J. Myers, Thurmont Grange, Maryland

Recipes for this photograph on pages 175, 230, 291.

GERMAN'S SWEET CHOCOLATE-CREAM CHEESE BROWNIES

Yields: 16 servings	Pan Size: 9 x 9 inch	Preheat: 350°

1 bar German's chocolate	¾ c. sugar
5 tbsp. margarine	½ c. flour
3 oz. cream cheese, softened	¼ tsp. salt
¼ c. sugar	½ tsp. baking powder
1 tbsp. flour	1 tsp. vanilla extract
½ tsp. vanilla extract	¼ tsp. almond extract
3 eggs	½ c. chopped nuts

Melt chocolate with 3 tablespoons margarine in saucepan over low heat, stirring constantly. Cool. Cream remaining margarine with cream cheese and ¼ cup sugar in mixer bowl until light. Blend in 1 tablespoon flour, ½ teaspoon vanilla and 1 egg; set aside. Beat remaining 2 eggs in bowl until thick. Add ¾ cup sugar gradually, beating well. Add remaining ingredients and cooled chocolate. Reserve 1 cup batter for top. Spread remaining batter in greased baking pan. Spoon cream cheese mixture over chocolate layer. Drizzle with reserved chocolate mixture. Bake for 25 minutes.

Annette Sharpsteen, Lansing United Grange, New York

PEANUT BUTTER BROWNIES

Yields: 2½ to 3 dozen	Pan Size: 9 x 13 inch	Preheat: 350°

½ c. shortening	1 tsp. vanilla extract
3 c. sugar	4 c. flour
1½ c. packed brown sugar	1½ tsp. baking powder
1 c. peanut butter	1½ tsp. salt
6 eggs	1 c. chopped peanuts

Cream first 4 ingredients in bowl until light. Blend in eggs and vanilla. Add dry ingredients and peanuts; mix well. Spread in greased baking pan. Bake for 25 minutes. Cool. Cut into squares.

Thelma Walker, Whallonsbury Grange, New York

SOUR CREAM BROWNIES

Yields: 1½ dozen	Pan Size: 9 x 9 inch	Preheat: 400°

2 sticks butter	½ tsp. salt
¼ c. cocoa	2 eggs, well beaten
2 c. flour	½ c. sour cream
2 c. sugar	1 tsp. soda

Bring butter, cocoa and *1 cup water* to a boil in saucepan; mix well. Pour over mixture of flour, sugar and salt in bowl; beat until smooth. Add eggs, sour cream and soda; mix well. Spoon into greased baking pan. Bake for 20 minutes. Cool. Cut into squares.

Mrs. Richard R. Troutman, Marion Grange, Pennsylvania

Recipes for this photograph on pages 173, 202, 254.

CHEESECAKE BARS

Yields: 16 servings	Pan Size: 8x8 inch	Preheat: 350°

⅓ c. margarine, softened
⅓ c. packed brown sugar
1 c. flour
½ c. chopped walnuts
¼ c. sugar

8 oz. cream cheese, softened
1 egg
2 tbsp. milk
1 tbsp. lemon juice
½ tsp. vanilla extract

Cream margarine and brown sugar in mixer bowl until light and fluffy. Add flour and walnuts; mix until crumbly. Reserve 1 cup crumb mixture for topping. Press remaining crumbs into baking pan. Bake for 12 to 15 minutes or until brown. Cream sugar and cream cheese in mixer bowl until light and fluffy. Add remaining ingredients; mix until smooth. Pour over baked crust. Sprinkle with reserved crumbs. Bake for 25 minutes. Cool. Cut into squares. Store in refrigerator.

Irene M. Patterson, Quidnessett Grange, Rhode Island

CHERRY-COCONUT BARS

Yields: 1 dozen	Pan Size: 8x11 inch	Preheat: 350°

1 c. sifted flour
½ c. butter
3 tbsp. confectioners' sugar
2 eggs, lightly beaten
1 c. sugar
1 tsp. vanilla extract
¼ c. flour

½ tsp. baking powder
¼ tsp. salt
¾ c. chopped nuts
½ c. coconut
½ c. quartered maraschino
  cherries

Mix first 3 ingredients in bowl. Pat into baking pan. Bake for 25 minutes. Beat eggs, sugar and vanilla in bowl. Add mixture of flour, baking powder and salt; mix well. Stir in nuts, coconut and cherries. Pour over hot baked layer. Bake for 25 minutes. Cool. Cut into bars.

Lucinda Hollander, Rising Sun Grange, Wisconsin

MOCHA BARS

Yields: 6 dozen	Pan Size: 10x15 inch	Preheat: 350°

1 c. butter, softened
1 c. packed brown sugar
2¼ c. flour
1 tsp. instant coffee powder
½ tsp. baking powder

¼ tsp. salt
1 tsp. almond extract
6 oz. semisweet chocolate
  chips
½ c. chopped almonds

Cream butter and brown sugar in mixer bowl until light and fluffy. Add mixture of flour, coffee powder, baking powder and salt; mix well. Stir in flavoring, chocolate chips and almonds. Press into greased 10 x 15-inch baking pan. Bake at 350 degrees for 25 minutes. Cool. Cut into bars.

Barbara Barnett, Glade Valley Grange, Maryland

CHEWY COCONUT BARS

Yields: 2 dozen	Pan Size: 9 x 13 inch	Preheat: 350°

½ c. shortening	¼ c. flour
½ c. butter, softened	2 tsp. baking powder
1 c. packed brown sugar	1 tsp. salt
2 c. flour	2 tsp. vanilla extract
4 eggs, beaten	2 c. shredded coconut
1 c. light corn syrup	2 c. chopped nuts
1 c. packed brown sugar	

Cream shortening, butter and 1 cup brown sugar in mixer bowl until light and fluffy. Add 2 cups flour; mix until crumbly. Press into baking pan. Bake for 10 minutes. Combine remaining ingredients in bowl; beat until smooth. Spread over baked layer. Bake for 25 minutes longer. Cool. Cut into bars.

Helen Hytien, South Fork Grange, Washington

DATE-NUT BARS

Yields: 2 dozen	Pan Size: 8 x 8 inch	Preheat: 350°

1 egg, beaten	1 c. chopped dates
1 c. packed brown sugar	1 c. chopped nuts
5 tbsp. flour	Confectioners' sugar
¼ tsp. soda	

Combine egg, brown sugar, flour and mixture of soda dissolved in *1 tablespoon boiling water* in bowl; mix well. Stir in dates and nuts; batter will be stiff. Spread in greased and floured baking pan. Bake for 25 to 30 minutes or until brown. Cut into squares while warm. Roll in confectioners' sugar.

Katharine Black, Priest Lake Grange, Idaho

JAN HAGEL (HOLLAND) Almond Cookies

Yields: 3 dozen	Pan Size: cookie sheet	Preheat: 350°

1 stick butter, softened	2 c. flour
1 stick margarine, softened	1 tbsp. sugar
1 c. sugar	¼ tsp. cinnamon
2 eggs, separated	½ c. sliced almonds
⅛ tsp. almond extract	

Cream butter, margarine and 1 cup sugar in mixer bowl until light and fluffy. Blend in egg yolks and almond flavoring. Add flour; mix well. Spread on greased cookie sheet. Spread with stiffly beaten egg whites. Sprinkle with mixture of 1 tablespoon sugar and cinnamon. Top with almonds. Bake for 25 minutes. Cool for 10 minutes. Cut into 2-inch bars.

Grada den Hartog, Friend of Mifflin Grange, Pennsylvania

KRINGLE (SWEDEN)

Yields: 12 servings	Pan Size: cookie sheet	Preheat: 350°

½ c. margarine, softened	3 eggs
1 c. flour	½ tsp. almond flavoring
½ c. butter	Almonds
1 c. flour	

Cut margarine into 1 cup flour in bowl until crumbly. Add *1 tablespoon water*; mix into dough. Pat into two 3-inch wide strips on cookie sheet. Bring *1 cup water* and butter to a boil in saucepan; remove from heat. Stir in 1 cup flour. Add eggs 1 at a time, mixing well after each addition. Blend in almond flavoring. Spread evenly over dough strips. Bake for 55 minutes or until crisp and light brown. Cool. Frost with favorite confectioners' sugar frosting flavored with additional almond flavoring. Sprinkle with almonds. Cut into pieces.

Mildred Otte
Nebraska Director of Women's Activities

LEMON GEMS

Yields: 2½ dozen	Pan Size: 9 x 13 inch	Preheat: 350°

2 c. flour	1½ c. sugar
½ c. sugar	4 eggs
1 tbsp. lemon rind	½ c. lemon juice
1 c. butter	½ tsp. baking powder
⅓ c. flour	Confectioners' sugar

Combine first 3 ingredients in bowl. Cut in butter until crumbly. Pat into baking pan. Bake for 20 to 25 minutes or until light brown. Combine remaining flour, sugar, eggs, lemon juice and baking powder in blender container. Process until smooth. Pour over baked layer. Bake for 20 to 25 minutes longer or until light brown. Cool in pan. Dust with confectioners' sugar. Cut into diamond shapes or squares.

Clara Fenton, Pleasant Valley Grange, Washington

LEMON BARS

Yields: 15 servings	Pan Size: 9 x 13 inch	Preheat: 350°

1 c. butter, softened	**6 tbsp. lemon juice**
½ c. confectioners' sugar	**Grated rind of 1 lemon**
2 c. flour	**¼ c. flour**
4 eggs	**1 tsp. baking powder**
2 c. sugar	**Confectioners' sugar**

Cream butter and confectioners' sugar in mixer bowl until light and fluffy. Blend in 2 cups flour. Press into greased pan. Bake for 20 minutes. Cool. Beat eggs lightly in bowl. Add sugar, lemon juice, lemon rind, ¼ cup flour and baking powder; mix well. Spread over baked layer. Bake for 25 minutes. Sprinkle with confectioners' sugar immediately. Cool on wire rack. Cut into squares.

Congressman Phillip M. Crane, Illinois
Member of Bicentennial Commission

LEMON-COCONUT SQUARES

Yields: 2 dozen	Pan Size: 9 x 13 inch	Preheat: 275°

½ c . butter, softened	**¼ tsp. salt**
½ c. packed brown sugar	**½ tsp. vanilla extract**
1½ c. flour	**1½ c. coconut**
2 eggs, beaten	**1 c. chopped pecans**
1 c. packed brown sugar	**1 c. confectioners' sugar**
2 tbsp. flour	**1 tbsp. melted butter**
½ tsp. baking powder	**Juice of 2 lemons**

Cream softened butter and ½ cup brown sugar in mixer bowl until light and fluffy. Add 1½ cups flour; mix until crumbly. Press into buttered baking dish. Bake for 10 minutes. Blend eggs and 1 cup brown sugar in mixer bowl. Add 2 tablespoons flour, baking powder, salt and vanilla; mix well. Stir in coconut and pecans. Pour over baked layer. Increase temperature to 350 degrees. Bake for 20 minutes. Combine remaining ingredients in bowl. Spread on warm layers. Cool. Cut into squares.

Edna M. Hodson, Twin Valley Grange, Ohio

MARZIPAN BARS

Yields: 3 dozen	Pan Size: 9 x 13 inch	Preheat: 350°

1 egg white	2 c. flour
1½ c. ground almonds	2 tsp. baking powder
2½ c. confectioners' sugar	½ tsp. vanilla extract
1 c. margarine	1 egg

Mix egg white with almonds and 2 cups confectioners' sugar in bowl. Stir in *2 tablespoons water*; set aside. Cut margarine into flour, baking powder and ½ cup confectioners' sugar in bowl until crumbly. Stir in mixture of vanilla and egg. Reserve ¾ cup dough. Press remaining dough in baking pan. Spread almond mixture on dough. Roll reserved dough on floured surface; cut into strips. Arrange over filling. Bake for 35 minutes.

Vivian Weber, Lincoln Grange, Oregon

MAZURKA (POLAND)

Yields: 2 dozen	Pan Size: 8 x 8 inch	Preheat: 325°

1 c. butter, softened	¼ tsp. allspice
1 c. sugar	⅛ tsp. cardamon
2 egg yolks	½ c. raspberry jam
1 tsp. vanilla extract	1 c. chopped walnuts
2 c. flour	

Cream butter in mixer bowl until light. Add sugar gradually, beating until fluffy. Blend in egg yolks and vanilla. Add sifted mixture of flour and spices. Press half the mixture into greased baking pan. Spread with jam. Mix half the walnuts into remaining dough. Spread over jam. Sprinkle with remaining walnuts; press in lightly. Bake for 1 hour or until light brown. Cool. Cut into small squares.

Nancy McKenzie, Friend of Rockwall Grange, Oregon

MUSTER BREAD

Yields: 4 dozen	Pan Size: cookie sheet	Preheat: 350°

1 c. molasses	1 tsp. ginger
1 c. sugar	1 tsp. salt
1 c. melted shortening	¼ tsp. cloves
1 c. sour milk	½ tsp. allspice
2 tsp. (rounded) soda	4 c. (or more) flour

Combine first 3 ingredients in bowl. Add mixture of sour milk and soda. Sift in remaining ingredients; mix well. Add enough additional flour to make stiff dough. Roll into cookie sheet-sized rectangle on floured surface. Slide onto cookie sheet. Bake for 10 minutes. Cool for several minutes. Cut into squares.

Isabel Bartz, Bartlett Grange, New Hampshire

FROSTED NUT COOKIES

Yields: 4 dozen	Pan Size: 11x15 inch	Preheat: 350°

1½ c. shortening	½ tsp. salt
2 c. packed brown sugar	1 tsp. baking powder
2 eggs, well beaten	1 c. chopped English walnuts
½ tsp. vanilla extract	½ tsp. vanilla extract
1½ c. sifted flour	2 egg whites

Cream shortening and 1 cup brown sugar in bowl. Beat in eggs and ½ teaspoon vanilla. Add dry ingredients. Spread on baking sheet. Sprinkle with walnuts. Fold 1 cup brown sugar and ½ teaspoon vanilla gently into stiffly beaten egg whites. Spread over cookie dough. Bake for 25 minutes. Cool. Cut into bars.

Jean M. Spilman, Fair Valley Grange, California

MALTED OATMEAL BARS

Yields: 2 dozen	Pan Size: 9x9 inch	Preheat: 350°

½ c. margarine, softened	¼ tsp. salt
1 c. sugar	½ c. chocolate-flavored
2 eggs	malted milk powder
1 tsp. vanilla extract	¾ c. quick-cooking oats
½ c. flour	½ c. chopped nuts

Cream margarine and sugar in bowl until light and fluffy. Add eggs and vanilla; mix well. Sift in flour, salt and chocolate powder; mix well. Stir in oats and nuts. Spread in greased baking pan. Bake for 35 minutes. Cool. Cut into bars.

Frances Skillman, Bean Grange, Kansas

ORANGE DREAM BARS

Yields: 3 dozen	Pan Size: 9x13 inch	Preheat: 350°

½ c. margarine, softened	2 eggs, beaten
½ c. packed brown sugar	Pinch of salt
1 c. flour	2 tbsp. orange juice
1 c. packed brown sugar	1 tbsp. lemon juice
2 tbsp. flour	1 tbsp. each orange
¼ tsp. vanilla extract	and lemon rind
1 c. each chopped nuts, coconut	1½ c. confectioners' sugar

Cream margarine and brown sugar in bowl until light and fluffy. Add flour; mix well. Spread in greased baking pan. Bake for 15 minutes. Combine next 7 ingredients. Pour over baked layer. Bake for 25 minutes. Blend juices, rinds and confectioners' sugar in bowl. Spread over warm cookie layer. Cut into bars.

Dora Steincross, Blue Mound Grange, Missouri

PECAN-CARAMEL BARS

Yields: 10 to 12 servings	Pan Size: 9 x 13 inch	Preheat: 375°

⅔ c. margarine, softened
½ c. packed brown sugar
1½ c. flour
28 caramels
¼ c. margarine

2 eggs, slightly beaten
¼ c. sugar
½ tsp. vanilla extract
¼ tsp. salt
1 c. chopped pecans

Cream ⅔ cup margarine and brown sugar in bowl until fluffy. Mix in flour. Press into baking pan. Bake for 15 minutes. Melt caramels and ¼ cup margarine in ¼ cup water in saucepan over low heat. Pour over eggs, sugar, vanilla and salt in bowl; mix well. Stir in pecans. Pour over baked layer. Bake for 15 minutes. Cool. Cut into bars.

Lyndy Cline, Ashley Grange, Ohio

RAISIN SPICE SQUARES

Yields: 2 dozen	Pan Size: 9 x 13 inch	Preheat: 350°

1 c. raisins
1 egg
½ c. shortening
1 c. sugar
2 c. sifted flour
1 tsp. soda

1 tsp. each cinnamon, nutmeg
½ tsp. salt
½ c. chopped walnuts
2 c. confectioners' sugar
2 tbsp. orange juice
1 tbsp. butter, melted

Simmer raisins and *2 cups water* in saucepan for 10 minutes. Pour into large bowl. Cool to lukewarm. Add egg, shortening and sugar; mix well. Add dry ingredients; mix well. Stir in walnuts. Pour into greased baking pan. Bake for 25 minutes. Cool on wire rack. Beat confectioners' sugar, orange juice and melted butter in bowl until smooth. Spread on cookie layer. Cut into squares.

Alice Beatty, Bell Township Grange, Pennsylvania

RHUBARB DREAM BARS

Yields: 2 dozen	Pan Size: 9 x 13 inch	Preheat: 350°

2 c. flour
10 tbsp. confectioners' sugar
1 c. margarine
4 eggs, beaten

2 c. sugar
½ c. flour
¾ tsp. salt
4 c. chopped rhubarb

Mix first 3 ingredients in bowl until crumbly. Reserve ½ cup mixture. Press remaining mixture into pan. Bake for 15 minutes. Combine eggs, sugar, ½ cup flour and salt; mix well. Stir in rhubarb. Spread over baked layer. Sprinkle with reserved crumbs. Bake for 1 hour. Garnish with confectioners' sugar. Cool on wire rack. Cut into bars.

Arlene Petersen
Iowa Director of Women's Activities

SUNFLOWER SEED-RAISIN SQUARES

Yields: 1 to 1½ dozen	Pan Size: 9 x 13 inch	Preheat: 375°

1 c. raisins	1½ c. all-purpose flour
½ c. oil	1 tsp. soda
1 c. packed brown sugar	1 tsp. cinnamon
1 egg	½ tsp. each nutmeg, cloves
½ c. whole wheat flour	½ c. sunflower seed

Bring raisins and *1 cup water* to a boil in saucepan. Stir in oil. Cool to lukewarm. Stir in brown sugar and egg. Add dry ingredients; mix well. Stir in sunflower seed. Pour into greased baking pan. Bake for 15 to 20 minutes or until brown. Cool on wire rack. Spread with cream cheese frosting. Cut into squares.

Mary F. Crockett, Princeton Grange, Maine

JIFFY WALNUT BARS

Yields: 2 dozen	Pan Size: 9 inch	Preheat: 375°

½ c. butter, softened	1 tsp. baking powder
3 tbsp. confectioners' sugar	¼ tsp. salt
1 c. sifted flour	1 c. chopped walnuts
2 eggs	½ c. quick-cooking oats
½ tsp. vanilla extract	½ c. flaked coconut
2 tbsp. flour	1 c. packed brown sugar

Cream butter and confectioners' sugar in bowl until light and fluffy. Mix in 1 cup flour gradually. Pat into pan. Bake for 15 minutes. Beat eggs and vanilla in bowl. Add mixture of 2 tablespoons flour, baking powder and salt; mix well. Stir in remaining ingredients. Spread over baked layer. Bake for 25 minutes longer. Cool. Cut into bars.

CINNAMON DISCS

Yields: 4 dozen   Pan Size: cookie sheet   Preheat: 375°

1 c. shortening	2 tsp. baking powder
2 c. sugar	½ tsp. salt
2 eggs	⅔ c. chopped nuts
2 tsp. vanilla extract	4 tsp. cinnamon
2 c. sifted flour	

Cream shortening and sugar in bowl until light and fluffy. Beat in eggs and vanilla. Add sifted dry ingredients; mix well. Chill in refrigerator. Shape by tablespoonfuls into balls. Roll in mixture of nuts and cinnamon. Place 2 inches apart on cookie sheet. Bake for 12 to 15 minutes or until golden. Cool on wire rack.

Doris Schar, Canaan Grange, Ohio

COCONUT ANGEL COOKIES

Yields: 6 dozen   Pan Size: cookie sheet   Preheat: 350°

1 c. shortening	2½ c. flour
½ c. packed brown sugar	1 tsp. cream of tartar
½ c. sugar	1 tsp. soda
1 egg, beaten	½ tsp. salt
1 tsp. vanilla extract	1 c. flaked coconut

Cream shortening, brown sugar and sugar in bowl until light and fluffy. Add egg, vanilla and sifted dry ingredients; mix well. Stir in coconut. Shape into balls. Dip in water; coat with additional sugar. Place on baking sheet. Flatten slightly with fork. Bake for 15 minutes or until light brown.

Mrs. William K. Whittaker, Leon Valley Grange, Texas

COFFEE COOKIES

Yields: 12 dozen   Pan Size: cookie sheet   Preheat: 400°

2 c. shortening	2 tsp. cinnamon
3 c. packed brown sugar	6 c. flour
4 eggs	1¼ c. cold coffee
2 tsp. soda	2 c. chopped nuts
2 tsp. nutmeg	

Cream shortening and brown sugar in bowl until light and fluffy. Mix in eggs. Add soda, nutmeg and cinnamon; mix well. Add flour alternately with coffee, beating well after each addition. Stir in nuts. Drop by teaspoonfuls onto greased cookie sheet. Bake for 8 to 10 minutes or until light brown.

Barbara Jones, Friend of Kamiah Grange, Idaho

CREAM WAFERS (SWEDEN)

Yields: 5 dozen	Pan Size: baking sheet	Preheat: 375°

1 c. butter, softened	**¼ c. butter, softened**
⅓ c. whipping cream	**¾ c. confectioners' sugar**
2 c. flour	**1 tsp. vanilla extract**
Sugar	

Combine 1 cup butter, cream and flour in bowl; mix until smooth. Chill, covered, in refrigerator. Roll ⅓ at a time ⅛ inch thick on floured surface. Cut with 1½-inch cutter. Coat with sugar. Place on cookie sheet. Prick 4 times with fork. Bake for 7 to 9 minutes or until light brown. Remove to wire rack to cool. Combine remaining ingredients in bowl; cream until smooth. Spread on half the cookies; top with remaining cookies.

Cindy L. Greer, Marvel Grange, Colorado

CHOCOLATE BLOSSOMS

Yields: 5 dozen	Pan Size: cookie sheet	Preheat: 350°

½ c. shortening	**1 tsp. vanilla extract**
½ c. peanut butter	**1⅔ c. flour**
½ c. sugar	**½ tsp. salt**
½ c. packed brown sugar	**1 tsp. soda**
1 egg	**Additional sugar**
2 tbsp. milk	**60 milk chocolate stars or kisses**

Cream shortening and peanut butter in bowl until light and fluffy. Add sugar, brown sugar, egg, milk and vanilla; mix well. Add dry ingredients; mix well. Shape by rounded teaspoonful into balls. Roll in additional sugar. Place on cookie sheet. Bake for 8 minutes. Press milk chocolate star or kiss on top of each cookie. Bake for 2 to 5 minutes longer. Remove to wire rack to cool.

Mrs. Chester Noh, Fairview Grange, Idaho

ANITA'S CHRISTMAS COOKIES

Yields: 12 dozen   Pan Size: cookie sheet   Preheat: 350°

4 c. candied fruit	**2 tsp. baking powder**
2 c. butter, softened	**4 tsp. salt**
2 c. sugar	**6 c. flour**
2 c. packed brown sugar	**½ c. milk**
6 eggs	**1 lb. walnuts, chopped**
2 tsp. vanilla extract	**2 c. flour**
2 tsp. soda	

Steam candied fruit for 3 minutes to remove excess sugar; drain and cool. Cream butter, sugar and brown sugar in mixer bowl until light and fluffy. Beat in eggs. Add vanilla, soda, baking powder and salt, beating constantly. Add 6 cups flour and milk alternately, ½ at a time beating constantly. Add candied fruit and walnuts; mix well. Beat in 2 cups flour gradually. Shape into 1½-inch logs. Chill, wrapped in waxed paper, for several hours. Slice ¼ inch thick. Place on lightly greased cookie sheet. Bake for 10 minutes. Cool on wire rack.

Anita Webster, Sunnyside Grange, Washington

FRUITCAKE COOKIES

Yields: 3½ to 4 dozen   Pan Size: cookie sheet   Preheat: 375°

½ c. margarine, softened	**¾ c. drained crushed pineapple**
1 c. packed brown sugar	**2 c. flour**
1 egg	**½ tsp. soda**
1 tsp. vanilla extract	**1 tsp. baking powder**
¾ c. chopped maraschino	**½ tsp. salt**
cherries	**⅓ c. chopped nuts**
⅓ c. raisins	

Cream margarine, brown sugar, egg and vanilla in bowl until light and fluffy. Add cherries, raisins and pineapple; mix well. Add dry ingredients; mix well. Stir in nuts. Drop by teaspoonfuls onto cookie sheet. Bake for 10 to 12 minutes or until golden. Cool on wire rack.

Beatrice C. Hatch, Stafford Grange, New York

PEPPARKAKOR (SWEDEN) Ginger Snaps

Yields: 4 to 6 dozen   Pan Size: cookie sheet   Preheat: 375°

1 c. sugar	**½ tsp. cloves**
1 c. maple syrup	**1 c. margarine**
2 tsp. cinnamon	**5 c. flour**
2 tsp. ginger	**½ tsp. soda**

Bring sugar, syrup, spices and *5 tablespoons water* to a boil in saucepan. Cook for 5 minutes. Stir in margarine. Cool. Add flour and soda; mix well. Chill for several hours to overnight. Roll on floured surface. Cut with cookie cutter. Place on baking sheet. Bake for 8 to 10 minutes or until brown. Cool on wire rack.

Anna Hesselman, Vashon Maury Grange, Washington

HARD TACKS (GERMANY)

Yields: 36 dozen	Pan Size: cookie sheet	Preheat: 350°

6 qt. flour	**1 lb. butter**
4 tsp. soda	**2 qt. thick molasses**
4 tsp. baking powder	**3 qt. pecans**
4 tsp. cloves	**1 qt. raisins**
4 lb. brown sugar	**2 to 4 qt. flour**

Divide 6 quarts flour into 6 portions. Divide soda, baking powder and spices evenly between the portions; mix well. Heat brown sugar, butter, molasses and *1 cup water* in saucepan until butter melts; mix well. Pour over pecans and raisins in large bowl. Add flour mixture; mix well. Divide into 5 portions. Knead each portion on floured surface, kneading in enough additional flour to make a stiff, easily handled dough. Shape into long rolls. Chill overnight. Cut into ¼-inch slices. Place on cookie sheet. Bake for 10 minutes or until light brown. Remove to wire rack to cool completely. Store in airtight container.
Note: I store these cookies in a 50-pound lard can.

Nellie Bell, Alamo Grange, Texas

GRANDMA'S HAZELNUT COOKIES

Yields: 1½ to 2 dozen	Pan Size: cookie sheet	Preheat: 375°

1 c. sifted flour	**⅛ tsp. salt**
½ c. butter, softened	**1 tsp. vanilla extract**
1 c. finely chopped hazelnuts	**Confectioners' sugar**
2 tbsp. sugar	

Combine flour, butter, hazelnuts, sugar, salt and vanilla in bowl; mix well with hands. Chill for 30 minutes. Shape into 1¼-inch balls. Place 1 inch apart on cookie sheet. Bake for 15 to 20 minutes or until set. Do not brown. Let stand for 1 minute. Remove to wire rack to cool for several minutes. Roll warm cookies in confectioners' sugar. Cool completely. Roll in confectioners' sugar again.

Virginia Luethe, Skyline Grange, Oregon

RAISIN JUMBO COOKIES

Yields: 3½ dozen	Pan Size: cookie sheet	Preheat: 375°

2 c. raisins
1 c. shortening
1½ c. sugar
2 eggs, lightly beaten
1 tsp. vanilla extract
4 c. flour

¾ tsp. baking powder
¾ tsp. soda
1 tsp. salt
½ tsp. each cinnamon, nutmeg
½ c. chopped pecans

Combine raisins and *1 cup water* in saucepan. Cook for 3 minutes. Cool. Cream shortening and sugar in mixer bowl until light and fluffy. Blend in eggs and vanilla. Stir in raisins with liquid. Add sifted dry ingredients gradually, mixing well after each addition. Stir in pecans. Drop by tablespoonfuls 1 inch apart onto greased cookie sheet. Bake for 12 to 15 minutes or until brown. Remove to wire rack to cool.

Margaret Miller
Colorado Director of Women's Activities

KOLACHE (POLAND)

Yields: 8 dozen	Pan Size: cookie sheet	Preheat: 375°

1 c. cream
1 c. butter
2 cakes yeast
3 egg yolks, beaten
1 tsp. vanilla extract
4 c. flour
5 tbsp. sugar

1 lb. nuts, ground
¾ c. sugar
½ tsp. grated lemon rind
1 tsp. vanilla extract
Milk
Confectioners' sugar

Bring cream just to the simmering point in saucepan. Add butter, stirring until butter melts. Cool to lukewarm. Mix with yeast in bowl. Let stand for several minutes. Blend in egg yolks and 1 teaspoon vanilla. Add flour and 5 tablespoons sugar; mix well. Knead on floured surface until smooth and elastic. Place in greased bowl, turning to grease surface. Cover with waxed paper and damp towel. Chill overnight. Combine nuts, ¾ cup sugar, lemon rind and 1 teaspoon vanilla in bowl. Add enough milk to make of spreading consistency; mix well. Divide chilled dough into 4 portions. Roll each portion thinly on floured surface. Spread with nut mixture. Cut each into 24 wedges. Roll up to enclose filling. Roll in confectioners' sugar. Place on greased cookie sheet. Bake until light brown. Remove to wire rack to cool.

Mary Morse
Secretary, New York State Grange

HOLIDAY MACAROONS

Yields: 2 dozen	Pan Size: cookie sheet	Preheat: 325°

2 eggs
¾ c. sugar
⅓ c. flour
¼ tsp. baking powder
⅛ tsp. salt

1 tbsp. butter, melted
1 tsp. vanilla extract
1 tsp. grated lemon rind
2⅔ c. flaked coconut

Beat eggs in bowl until light. Add sugar gradually; beat for about 5 minutes or until thick. Add sifted dry ingredients; mix well. Stir in remaining ingredients. Drop by teaspoonfuls onto greased and floured cookie sheet. Decorate with candied cherries. Bake for 15 minutes. Cool completely. Store in tightly covered container.

Pauline Cuykendall, Auburn Grange, New York

MERINGUE KISSES

Yields: 4 dozen	Pan Size: cookie sheet	Preheat: 300°

3 egg whites, at room
   temperature
⅛ tsp. cream of tartar
⅛ tsp. salt

¾ c. sugar
1 tsp. vanilla extract
12 oz. miniature semisweet
   chocolate chips

Beat egg whites, cream of tartar and salt in mixer bowl until soft peaks form. Add sugar 1 tablespoon at a time, beating until stiff peaks form. Fold in vanilla and chocolate chips. Spoon into pastry bag with 1-inch opening. Pipe onto parchment-lined cookie sheet, swirling to form peaks. Bake for 25 minutes or until lightly brown and firm. Cool on wire rack. Store in airtight container.

Sharon Woods, Mohawk Grange, Oregon

SPICY NUT TRIANGLES

Yields: 4 dozen	Pan Size: 10x15 inch	Preheat: 275°

1 c. butter, softened
1 c. sugar
1 egg, separated

2 c. sifted flour
1 tsp. cinnamon
1 c. finely chopped nuts

Cream butter and sugar in bowl until light and fluffy. Beat in egg yolk. Add sifted flour and cinnamon gradually, stirring constantly. Spread in pan. Brush with lightly beaten egg white, smoothing surface with fingertips. Sprinkle with nuts. Press nuts gently into dough. Bake for 1 hour. Cut immediately into 4 lengthwise and 6 crosswise strips. Cut each strip in half diagonally.

Mrs. Lewis W. Pyle, Chester Valley Grange, Pennsylvania

MOLASSES COOKIES (GERMANY)

Yields: 5 to 6 dozen	Pan Size: cookie sheet	Preheat: 350°

1 tsp. (heaping) salt	2 tsp. (heaping) soda
1 c. packed brown sugar	¼ c. vinegar
1 c. lard	1 tbsp. ginger
1 c. molasses	6 c. flour
2 eggs, beaten	

Cream salt, brown sugar and lard in mixer bowl until light and fluffy. Blend in molasses and eggs. Add soda dissolved in *½ cup hot water* and remaining ingredients in order listed; mix well. Chill for several hours to overnight. Roll ¼ inch thick on floured surface. Cut into 3-inch circles. Place on greased cookie sheet. Bake for 9 minutes or until brown. Cool on wire rack. Frost with confectioners' sugar frosting. *Note:* This recipe is from my German Great-Grandmother and is a Christmas tradition. The original recipe called for "settled" flour.

Martha E. Laupp, Home Grange, Michigan

OLD-FASHIONED OATMEAL COOKIES

Yields: 5 to 6 dozen	Pan Size: cookie sheet	Preheat: 350°

½ c. butter, softened	3 c. old-fashioned oats
1 c. sugar	2⅔ c. flour
1 c. packed brown sugar	½ tsp. salt
3 eggs, separated	1 tsp. cinnamon
1 c. sour cream	2 c. raisins
1 tsp. soda	½ c. chopped nuts

Cream butter, sugar and brown sugar in bowl until light and fluffy. Add egg yolks and sour cream mixed with soda; mix well. Stir in oats. Add sifted flour, salt and cinnamon; mix well. Fold in stiffly beaten egg whites gently. Stir in raisins and nuts. Drop by rounded teaspoonfuls onto greased cookie sheet. Bake for 12 to 15 minutes.

Lauretta Wunderlich, Salt Valley Grange, Nebraska

OATMEAL LACE COOKIES

Yields: 3 dozen	Pan Size: cookie sheet	Preheat: 350°

½ c. melted butter	¼ tsp. baking powder
1 c. sugar	¼ tsp. salt
1 c. quick-cooking oats	½ tsp. vanilla extract
3 tbsp. flour	1 egg

Combine all ingredients in bowl in order listed; mix well. Drop by tablespoonfuls 2 to 3 inches apart on foil-lined cookie sheet. Bake for 8 minutes or until light brown. Cool completely in pan. Peel from foil.

Janet M. Porter, Beavercreek Grange, Oregon

ALL-AMERICAN PEANUT BUTTER COOKIES

Yields: 4 dozen	Pan Size: cookie sheet	Preheat: 350°

½ c. butter, softened
1 c. peanut butter
½ c. sugar
½ c. packed brown sugar
½ tsp. vanilla extract

1 egg
1½ c. flour
¾ tsp. soda
½ tsp. baking powder
¼ tsp. salt

Cream butter, peanut butter, sugar, brown sugar, vanilla and egg in bowl until light and fluffy. Add sifted dry ingredients; mix well. Shape into 1-inch balls. Place 2 inches apart on cookie sheet. Flatten in criss-cross pattern with fork. Bake for 10 minutes or until lightly browned.

Charlotte W. Lincoln, Ira Valley Grange, Vermont

RUSSIAN ROLLS

Yields: 12 dozen	Pan Size: cookie sheet	Preheat: 350°

2 pkg. dry yeast
1 lb. butter, softened
6 eggs, lightly beaten
6 c. flour
½ tsp. salt
1 tsp. vanilla extract

4 c. ground walnuts
2 eggs
½ tsp. vanilla extract
Milk
Honey
Sugar

Dissolve yeast in *½ cup warm water*. Blend butter and 6 eggs in mixer bowl. Add flour, salt, 1 teaspoon vanilla and yeast; mix well. Chill, covered, for 2 hours to overnight. Combine walnuts, 2 eggs and ½ teaspoon vanilla in bowl. Add enough milk and honey to moisten; mix well. Divide dough into four portions. Roll each very thin on sugared surface. Cut into 2-inch squares. Place 1 teaspoon walnut filling on each square. Roll diagonally to enclose filling. Shape into crescents on greased cookie sheet. Bake for 15 minutes or until golden brown. Remove to wire rack to cool. Store in covered container in cool place.
Note: This recipe was given to my father 40 years ago by a Siberian immigrant whose family made the cookies at Christmas. The original recipe called for farm-fresh butter and a 5-cent cake of yeast.

Mary-Lee Steel, Frankfort Springs Grange, Pennsylvania

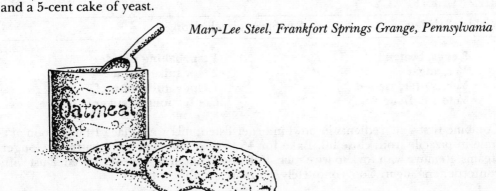

PECAN HONEYBALLS

Yields: 10½ dozen   Pan Size: cookie sheet   Preheat: 300°

1 c. shortening	2 tsp. vanilla extract
¼ c. honey	2 c. finely chopped pecans
2 c. sifted flour	Confectioners' sugar
½ tsp. salt	

Cream shortening and honey in mixer bowl until light and fluffy. Sift flour and salt together twice. Add to creamed mixture gradually, mixing well after each addition. Mix in vanilla and pecans. Chill in refrigerator. Shape by ½ teaspoonfuls into small balls; place on greased cookie sheet. Bake for 30 to 45 minutes or until light brown. Roll in confectioners' sugar.

Jim Buck Ross
Commissioner, Mississippi Department of Agriculture and Commerce

PFEFFERNÜSSE (GERMANY) Peppernuts

Yields: 10 dozen   Pan Size: cookie sheet   Preheat: 300°

2 eggs	½ tsp. allspice
¾ c. packed brown sugar	½ tsp. soda
¾ c. sugar	¼ tsp. pepper
3¼ c. flour	2 tbsp. melted butter
1 tsp. cinnamon	¼ c. honey
½ tsp. cloves	

Beat eggs in mixer bowl. Add sugars. Beat for 15 minutes. Add mixture of dry ingredients gradually, beating constantly. Mix in butter and honey. Knead for 1 minute on lightly floured surface. Shape into ½-inch balls. Place 1 inch apart on greased cookie sheet. Keep unused dough covered with plastic wrap. Bake for 10 to 15 minutes or until firm. Cool on wire rack. Store in airtight container.

Photograph for this recipe on page 238.

PIZZELLE (ITALY)

Yields: 2 dozen   Pan Size: pizzelle iron

3 eggs, beaten	1 tsp. baking powder
¾ c. sugar	2 tsp. anise extract
¾ c. butter, melted	1 tsp. vanilla extract
¾ to 1 c. flour	Confectioners' sugar

Combine first 7 ingredients in bowl in order listed; mix well. Place 1 tablespoon at a time in pizzelle iron; close lid. Bake for 45 to 60 seconds or until batter no longer steams. Remove with fork to wire rack. Roll into cylinder or cone if desired. Dust with confectioners' sugar. Cool completely. Store in airtight container.

Genevieve F. Murphy, Henlopen Grange, Delaware

Candies

ALMOND BRITTLE

Yields: 1 pound	Pan Size: 2 quart

1 c. butter
1 c. sugar

2 c. raw almonds

Melt butter in saucepan over low heat. Add sugar and almonds. Cook over medium heat to deep caramel color, stirring constantly. Pour onto baking sheet, spreading thin. Let stand until cool. Break into bite-sized pieces.
Note: Use copper bottomed saucepan for best results.

Margaret James, San Luis Obispo Grange, California

ENGLISH ALMOND TOFFEE

Yields: 1 pound   Pan Size: baking sheet

⅔ c. butter	⅔ c. slivered blanched almonds
½ c. sugar	6 oz. semisweet chocolate chips
½ tsp. salt	½ c. chopped almonds
¼ tsp. soda	

Combine butter, sugar, salt and ⅓ *cup water* in saucepan. Bring to a boil over low heat, stirring constantly. Cook to 236 degrees on candy thermometer, soft-ball stage; do not stir. Cook to 290 degrees on candy thermometer, soft-crack stage, stirring constantly. Remove from heat. Stir in soda and ⅔ cup almonds. Spread ¼ inch thick on baking sheet. Sprinkle chocolate chips over top; spread chocolate as it melts. Sprinkle with ½ cup almonds. Let stand until cool. Break into bite-sized pieces.

Paige Wells, Klondike-Piney Grange, Wyoming

BLACK WALNUT BRITTLE

Yields: 1¼ pounds

½ c. corn syrup	3 tbsp. butter
2 c. sugar	1 c. black walnut pieces
¼ tsp. salt	1 tsp. vanilla extract

Combine corn syrup, sugar, salt, butter and ⅓ *cup water* in saucepan. Bring to a boil over medium heat. Cook until sugar dissolves, stirring constantly. Add black walnuts. Cook over medium heat to 300 degrees on candy thermometer, hard-crack stage, stirring constantly. Stir in vanilla. Pour onto buttered baking sheet. Cool until set. Break into pieces.

Lucille Pierson, Leonidas Grange, Michigan

BUDDY'S DELIGHT

Yields: 3 pounds   Pan Size: saucepan

2 c. packed brown sugar	1 tbsp. butter
2 c. sugar	½ c. cream
1½ c. light corn syrup	1 c. chopped nuts

Combine brown sugar, sugar, corn syrup, butter and cream in saucepan. Cook over medium heat to 234 to 240 degrees on candy thermometer, soft-ball stage, stirring constantly. Remove from heat. Beat until creamy. Stir in nuts. Pour into buttered pan. Let stand until completely cool. Cut into squares.

Irene Smazal, Lookout Mt. Grange, Oregon

CARAMELS

Yields: 3½ pounds	Pan Size: 8x12 inch

1 c. butter	**2 c. light corn syrup**
1 can sweetened condensed milk	**1 lb. brown sugar**

Combine all ingredients in saucepan. Boil for 15 minutes or to 242 degrees on candy thermometer, firm-ball stage, stirring constantly. Pour into buttered pan. Let stand until completely cool. Invert onto waxed paper. Cut with scissors. Wrap individual pieces in plastic wrap.

Velma Adams, Wilmington Grange, Pennsylvania

SURPRISE CHERRY BALLS

Yields: 32 servings

¼ c. butter, softened	**32 maraschino cherries**
½ c. peanut butter	**5 sq. semisweet chocolate, melted**
2 c. confectioners' sugar	**Chopped walnuts**
1 tbsp. cream	

Cream butter and peanut butter in mixer bowl until light. Add confectioners' sugar gradually, beating until fluffy. Blend in cream. Shape heaping teaspoonful around each cherry. Let stand for several minutes. Dip in melted chocolate. Roll in walnuts. Let stand on waxed paper-lined surface until firm.

Mary Grudowski, Wesley Grange, Pennsylvania

CHOCOLATE BALLS

Yields: 7 dozen	Pan Size: 1 quart

2 sticks margarine	**1 c. crushed graham crackers**
1 12-oz. jar chunky	**1 lb. confectioners' sugar**
peanut butter	**12 oz. chocolate chips**
1 tsp. vanilla extract	**2 to 3 tbsp. melted paraffin**

Melt margarine in saucepan. Remove from heat. Add peanut butter, vanilla, graham cracker crumbs and confectioners' sugar, mixing well after each addition. Shape by teaspoonfuls into balls. Place on waxed paper-lined baking sheet. Chill for 30 minutes. Melt chocolate with paraffin in saucepan; mix well. Dip candies into melted chocolate. Let stand on baking sheet until firm.

Kathryn Warren, Benton Grange, New York

DATE LOAF

Yields: 2 pounds	Pan Size: 3 quart

1 c. milk	1 c. chopped English walnuts
2 c. sugar	1 tsp. vanilla extract
1 tbsp. butter	1 tbsp. confectioners' sugar
1 lb. dates, chopped	1 tbsp. cornstarch

Combine milk, sugar and butter in saucepan. Cook over medium heat to 234 to 240 degrees on candy thermometer, soft-ball stage, stirring constantly. Remove from heat. Stir in dates, walnuts and vanilla. Beat until very thick. Sprinkle mixture of confectioners' sugar and cornstarch on platter. Spread date mixture on platter. Let stand until firm. Cut into squares.

Maryalice Roush, Smithville Grange, Ohio

PERFECT DIVINITY

Yields: 1 pound	Pan Size: 2 quart

2 c. sugar	2 egg whites
½ c. light corn syrup	1 tsp. vanilla extract
½ tsp. salt	½ c. chopped nuts

Combine sugar, corn syrup, salt and *½ cup hot water* in saucepan. Bring to a boil, stirring to dissolve sugar. Cook to 250 degrees on candy thermometer, hard-ball stage. Do not stir. Wipe crystals from side of pan frequently with fork wrapped in damp cloth. Add hot syrup gradually to stiffly beaten egg whites in mixer bowl, beating constantly. Beat for 5 minutes at high speed. Add vanilla. Beat until soft peaks form and mixture loses its luster. Stir in nuts. Drop by teaspoonfuls onto waxed paper-lined pan. Cool completely.

Martha Healy, Chumstick Grange, Washington

FRUIT BALLS

Yields:	

1 c. figs	1 c. chopped walnuts
1 c. dates	Confectioners' sugar
1 c. raisins	

Put all ingredients through food chopper, mix well. Shape into 1-inch balls. Roll in confectioners' sugar.

Ruth Tweedie, Walton Grange, New York

FOOLPROOF CHOCOLATE FUDGE

Yields: 2 pounds   Pan Size: 8x8 inch

18 oz. semisweet chocolate chips
1   14-oz. can sweetened
    condensed milk

1½ tsp. vanilla extract
½ c. chopped nuts

Melt chocolate chips with condensed milk in heavy saucepan; mix well. Remove from heat. Stir in vanilla and nuts. Spread in waxed paper-lined pan. Chill for 2 hours or until set. Invert onto cutting board; remove waxed paper. Cut into squares. Store in airtight container at room temperature.

Diana N. Smith, Farmingdale Junior Grange, New York

MILLION-DOLLAR FUDGE

Yields: 5½ pounds   Pan Size: 10x15 inch

4 c. sugar
2 sticks butter
1 can evaporated milk
Dash of salt

24 oz. chocolate chips
7 oz. marshmallow creme
1½ c. chopped nuts
1 tsp. vanilla extract

Bring sugar, butter, evaporated milk and salt to a rolling boil in saucepan. Boil for 8 minutes, stirring constantly; remove from heat. Add chocolate chips. Beat with electric mixer until smooth. Add remaining ingredients; mix well. Pour into buttered pan. Let stand until cool. Cut into 1-inch squares.

Virginia L. Hill, Broad Hollow Grange, Illinois

TWO-FLAVOR FUDGE

Yields: 2½ pounds   Pan Size: 9 x 9 inch

2 c. packed brown sugar
1 c. sugar
1 c. evaporated milk
½ c. butter
7 oz. marshmallow creme

6 oz. butterscotch chips
6 oz. chocolate chips
1 c. chopped nuts
1 tsp. vanilla extract

Combine brown sugar, sugar, evaporated milk and butter in saucepan. Bring to a boil over medium heat. Cool for 15 minutes, stirring occasionally; remove from heat. Add marshmallow creme, butterscotch and chocolate chips; stir until melted. Stir in nuts and vanilla. Pour into buttered pan. Chill until firm. Cut into bite-sized pieces.

Karen Miles, Milbrook Grange, Illinois

WHITE FUDGE

Yields: 3 dozen pieces	Pan Size: 2 quart

2¼ c. sugar	¼ c. butter
Pinch of salt	5 oz. marshmallow creme
1 5-oz. can evaporated milk	½ c. chopped nuts

Combine sugar, salt, evaporated milk and butter in saucepan. Bring to a boil, stirring constantly with wooden spoon. Cook to 240 degrees on candy thermometer, soft-ball stage. Remove from heat. Stir in marshmallow creme and nuts. Pour into buttered 8-inch square dish. Let stand until firm. Cut into squares.

A. Elaine Cook, Brandywine Grange, Pennsylvania

ORANGE CARAMEL FUDGE

Yields: 2 pounds

3 c. sugar	⅓ to ½ c.
¼ c. butter	orange
1 lg. can	rind
evaporated	1 c. chopped
milk	walnuts
1 c. sugar	

Cook first 3 ingredients over medium heat until sugar dissolves, stirring constantly. Cook to 234 degrees on candy thermometer, stirring occasionally. Caramelize 1 cup sugar in skillet over medium heat. Stir in cooked mixture gradually. Add remaining ingredients. Beat until mixture loses its gloss. Spread in buttered pan. Cool. Cut into squares.

MOUNDS CANDY BALLS

Yields: 2 dozen

¼ c. mashed potatoes	1½ c. coconut
1¾ c. confectioners' sugar	½ tsp. salt
1 tbsp. butter, softened	1 sq. unsweetened chocolate
½ tsp. vanilla extract	½ to ¾ c. chocolate chips

Combine potatoes, confectioners' sugar, butter, vanilla, coconut and salt in bowl; mix well. Shape into balls. Place on baking sheet. Chill until firm. Melt unsweetened chocolate and chocolate chips in double boiler; blend well. Dip chilled candies into chocolate; place on waxed paper. Let stand until set.

Arlene Burda
Minnesota Director of Women's Activities

ICE CREAM CANDY

Yields: 1½ pounds   Pan Size: 3 quart

3 c. sugar
½ tbsp. vinegar
¼ tsp. cream of tartar

Vanilla, orange or lemon
   extract to taste
Butter

Combine sugar, vinegar, cream of tartar and *½ cup boiling water* in saucepan. Cook over medium heat to 300 to 310 degrees on candy thermometer, hard-crack stage. Do not stir. Pour onto buttered platter. Let stand until cool enough to handle, folding edges toward center as they cool. Pull with buttered hands until white and glossy, adding flavoring during pulling. Cut into bite-sized pieces.

Marian M. Boyce, Townsend Grange, New York

LOG ROLL

Yields: 15 servings

1 lb. graham crackers, crushed
1 lb. walnuts, chopped
1 lb. miniature marshmallows

1 lb. dates, chopped
½ pt. whipping cream, whipped

Reserve ½ cup graham cracker crumbs. Combine remaining crumbs, walnuts, marshmallows and dates in bowl; mix well. Stir in cream. Shape into roll; coat with reserved crumbs. Wrap in foil. Chill for 24 hours. Cut into slices.

Margaret L. Wagner, Priest Lake Grange, Idaho

PEANUT BRITTLE

Yields: 2 pounds   Pan Size: 3 quart

2 c. sugar
1 c. light corn syrup
½ tsp. salt

2 tbsp. butter
1½ c. raw Spanish peanuts
1 tsp. soda

Combine sugar, corn syrup and *1 cup water* in saucepan. Cook to 234 to 240 degrees on candy thermometer, soft-ball stage, stirring constantly. Add salt, butter and peanuts. Cook to 300 to 310 degrees on candy thermometer, hard-crack stage, stirring frequently; remove from heat. Stir in soda. Pour onto buttered platter. Cool for 2 hours. Break into bite-sized pieces.

Janet Wheeler, Friend of Priest Lake Grange, Idaho

PENUCHE

Yields: 1½ pounds	Pan Size: 8x8 inch

16 oz. light brown sugar
¾ c. milk
2 tbsp. (rounded) butter
Pinch of salt

2 tbsp. marshmallow creme
½ c. chopped nuts
½ tsp. vanilla extract

Combine brown sugar, milk, butter and salt in saucepan; mix well. Cook over low heat until brown sugar is completely dissolved, stirring constantly. Cook, uncovered, over medium heat to 234 to 240 degrees on candy thermometer, soft-ball stage. Let stand until lukewarm; do not stir. Beat until mixture thickens and loses its luster. Stir in remaining ingredients. Pour into buttered pan. Let stand until firm. Cut into squares.

Sue Gran, Ekonk Grange, Connecticut

SPICED PECANS

Yields: 8 ounces	Pan Size: cookie sheet	Preheat: 300°

1 egg white
2 c. pecan halves
½ c. sugar

½ tsp. salt
½ tsp. each cloves, nutmeg
1 tsp. cinnamon

Beat egg white with *1 tablespoon water* in bowl until frothy. Stir in pecans. Sift mixture of remaining ingredients over pecans; mix well. Spread on cookie sheet. Bake for 30 minutes, stirring every 10 minutes.

Isabelle S. Covington, West Suffield Grange, Connecticut

POPCORN BALLS

Yields: 16 cups

½ c. light corn syrup
1½ c. sugar
1 c. margarine

1 tsp. vanilla extract
¼ tsp. almond extract
4 qt. popped popcorn

Combine corn syrup, sugar and margarine in saucepan. Cook to 250 to 268 degrees on candy thermometer, hard-ball stage, stirring constantly; remove from heat. Stir in flavoring. Pour over popcorn; stir to coat evenly. Shape into balls.

Ruth Thames, Shive Grange, Texas

Pies

CONNECTICUT APPLE PIE

Yields: 7 servings	Pan Size: 9 inch	Preheat: 350°

Connecticut apples, peeled, sliced	**¾ c. butter, melted**
2 tsp. sugar	**1 c. flour**
1 tsp. each cinnamon, nutmeg	**1 c. sugar**
	Pinch of salt

Fill pie plate ¾ full with apples. Sprinkle with 2 teaspoons sugar, cinnamon and nutmeg. Sprinkle mixture of butter, flour, 1 cup sugar and salt over apples. Bake for 30 to 40 minutes or until golden brown. Serve warm.

William A. O'Neill
Governor of Connecticut

DEEP-DISH STREUSEL APPLE PIE

Yields: 8 to 10 servings	Pan Size: 6x10 inch	Preheat: 375°

8 c. sliced peeled tart apples	**2 c. flour**
¾ c. sugar	**1 c. packed brown sugar**
½ c. raisins	**½ tsp. salt**
1 tbsp. flour	**1 tsp. apple pie spice**
2 tsp. apple pie spice	**1 c. butter**

Combine apples, sugar, raisins, 1 tablespoon flour and 2 teaspoons apple pie spice in bowl; toss lightly. Spoon into baking dish. Combine 2 cups flour, brown sugar, salt and 1 teaspoon apple pie spice in bowl. Cut in butter until crumbly. Sprinkle over apples. Bake for 10 minutes. Reduce temperature to 350 degrees. Bake for 30 minutes.

Photograph for this recipe on page 271.

DUTCH APPLE TART

Yields: 6 servings	Pan Size: 9 inch	Preheat: 400°

¾ to 1 c. sugar	**1 unbaked pie shell**
2 tbsp. flour	**¼ c. heavy cream**
½ tsp. cinnamon	**2 tbsp. butter**
7 tart cooking apples, peeled	

Combine sugar, flour and cinnamon in small bowl; mix well. Slice 2 apples thinly. Place in pie shell. Sprinkle with half the cinnamon mixture. Cut remaining apples into halves; remove cores. Place apples cut side down in prepared pie shell. Sprinkle with remaining cinnamon mixture. Pour cream carefully around center apple. Dot with butter. Bake for 45 minutes or until apples are tender.

Elizabeth M. Almgren, Pleasant Hill Grange, Pennsylvania

PENNSYLVANIA DUTCH APPLE PIE

Yields: 6 to 8 servings	Pan Size: 10 inch	Preheat: 450°

1 egg	**1 c. sour cream**
1 c. sugar	**4 c. finely chopped apples**
1 tsp. cinnamon	**1 unbaked pie shell**
¾ tsp. salt	

Combine egg, sugar, cinnamon, salt and sour cream in bowl; mix well. Pour over apples in bowl; stir gently. Pour into pie shell. Bake for 15 minutes. Reduce temperature to 350 degrees. Bake for 30 minutes or until knife inserted in center comes out clean. Serve hot or cold.

Frances D. Murphy, Lookout Mt. Grange, Oregon

SWEDISH APPLE PIE

Yields: 6 to 8 servings	Pan Size: 9 inch	Preheat: 350°

Sliced apples
1 tbsp. sugar
1 tsp. cinnamon
1 tsp. nutmeg
1 c. flour

1 c. sugar
1 egg
¾ c. melted butter
1 c. chopped nuts

Fill pie plate with sliced apples. Sprinkle with mixture of 1 tablespoon sugar, cinnamon and nutmeg. Combine remaining ingredients in bowl; mix well. Pour over apples. Bake for 45 minutes.

Elois Wallace, Pemigewasset Valley Pomona Grange, New Hampshire

BANANA CREAM PIE

Yields: 6 servings	Pan Size: 9 inch	Preheat: 375°

2 c. milk
1 c. sugar
2 eggs, separated
¼ c. cornstarch
¼ tsp. salt
½ c. milk

1 tbsp. vanilla extract
1 tbsp. butter
2 bananas
1 baked pie shell
⅓ tsp. cream of tartar
2 tbsp. sugar

Combine 2 cups milk and sugar in top of double boiler. Add egg yolks and paste of cornstarch, salt and ½ cup milk; mix well. Cook until thickened, stirring constantly. Stir in vanilla and butter. Pour over sliced bananas in pie shell. Beat egg whites with cream of tartar and 2 tablespoons sugar until stiff peaks form. Spread over pie, sealing to edge. Bake until golden brown.

Ruth Logan, Williamsfield Grange, Ohio

BERRIES AND CREAM PIE

Yields: 6 to 8 servings	Pan Size: 9 inch	Preheat: 400°

4 c. fresh berries
1 unbaked pie shell
¾ c. sugar
¼ c. flour

¼ tsp. salt
½ tsp. cinnamon
1 c. cream

Place berries in pie shell. Pour mixture of remaining ingredients over berries. Bake for 35 to 45 minutes or until light brown. Serve warm.

Dorothy Groves, Lincoln Grange, Oregon

BANANA SPLIT PIE

Yields: 6 to 8 servings	Pan Size: 9 inch

2 c. milk	½ tsp. salt
½ c. sugar	¼ c. cornstarch
½ tsp. salt	1 baked pie shell
¼ c. cornstarch	Pineapple slices
¼ c. milk	Bananas, sliced
1 tbsp. butter	Maraschino cherries,
1 20-oz. can crushed pineapple	cut into quarters
½ c. sugar	

Combine 2 cups milk, sugar and ½ teaspoon salt in saucepan. Bring to a boil. Add ¼ cup cornstarch dissolved in ¼ cup milk. Cook over medium heat until thickened, stirring constantly. Remove form heat. Stir in butter; cool. Combine pienapple, ½ cup sugar and ½ teaspoon salt in saucepan. Bring to a boil. Add ¼ cup cornstarch dissolved in ¼ cup cold water. Cook over medium heat until thickened and clear, stirring constantly. Remove from heat; cool. Pour cream filling into pie shell. Top with pineapple filling. Arrange pineapple, bananas and maraschino cherries over filling. Chill until serving time. Garnish with whipped cream.

Anita Bender, Sauvie Island Grange, Oregon

BERRY TART

Yields: 12 to 18 servings	Pan Size: 10x15 inch	Preheat: 350°

1½ c. berries, mashed	6½ c. flour
1½ c. sugar	4 tsp. baking powder
3 tbsp. cornstarch	1 tsp. salt
2 tbsp. lemon juice	1 c. milk
1½ c. whole berries	2 c. confectioners' sugar
1 c. sugar	2 tbsp. shortening
1 c. shortening	1 tsp. vanilla extract
3 eggs	2 to 4 tbsp. milk
2 tsp. vanilla extract	

Combine mashed berries and 1½ cups sugar in saucepan. Bring to a boil. Add mixture of cornstarch and ½ cup water. Cook until thickened. Stir in lemon juice and whole berries. Let stand until almost cool. Cream 1 cup sugar and 1 cup shortening in bowl until light and fluffy. Add eggs and 2 teaspoons vanilla. Add mixture of flour, baking powder and salt to creamed mixture alternately with 1 cup milk, beating well after each addition. Reserve 1 cup dough. Pat remaining dough in greased baking pan. Pour berry filling over top. Crumble reserved dough over berries. Bake for 35 minutes. Drizzle warm tart with mixture of confectioners' sugar, 2 tablespoons shortening, 1 teaspoon vanilla and milk.

Carole Zimmerman, Ackly Grange, Pennsylvania

BLACKBERRY PIES

Yields: 2 pies   Pan Size: 9 inch

1 c. sugar
3 tbsp. margarine
4 c. fresh blackberries

2 tbsp. cornstarch
1 sm. package blackberry gelatin
2 baked pie shells

Combine sugar, margarine and ½ cup water in saucepan. Simmer until sugar dissolves and margarine melts. Add blackberries gradually. Cook until heated through, stirring constantly. Blend enough cold water with cornstarch to make thin paste. Stir into blackberries. Cook until thickened, stirring constantly. Dissolve gelatin in 1 cup boiling water. Stir into berry mixture. Spoon into pie shells. Chill for 2 hours or until set.

Jenny Grobusky
Secretary, South Carolina State Grange

CAROLINA BLACK PEPPER PIE

Yields: 6 servings   Pan Size: 9 inch   Preheat: 425°

2 c. packed dark brown sugar
1 tbsp. flour
¼ tsp. freshly ground
   black pepper
2 eggs
2 tbsp. melted butter

¼ c. dark corn syrup
2 tsp. vanilla extract
1 c. heavy cream
1 partially baked pie shell
1 c. whipping cream, whipped

Combine brown sugar and flour in bowl. Stir in pepper, eggs, butter, corn syrup, vanilla and 1 cup cream. Pour into pie shell. Bake for 10 minutes. Reduce temperature to 325 degrees. Bake for 40 minutes. Cool completely. Spread whipped cream over pie before serving.

Betty King, Berea Grange, North Carolina

BLUEBARB PIE

Yields: 6 to 8 servings   Pan Size: 10 inch   Preheat: 400°

3 c. ½-inch slices rhubarb
2 c. blueberries
¼ c. unbleached flour
1 c. sugar

1 recipe 2-crust pie pastry
1 tbsp. butter
1 egg, beaten

Combine rhubarb, blueberries, flour and sugar in bowl; mix well. Pour into pastry-lined pie plate. Dot with butter. Top with remaining pastry; seal edge and cut vents. Brush with egg. Bake for 20 minutes. Reduce temperature to 350 degrees. Bake for 20 minutes longer. Cool for 30 minutes before serving.

Mary Ellen Dahlgreen, Chumstick Grange, Washington

DOUBLE-CRUST BLUEBERRY PIE

Yields: 6 to 8 servings	Pan Size: 9 inch	Preheat: 425°

4 c. blueberries
3 tbsp. Minute tapioca
¼ tsp. salt
2 tbsp. lemon juice

⅔ c. sugar
1 recipe 2-crust pie pastry
⅓ c. packed brown sugar
Butter

Combine blueberries, tapioca, salt, lemon juice and sugar in bowl; mix well. Pour into pastry-lined pie plate. Sprinkle with brown sugar. Dot with butter. Top with remaining pastry; seal edge and cut vents. Bake for 10 minutes. Reduce temperature to 375 degrees. Bake for 30 minutes.

Lorna Anderson, Mossyrock Grange, Washington

BROWN SUGAR PIE

Yields: 6 servings	Pan Size: 8 inch	Preheat: 425°

2 c. packed brown sugar
2 eggs, beaten
3 tbsp. flour
½ tsp. vanilla extract

½ tsp. vinegar
½ c. cream
1½ tbsp. butter
1 unbaked pie shell

Combine brown sugar and ¼ *cup water* in saucepan. Bring to a boil. Mix eggs, flour, vanilla, vinegar, cream and butter in bowl. Add to brown sugar mixture; mix well. Pour into pie shell. Bake for 10 minutes. Reduce temperature to 350 degrees. Bake until filling is set.

Phebe Harbaugh, Springboro Grange, Ohio

BUTTERMILK PIE

Yields: 6 servings	Pan Size: 10 inch	Preheat: 450°

3 eggs, separated
3 tbsp. butter, melted
½ c. sugar
2 tbsp. flour
¼ tsp. salt

1½ c. buttermilk
½ tsp. grated lemon rind
3 tbsp. lemon juice
¼ c. sugar
1 unbaked pie shell

Combine slightly beaten egg yolks, cooled butter, ½ cup sugar, flour and salt in bowl; mix well. Add buttermilk, lemon rind and lemon juice; mix well. Beat egg whites with ¼ cup sugar until soft peaks form. Fold into buttermilk mixture. Pour into pie shell. Bake for 10 minutes. Reduce temperature to 350 degrees. Bake for 20 to 25 minutes or until knife inserted in center comes out clean.

Cecile Mae Rudeen, Williamsfield Grange, Ohio

Recipes for this photograph on pages 266, 273, 278.

BUTTERMILK MERINGUE PIE

Yields: 6 servings   Pan Size: 9 inch   Preheat: 425°

¼ c. butter, softened	⅛ tsp. allspice
⅔ c. sugar	¼ tsp. salt
1 tsp. vanilla extract	2 c. buttermilk
3 eggs, separated	1 Sesame-Cheddar pie shell
¼ c. flour	¼ tsp. cream of tartar
½ tsp. grated lemon rind	⅓ c. sugar
½ tsp. nutmeg	

Cream butter and ⅔ cup sugar in mixer bowl until light and fluffy. Add vanilla and egg yolks 1 at a time, mixing well after each addition. Stir in flour, lemon rind, spices and salt. Pour into pie shell. Bake for 8 minutes. Reduce temperature to 325 degrees. Bake for 40 minutes or until set. Cool for 30 minutes. Beat egg whites with cream of tartar until soft peaks form. Add ⅓ cup sugar gradually, beating constantly until stiff peaks form. Spread over filling, sealing to edge. Bake at 375 degrees for 6 minutes or until golden. Cool. Chill until serving time.

Sesame-Cheddar Pie Shell

½ c. shortening	¼ c. shredded sharp
1 c. flour	Cheddar cheese
⅓ c. yellow cornmeal	1 tbsp. sugar
3 tbsp. toasted sesame seed	½ tsp. salt

Cut shortening into mixture of flour, cornmeal and sesame seed in bowl. Mix in cheese. Mix sugar, salt and *2 tablespoons cold water*. Add to cheese mixture; mix well. Roll between lightly floured waxed paper. Fit into pie plate; flute edge.

Photograph for this recipe on page 271.

BUTTERSCOTCH PIE

Yields: 6 servings   Pan Size: 9 inch

1 c. packed brown sugar	3 tbsp. flour
¼ c. butter	2 c. milk
1 egg, separated	1 baked pie shell
¼ tsp. salt	¼ c. sugar

Combine brown sugar and butter in heavy skillet. Cook until melted and dark, stirring constantly. Combine beaten egg yolk, salt, flour and milk in bowl; mix well. Add to syrup. Cook until thickened, stirring constantly. Pour into pie shell. Beat egg white with sugar in bowl until stiff peaks form. Spread over pie, sealing to edge. Bake until golden brown.

Ethel Jane Stevens, Beltsville Grange, Maryland

CARROT PIE

Yields: 6 to 8 servings	Pan Size: 9 inch	Preheat: 350°

1½ c. cooked chopped carrots	½ tsp. salt
1 c. sugar	1 tsp. cinnamon
3 eggs	¼ tsp. cloves
2 c. milk	1 unbaked pie shell

Combine first 7 ingredients in blender container. Process until smooth. Pour into pie shell. Bake for 45 minutes or until knife inserted in center comes out clean.

Gertie Banks, Eagle Cliff Grange, Washington

CHERRY PIE

Yields: 6 servings	Pan Size: 9 inch	Preheat: 425°

1 c. sugar	4 c. cherries
¼ c. cherry gelatin	1 tsp. almond extract
3 tbsp. cornstarch	1 recipe 2-crust pie pastry

Combine sugar, gelatin and cornstarch in saucepan. Stir in *1 cup hot water*. Cook until thickened, stirring constantly; remove from heat. Stir in cherries and flavoring. Pour into pastry-lined pie plate. Top with remaining pastry. Seal edges; cut vents. Bake for 45 minutes or until brown.

Blanche J. Evans, Log Cabin Grange, Ohio

CHESS PIE

Yields: 6 servings	Pan Size: 9 inch	Preheat: 400°

¼ c. butter, softened	½ c. milk
1 c. sugar	4 egg yolks
1 c. packed brown sugar	1½ c. milk
3 tbsp. flour	2 tsp. vanilla extract
¼ tsp. salt	1 unbaked pie shell

Cream butter, sugar and brown sugar in mixer bowl until light and fluffy. Add mixture of flour, salt and ½ cup milk; mix well. Blend in egg yolks, 1½ cups milk and vanilla. Pour into pie shell. Bake until pie begins to brown. Reduce temperature to 300 degrees. Bake for 25 minutes longer or until almost set. Cool before serving.

Viola Thompson, Lime Creek Grange, Michigan

CHOCOLATE ANGEL PIE

Yields: 9 servings	Pan Size: 9 inch	Preheat: 275°

2 egg whites	**1 c. chocolate chips**
⅛ tsp. cream of tartar	**3 tbsp. strong coffee**
½ c. sugar	**1 tsp. vanilla extract**
½ c. chopped pecans	**1 c. whipping cream**

Beat egg whites and cream of tartar until foamy. Add sugar 1 tablespoon at a time, beating until stiff peaks form. Spread over bottom and side of greased pie plate, shaping high edge. Sprinkle with pecans. Bake for 50 minutes or until light brown and crisp. Cool. Melt chocolate chips in double boiler over hot water. Blend in coffee. Cook for 5 minutes, stirring constantly. Stir in vanilla. Cool. Whip cream in bowl until stiff peaks form. Fold in chocolate mixture. Spoon into meringue pie shell. Chill for 2 hours or until set.

Elizabeth H. Dole
Secretary, U.S. Department of Transportation

CHOCOLATE SURPRISE PIE

Yields: 6 servings	Pan Size: 10 inch

¾ c. butter, softened	**¼ tsp. almond extract**
1¼ c. sugar	**1 c. finely chopped rinsed**
⅔ c. cocoa	**sauerkraut**
3 eggs	**1 baked 10-in. pie shell**
1 tsp. vanilla extract	**½ c. whipping cream, whipped**

Cream butter in mixer bowl until light. Beat in mixture of sugar and cocoa gradually. Add eggs 1 at a time, mixing well after each addition. Add flavorings; beat until thick. Stir in sauerkraut. Pour into pie shell. Chill for 3 hours or longer. Top with whipped cream.

CHOCOLATE CUSTARD PIE

Yields: 6 servings	Pan Size: 9 inch	Preheat: 325°

½ c. sugar
2 tbsp. cocoa
1 tbsp. flour
¼ tsp. salt

3 eggs, lightly beaten
2 c. milk
1 unbaked pie shell

Add mixture of dry ingredients to beaten eggs in bowl; mix well. Stir in milk. Pour into pie shell in metal pie plate. Bake for 1 hour or until set. Cool before serving.

Mrs. Roger Morse, Auburn Grange, New York

FUDGE MACAROON PIE

Yields: 8 servings	Pan Size: 9 inch	Preheat: 350°

3 sq. unsweetened chocolate
½ c. butter
3 eggs, lightly beaten
¾ c. sugar

½ c. flour
1 tsp. vanilla extract
⅔ c. sweetened condensed milk
2⅔ c. coconut

Melt chocolate and butter in saucepan over low heat. Add eggs, sugar, flour and vanilla; mix well. Pour into greased pie plate. Spoon mixture of sweetened condensed milk and coconut to within 1 inch of edge. Bake for 30 minutes.

Dorothy C. Gower, Medford Grange, New Jersey

COCONUT PIES

Yields: 12 servings	Pan Size: 9 inch	Preheat: 400°

3 eggs, separated
1 c. sugar
1 tbsp. cornstarch
2 c. milk

2 c. coconut
¼ c. margarine, melted
1½ tsp. vanilla extract
2 unbaked pie shells

Beat egg yolks in mixer bowl. Blend in sugar and cornstarch. Add milk gradually, mixing well. Beat egg whites until soft peaks form. Fold egg whites, coconut, margarine and vanilla gently into egg yolk mixture; mix well. Pour into pie shells. Bake for 20 minutes. Reduce temperature to 350 degrees. Cook until set.

Mrs. Henry Lee Blackburn, Ingold Grange, North Carolina

OLD-FASHIONED COCONUT CUSTARD PIE

Yields: 6 servings	Pan Size: 10 inch	Preheat: 350°

6 eggs, separated
1 c. sugar
2½ c. milk

½ c. coconut
1 unbaked pie shell

Beat egg yolks in mixer bowl. Add sugar 1 tablespoon at a time, beating constantly. Add milk; mix well. Stir in coconut. Beat egg whites for 1 minute. Fold gently into coconut mixture. Spoon into pie shell. Bake for 1 hour.

Arlene Heck, Ontelaunee Grange, Pennsylvania

COCONUT-CHEESE PIE

Yields: 6 servings	Pan Size: 9 inch	Preheat: 325°

1½ tbsp. butter, softened
2½ c. coconut
4 eggs
⅔ c. sugar

8 oz. cream cheese, softened
3 tbsp. lemon juice
5⅓ tbsp. coconut

Spread butter evenly over bottom and side of pie plate. Press 1½ cups coconut into butter, shaping into pie shell. Combine 1 cup coconut, eggs, sugar, cream cheese and lemon juice in blender container. Process until smooth. Pour into shell. Sprinkle remaining coconut around edge. Bake for 30 minutes, covering coconut with aluminum foil if necessary to prevent overbrowning. Serve warm or cold.

Virginia Davis, Quartz Hill Grange, California

CRANBERRY-APPLE-PINEAPPLE PIE

Yields: 6 servings	Pan Size: 8 inch	Preheat: 450°

1 c. chopped cranberries
1 c. chopped tart apples
¼ c. crushed pineapple

1 c. sugar
⅛ tsp. salt
1 recipe 2-crust pie pastry

Combine fruit, sugar and salt in bowl. Let stand for 2 hours to overnight. Pour into pastry-lined pie plate. Top with remaining pastry. Seal edges; cut vents. Bake for 10 minutes. Reduce temperature to 350 degrees. Bake for 30 minutes longer.

Barbara Filios, Morris Grange, New Jersey

CRANBERRY-NUT PIE

Yields: 8 servings	Pan Size: 9 inch	Preheat: 325°

2 c. cranberries
½ c. chopped nuts
½ c. sugar
¼ c. melted butter

2 eggs, beaten
1 c. sugar
1 c. sifted flour
½ c. melted butter

Place cranberries in greased pie plate. Sprinkle with nuts and ½ cup sugar. Drizzle with ¼ cup melted butter. Combine remaining ingredients in bowl; mix well. Pour over cranberries; do not mix. Bake for 40 to 50 minutes or until golden brown. Serve warm with ice cream or whipped cream.

Barbara L. Boyden, Moosup Valley Grange, Rhode Island

MARTHA WASHINGTON'S NUTMEG CUSTARD PIE

Yields: 8 servings	Pan Size: 9 inch	Preheat: 425°

1 unbaked pie shell
3 c. milk
1 bay leaf
1 3-in. cinnamon stick
3 eggs

3 egg yolks
½ c. sugar
1 tsp. vanilla extract
¾ tsp. nutmeg
⅛ tsp. salt

Prick pie shell with fork. Bake at 425 degrees for 7 minutes. Scald milk with bay leaf and cinnamon stick. Beat eggs and remaining ingredients in bowl until smooth. Strain milk into egg mixture; mix well. Pour into pie shell. Bake at 325 degrees for 55 minutes or until knife inserted in center comes out clean. Cool on wire rack. Serve at room temperature with whipped cream.

Photograph for this recipe on page 271.

EGG CUSTARD PIE

Yields: 8 servings	Pan Size: 10 inch	Preheat: 325°

3 c. milk
4 eggs, beaten
2 tbsp. flour
½ c. sugar

¼ tsp. salt
½ tsp. nutmeg
1 unbaked pie shell

Scald milk in saucepan. Stir a small amount of hot milk into eggs; stir eggs into hot milk. Add dry ingredients; mix well. Prick pie shell with fork. Pour custard into pie shell. Bake for 45 minutes to 1 hour or until knife inserted in center comes out clean. Cool. Chill until serving time.

Dorothy King
Lady Assistant Steward, National Grange

ELDERBERRY CRUMB PIE

Yields: 6 to 8 servings	Pan Size: 9 inch	Preheat: 375°

1 c. elderberries	1 unbaked pie shell
1 c. sugar	½ c. flour
3 tbsp. cornstarch	¼ c. sugar
⅛ tsp. salt	¼ tsp. cinnamon
2 c. elderberries	¼ c. butter
1 tbsp. butter	

Combine 1 cup elderberries, 1 cup sugar, cornstarch, salt and ⅔ *cup water* in saucepan. Simmer until thickened, stirring constantly. Stir in remaining berries and butter. Pour into pie shell. Mix remaining ingredients in bowl until crumbly. Sprinkle over pie. Bake for 30 minutes or until light brown.

Mrs. Charles Hileman, Sinking Valley Grange, Pennsylvania

JAPANESE FRUIT PIE

Yields: 6 to 8 servings	Pan Size: 9 inch	Preheat: 300°

1 stick margarine, melted, cooled	1 tsp. vanilla extract
1 c. sugar	½ c. chopped dates
2 eggs, beaten	½ c. coconut
½ tsp. vinegar	½ c. chopped nuts
	1 unbaked pie shell

Combine margarine, sugar, eggs, vinegar and vanilla in bowl; mix well. Stir in dates, coconut and nuts. Pour into pie shell. Bake for 45 to 50 minutes or until brown.

Joan Wade, Rushcreek Grange, Ohio

JELLY PATTIES

Yields: 6 servings	Pan Size: muffin pan	Preheat: 425°

½ c. sugar	Jelly
¼ c. butter, softened	1 recipe 2-crust rich pie pastry
1 egg	Whipped cream

Combine sugar, butter, egg and jelly in bowl; mix well. Place 2 tablespoonfuls into each of 6 pastry-lined muffin cups. Bake for 25 minutes or until set. Cool. Fill with whipped cream.

Roland G. Winters
Master, Michigan State Grange

OLD-FASHIONED LEMON PIE

Yields: 6 servings	Pan Size: 9 inch	Preheat: 375°

1½ c. sugar
1 tbsp. cornstarch
1 tbsp. flour
3 eggs
¼ c. milk

¼ c. melted butter
¼ c. lemon juice
2 tbsp. grated lemon rind
1 unbaked pie shell

Combine dry ingredients in bowl. Add eggs, milk, butter, lemon juice and lemon rind; mix well. Pour into pie shell. Bake for 30 to 40 minutes or until set. Serve with whipped cream if desired.

Ann Yandow, Blue Spruce Grange, Vermont

LEMON CHIFFON PIE

Yields: 6 to 7 servings	Pan Size: 9 inch	Preheat: 425°

1 tbsp. flour
1 c. sugar
1 tbsp. butter
1 c. milk

2 eggs, separated
Juice of 1 lemon
Grated rind of 1 lemon
1 unbaked pie shell

Combine flour, sugar, butter and milk in bowl; mix well. Add egg yolks, lemon juice and lemon rind; mix well. Fold in stiffly beaten egg whites. Spoon into pie shell. Bake for 15 minutes. Reduce temperature to 350 degrees. Bake for 35 minutes or until knife inserted near center comes out clean. Cool before serving.

Lenora A. Wilson, Goodwill Grange, West Virginia

OLD-FASHIONED TWO-CRUST LEMON PIE

Yields: 6 servings	Pan Size: 9 inch	Preheat: 375°

¼ c. cornstarch
1 tbsp. butter
1½ c. sugar
2 eggs, beaten
¼ c. lemon juice

2 tbsp. grated lemon rind
1 recipe 2-crust pie pastry
1 tbsp. milk
1 tbsp. sugar

Blend cornstarch and ¼ cup water in saucepan. Stir in 1½ cups boiling water. Cook over medium heat until thickened, stirring constantly. Cook for 1 minute; remove from heat. Stir in butter. Cool. Add 1½ cups sugar, eggs, lemon juice and lemon rind; mix well. Pour into pastry-lined pie shell. Top with remaining pastry. Seal edges; cut vents. Brush with milk. Sprinkle with 1 tablespoon sugar. Bake for 30 minutes. Increase temperature to 425 degrees. Bake for 10 minutes longer.

Beatrice S. Straw, North Scarboro Grange, Maine

VERMONT MAPLE BUTTERNUT PIE

Yields: 6 servings   Pan Size: 9 inch   Preheat: 350°

3 eggs, lightly beaten   ½ tsp. salt
1 c. sugar   1 tsp. vanilla extract
1 c. maple syrup   1 unbaked pie shell
½ c. chopped butternuts

Combine first 6 ingredients in bowl; mix well. Pour into pie shell. Bake for 40 minutes or until set.
Note: May substitute walnuts for butternuts.

Marjorie Van Alstyne, East Barnard Grange, Vermont

MAPLE-NUT MERINGUE PIE

Yields: 8 servings   Pan Size: 9 inch   Preheat: 375°

2 c. maple syrup   1 tsp. vanilla extract
1 tsp. salt   Dash of cinnamon
⅔ c. cornstarch   ½ c. chopped hickory nuts
3 eggs, separated   1 baked pie shell
2 tbsp. butter   6 tbsp. sugar

Bring syrup, salt and *1 cup water* to a boil in saucepan. Add cornstarch blended with ½ *cup water*. Cook, covered, over low heat for 5 minutes or until mixture comes to a boil. Stir a small amount of hot mixture into beaten egg yolks; stir egg yolks into hot mixture. Cook for 1 minute, stirring constantly; remove from heat. Stir in butter, vanilla, cinnamon and nuts. Pour into pie shell. Beat egg whites with sugar until stiff peaks form. Spread over pie, sealing to edge. Sprinkle with additional nuts. Bake for 10 minutes or until light brown.

Mrs. John Logan, Gustavus Grange, Ohio

OATMEAL PIE

Yields: 6 to 8 servings   Pan Size: 9 inch   Preheat: 350°

½ c. sugar   ¾ c. dark corn syrup
½ c. packed light brown   ¾ c. quick-cooking oats
  sugar   1 c. coconut
½ c. margarine   1 c. milk
2 eggs   1 unbaked pie shell
Pinch of salt

Combine sugar, brown sugar, margarine, eggs and salt in mixer bowl. Beat at medium speed until smooth. Add next 4 ingredients; mix well. Pour into pie shell. Bake for 45 minutes or until set.

Mrs. Ernest W. Hofman, Washington Grange, Pennsylvania

ORANGE-RAISIN PIE

Yields: 6 to 8 servings	Pan Size: 9 inch	Preheat: 425°

1 c. packed brown sugar	2 c. seedless raisins
2 tbsp. cornstarch	½ c. finely chopped pecans
6 oz. frozen orange juice	2 tsp. butter
concentrate	1 recipe 2-crust pie pastry

Combine brown sugar and cornstarch in saucepan. Blend in orange juice and *2 cups water*. Cook over medium heat until thickened and clear, stirring constantly. Stir in raisins, pecans and butter. Cool. Pour into pastry-lined pie plate. Top with remaining pastry. Bake for 20 minutes or until crust is brown.

Betty Deets
Illinois Director of Women's Activities

PEACH AND BLUEBERRY PIE

Yields: 8 servings	Pan Size: 9 inch	Preheat: 425°

2 c. sliced peaches	2 tbsp. butter
1 c. blueberries	½ tsp. salt
1 c. sugar	1 recipe 2-crust pie pastry
2 tbsp. Minute tapioca	1 egg yolk, beaten
2 tbsp. lemon juice	

Combine fruit, sugar, tapioca, lemon juice, butter and salt in bowl; mix lightly. Pour into pastry-lined pie plate. Top with remaining pastry. Seal edge; cut vents. Brush with mixture of egg yolk and *1 tablespoon water*. Bake for 45 to 50 minutes.

E. Margaret Lockcuff, Pine Run Grange, Pennsylvania

BAKED PEACH PIE

Yields: 6 servings	Pan Size: 9 inch	Preheat: 425°

4 or 5 lg. fresh peaches	2 eggs
1 unbaked pie shell	½ tsp. cinnamon
1 c. sugar	½ c. chopped nuts
2 tbsp. melted butter	

Cut peaches into halves; remove pits. Place cut side down in pie shell. Combine sugar, butter and eggs in bowl; mix well. Pour over peaches. Sprinkle with cinnamon and nuts. Bake for 15 minutes. Reduce temperature to 325 degrees. Bake for 45 minutes or until set.

Aldine Sparklin, Champion Grange, Ohio

PEACH PIE

Yields: 6 servings	Pan Size: 2 quart

1 c. sugar	1 c. fresh peach purée
3 tbsp. cornstarch	2 c. sliced fresh peaches
⅛ tsp. salt	1 baked pie shell

Combine sugar and cornstarch in saucepan. Stir in ½ cup water, salt and purée. Cook until thickened, stirring constantly. Cool. Arrange sliced peaches in pie shell. Pour cooked mixture over top. Chill. Serve with whipped cream or ice cream.

Elizabeth Wade, Naches Grange, Washington

ARIZONA CHUNKY PEANUT BUTTER PIE

Yields: 6 servings	Pan Size: 9 inch	Preheat: 400°

1 c. light corn syrup	3 eggs, lightly beaten
1 c. sugar	½ tsp. vanilla extract
⅓ c. chunky peanut butter	1 unbaked pie shell

Combine first 5 ingredients in mixer bowl; mix well. Pour into pie shell. Bake for 15 minutes. Reduce temperature to 350 degrees. Bake for 30 to 35 minutes or until edges are set.

Bobbie Buckell, Friend of Upper Sound Grange, Washington

PEANUT STREUSEL PIE

Yields: 6 to 8 servings	Pan Size: 9 inch	Preheat: 350°

⅓ c. peanut butter	3 eggs, separated
¾ c. confectioners' sugar	2 tbsp. butter
1 baked pie shell	½ tsp. vanilla extract
⅓ c. flour	¼ tsp. cream of tartar
½ c. sugar	½ c. sugar
⅛ tsp. salt	1 tsp. cornstarch
2 c. milk, scalded	

Combine peanut butter and confectioners' sugar in bowl; mix until crumbly. Sprinkle ⅔ of the mixture in pie shell. Combine flour, ½ cup sugar and salt in double boiler. Stir in milk. Cook over boiling water until thickened, stirring constantly. Stir a small amount of hot mixture into egg yolks; stir egg yolks into hot mixture. Cook for several minutes longer. Remove from heat. Add butter and vanilla. Pour into pie shell. Beat egg whites until stiff peaks form. Add cream of tartar and mixture of ½ cup sugar and cornstarch gradually, beating constantly until very stiff peaks form. Spread over pie, sealing to edge. Sprinkle with remaining peanut butter mixture. Bake for 10 minutes or until golden.

Barbara Weed, Five Mile Prairie Grange, Washington

PEAR PIE

Yields: 6 servings	Pan Size: 9 inch	Preheat: 350°

2 eggs
½ c. sugar
1 c. sour cream
¼ tsp. salt
1 tsp. vanilla extract
2 tbsp. flour

1 unbaked pie shell
3 c. sliced pears
1 c. flour
½ c. sugar
¼ c. melted butter

Combine first 6 ingredients in mixer bowl. Beat until smooth. Pour half the mixture into pie shell. Arrange pears in pie shell. Pour remaining sour cream mixture over pears. Combine remaining ingredients in bowl; mix until crumbly. Sprinkle over pie. Bake for 1 hour.

Pauline Tipton, Lookout Mt. Grange, Oregon

PECAN PIE

Yields: 8 servings	Pan Size: 9 inch	Preheat: 450°

½ c. butter, softened
¾ c. packed light brown
   sugar
1 c. dark corn syrup
½ tsp. salt

1 tsp. vanilla extract
3 eggs
1 tbsp. (rounded) flour
1 c. chopped pecans
1 unbaked pie shell

Cream butter and brown sugar in mixer bowl until light and fluffy. Blend in corn syrup, salt and vanilla. Add eggs and flour; mix well. Stir in pecans. Pour into pie shell. Bake for 10 minutes. Reduce temperature to 350 degrees. Bake for 30 minutes or until filling is set and crust is brown.

Virginia Wilber, Summit Grange, New York

PEPPERMINT STICK PIE

Yields: 6 servings	Pan Size: 9 inch

1 env. unflavored gelatin
2 eggs, separated
¼ c. sugar
¼ c. crushed peppermint candy

¼ tsp. salt
1½ c. milk, scalded
¼ c. sugar
1 baked pie shell

Soften gelatin in ¼ *cup cold water*. Combine egg yolks, ¼ cup sugar, candy and salt in bowl. Stir in a small amount of hot milk; stir egg yolk mixture into hot milk in double boiler. Cook over simmering water for 5 to 8 minutes or until thickened, stirring constantly. Stir in gelatin. Chill until partially set. Beat egg whites until foamy. Add ¼ cup sugar gradually, beating until stiff peaks form. Fold into chilled mixture. Pour into pie shell. Chill until firm.

Frances Durward, Upper Sound Grange, Washington

PINEAPPLE-COTTAGE CHEESE PIE

Yields: 8 servings	Pan Size: 9 inch	Preheat: 450°

2 c. flour	1½ c. cottage cheese
¼ tsp. salt	½ c. sugar
⅔ c. shortening	3 eggs, lightly beaten
1¼ c. crushed pineapple	¼ tsp. salt
⅓ c. sugar	½ tsp. vanilla extract
1 tbsp. cornstarch	¼ c. cream

Combine flour and ¼ teaspoon salt in bowl. Cut in shortening until crumbly. Add *5 tablespoons ice water*; mix well. Roll half the dough thin on floured surface; fit into pie plate. Reserve remaining dough in refrigerator for another pie. Combine pineapple, ⅓ cup sugar and cornstarch in saucepan. Cook until thickened, stirring constantly. Cool. Pour into prepared pie plate. Beat cottage cheese in bowl until smooth. Add next 5 ingredients; mix well. Pour over pineapple. Sprinkle with cinnamon if desired. Bake for 15 minutes. Reduce temperature to 325 degrees. Bake for 45 minutes.

Miriam Stapleton, Henrietta Grange, New York

HAWAIIAN PINEAPPLE PIE

Yields: 6 servings	Pan Size: 9 inch	Preheat: 350°

3 eggs, well beaten	1 c. light corn syrup
2 tbsp. (heaping) flour	1 tsp. pineapple flavoring
1 c. sugar	1 unbaked pie shell
1 c. crushed pineapple	¼ c. melted margarine
1 c. coconut	

Combine eggs, flour and sugar in bowl; mix well. Add pineapple, coconut, corn syrup and flavoring; mix well. Pour into pie shell. Drizzle with margarine. Bake until knife inserted in center comes out clean.

Hazel Leiber, Elk Grove Grange, California

MOTHER'S PUMPKIN PIE

Yields: 6 to 8 servings	Pan Size: 9 inch	Preheat: 400°

¾ c. packed brown sugar	1 tsp. cinnamon
1 tbsp. flour	1 c. pumpkin
½ tsp. salt	1½ c. rich milk
¼ tsp. each nutmeg, allspice,	2 eggs, well beaten
ginger and cloves	1 unbaked pie shell

Combine brown sugar, flour, salt and spices in bowl. Mix in pumpkin, milk and eggs. Pour into pie shell. Bake for 10 minutes. Reduce temperature to 300 degrees. Bake for 30 minutes.

Paul M. Dunkle, Saltcreek Valley Grange, Ohio

PUMPKIN-PECAN PIE

Yields: 7 servings	Pan Size: 9 inch	Preheat: 350°

 4 eggs, lightly beaten
 2 c. mashed cooked
   pumpkin
 1 c. sugar
 ½ c. dark corn syrup

 1 tsp. vanilla extract
 ½ tsp. cinnamon
 ¼ tsp. salt
 1 unbaked pie shell
 1 c. chopped pecans

Combine eggs, pumpkin, sugar, corn syrup, vanilla, cinnamon and salt in bowl; mix well. Spoon into pie shell. Top with pecans. Bake for 40 minutes or until set.

Nancy Reagan
The White House

RAISIN-RICOTTA PIE

Yields: 8 servings	Pan Size: 9 inch	Preheat: 350°

 ⅓ c. margarine, softened
 1 c. ricotta cheese
 ½ c. sugar
 ½ c. packed brown sugar
 4 eggs

 ½ tsp. salt
 1 tsp. vanilla extract
 1 c. raisins, chopped
 1 unbaked pie shell

Beat margarine and ricotta cheese in bowl until smooth. Beat in sugar and brown sugar. Add eggs 1 at a time, beating well after each addition. Stir in salt, vanilla and raisins. Pour into pie shell. Bake for 45 minutes or until center is set. Cool completely. Garnish with whipped cream if desired.

Mary E. Herron, Fairview Grange, West Virginia

SOUR CREAM-RAISIN PIE

Yields: 6 servings	Pan Size: 9 inch	Preheat: 375°

 1 c. raisins
 1 tsp. soda
 1 c. sugar
 3 tbsp. cornstarch
 1 c. milk

 2 eggs, separated
 1 c. sour cream
 1 tbsp. butter
 1 baked pie shell
 Sugar to taste

Pour *1 cup hot water* over raisins and soda in saucepan. Add mixture of sugar, cornstarch, milk and egg yolks. Cook over medium heat until thickened, stirring constantly. Stir in sour cream. Cook until heated through. Stir in butter. Pour into pie shell. Beat egg whites with sugar to taste until stiff peaks form. Spread over pie, sealing to edge. Bake until golden brown.

Helen M. Frank, Adirondack Grange, New York

SO-DIFFERENT RHUBARB PIE

Yields: 6 servings   Pan Size: 10 inch   Preheat: 400°

3 eggs, separated   ¼ tsp. salt
1½ c. sugar   ½ c. sugar
3 tbsp. flour   3 c. chopped rhubarb
3 tbsp. butter   1 unbaked pie shell

Combine egg yolks and next 4 ingredients in bowl; mix well. Beat egg whites with ½ cup sugar until stiff peaks form. Fold gently into egg yolk mixture. Fold in rhubarb. Spoon into pie shell. Bake for 10 minutes. Reduce temperature to 325 degrees. Bake for 45 minutes longer.

Phyllis Young, Central Mesa Grange, Idaho

CUSTARD RHUBARB PIE

Yields: 6 servings   Pan Size: 9 inch   Preheat: 300°

3 eggs, beaten   ¼ c. melted margarine
1 c. sugar   3 stalks rhubarb, cut into 1-in.
1 tbsp. flour   pieces
½ tsp. vanilla extract   1 unbaked pie shell

Combine eggs, sugar, flour, vanilla and margarine in bowl; mix well. Pour over rhubarb in pie shell. Bake for 30 minutes or until set.

Shirley Eddy, Zion-Oak Grange, Arkansas

RHUBARB-ORANGE PIE

Yields: 6 servings   Pan Size: 9 inch   Preheat: 425°

4 c. 1-in. pieces rhubarb   ¼ tsp. nutmeg
1 lg. orange, peeled,   ⅓ c. flour
  sectioned   1 unbaked pie shell
¾ c. packed brown sugar   ⅓ c. melted butter
¾ c. sugar

Combine rhubarb, orange, brown sugar, sugar, nutmeg and flour in bowl; mix well. Pour into pie shell. Drizzle with butter. Bake for 40 to 50 minutes or until set.

Mrs. Ross Eby, Smithville Grange, Ohio

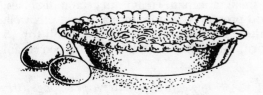

SHOOFLY PIES

Yields: 12 servings	Pan Size: two 9 inch	Preheat: 450°

¼ c. shortening
2 c. flour
1½ c. packed light brown
  sugar

2 tsp. soda
2 c. dark corn syrup
2 eggs
2 unbaked pie shells

Cut shortening into flour and brown sugar in bowl until crumbly. Reserve 2 cups crumbs for topping. Dissolve soda in *2 cups boiling water* in bowl. Add corn syrup, remaining crumb mixture and eggs; mix well. Pour into pie shells. Top with reserved crumbs. Bake for 10 minutes. Reduce temperature to 375 degrees. Bake for 30 minutes or until set.

Betty Stanton, Charlesville Grange, Pennsylvania

LEMON SHOOFLY PIES

Yields: 12 servings	Pan Size: two 9 inch	Preheat: 375°

1 c. molasses
1 c. sugar
¼ c. flour
1 egg
Juice of 2 lemons
Grated rind of 2 lemons

2 unbaked pie shells
1 c. shortening
3 c. flour
1 c. sugar
1 tsp. soda

Combine molasses, 1 cup sugar, ¼ cup flour, egg, lemon juice, lemon rind and *1½ cups boiling water* in bowl; mix well. Pour into pie shells. Cut shortening into remaining ingredients in bowl until crumbly. Sprinkle evenly over pies. Bake for 30 to 35 minutes or until set.

Ruth Robert, Washington Grange, Pennsylvania

INDIAN SUMMER STRAWBERRY CHIFFON PIE

Yields: 8 servings	Pan Size: 9 inch

1 env. unflavored gelatin
1½ c. Smucker's strawberry
  preserves
3 tbsp. lemon juice

Pinch of salt
3 egg whites, stiffly beaten
1 c. whipping cream, whipped
1 baked pie shell

Soften gelatin in *2 tablespoons cold water* in small saucepan. Heat until gelatin dissolves, stirring constantly; remove from heat. Add preserves, lemon juice and salt; mix well. Chill for 30 minutes. Fold into egg whites. Fold in whipped cream. Chill for 15 minutes. Spoon into pie shell. Chill until firm. Garnish with additional whipped cream and mint sprigs.

Photograph for this recipe on page 101.

FRESH STRAWBERRY PIE WITH COCONUT-SHORTBREAD CRUST

Yields: 7 servings   Pan Size: 9 inch   Preheat: 350°

⅓ c. butter, softened
3 tbsp. sugar
1 egg yolk
1 c. flour
1 c. coconut
1 c. chopped strawberries

1 c. sugar
3 tbsp. cornstarch
1 tbsp. lemon juice
2 pt. strawberries, cut
  into halves

Cream butter and 3 tablespoons sugar in mixer bowl until light and fluffy. Blend in egg yolk. Add flour; mix well. Mix in coconut. Press over bottom and side of pie plate. Chill for 30 minutes. Bake for 25 to 30 minutes or until brown. Cool. Combine chopped strawberries and ⅞ *cup water* in saucepan. Cook until strawberries are tender. Add mixture of 1 cup sugar and cornstarch; mix well. Cook until thickened and clear, stirring constantly. Stir in lemon juice. Cool. Spoon into crust. Top with strawberry halves. Chill until serving time. Garnish with whipped cream.

Cy Carpenter
President, National Farmers Union

STRAWBERRY PIE

Yields: 6 to 8 servings   Pan Size: 9 inch

8 oz. cream cheese, softened
½ c. confectioners' sugar
1 c. whipping cream,
  whipped

1 baked pie shell
2 lb. large strawberries
½ sm. jar currant jelly,
  melted

Beat cream cheese and confectioners' sugar in mixer bowl until light and fluffy. Add whipped cream; mix until smooth. Spoon into pie shell. Place strawberries stem end down on filling. Spoon melted jelly evenly over strawberries. Chill until serving time.

Dorothy Hyatt, Mica Flats Grange, Idaho

OLD-FASHIONED SWEET POTATO PIE

Yields: 6 servings   Pan Size: 9 inch   Preheat: 425°

¼ c. butter, softened
½ c. packed brown sugar
1 c. mashed cooked sweet potato
3 eggs, lightly beaten
⅓ c. corn syrup

⅓ c. milk
½ tsp. salt
1 tsp. vanilla extract
1 unbaked pie shell

Cream butter and brown sugar in bowl until light and fluffy. Blend in sweet potato and eggs. Add next 4 ingredients; mix well. Pour into pie shell. Bake for 10 minutes. Reduce temperature to 325 degrees. Bake for 35 to 45 minutes or until set.

Danny Flubart, Brandywine Grange, Maryland

AMISH VANILLA PIES

Yields: 12 servings	Pan Size: two 9 inch	Preheat: 375°

1 c. packed brown sugar	½ c. shortening
1 c. dark molasses	2 c. flour
2 tbsp. flour	1 c. packed brown sugar
1 egg, beaten	1 tsp. baking powder
2 tsp. vanilla extract	1 tsp. soda
2 unbaked pie shells	

Combine 1 cup brown sugar, molasses, 2 tablespoons flour, egg, vanilla and *1 cup water* in saucepan; mix well. Cook until thickened, stirring constantly. Pour into pie shells. Cut shortening into mixture of remaining ingredients in bowl until crumbly. Sprinkle over pies. Bake for 40 to 45 minutes or until set.

Mrs. Lee F. Finkenbinder, Mifflin Grange, Pennsylvania

VINEGAR PIE

Yields: 6 servings	Pan Size: 9 inch	Preheat: 400°

⅓ c. shortening	2 eggs, separated
1 c. flour	2 tbsp. vinegar
Dash of salt	2 tbsp. butter
1 c. sugar	½ tsp. lemon extract
2 tbsp. cornstarch	4 to 6 tbsp. sugar

Cut shortening into flour and salt in bowl until crumbly. Add *⅓ cup water*; mix well. Roll on floured surface. Fit into pie plate. Prick bottom and side. Bake until brown. Cool. Mix sugar and cornstarch in double boiler. Add *1 cup water* gradually. Add egg yolks 1 at a time, mixing well after each addition. Stir in vinegar. Cook until thickened, stirring constantly; remove from heat. Stir in butter and extract. Cool. Pour into pie shell. Beat egg whites and sugar until stiff peaks form. Spread over pie; seal to edge. Bake until light brown.

Dorothy Eudy, Columbus Grange, Indiana

TASSIES

Yields: 48 servings	Pan Size: miniature muffin	Preheat: 350°

2 c. flour	2 tbsp. melted butter
1 c. butter, softened	½ tsp. vanilla extract
8 oz. cream cheese, softened	Pinch of salt
2 c. packed brown sugar	1 c. chopped nuts
2 eggs	

Combine flour, softened butter and cream cheese in bowl; mix well. Shape into 48 balls. Press over bottom and side of miniature muffin cups. Combine remaining ingredients in bowl; mix well. Spoon into tart shells. Bake for 30 minutes.

Anne M. Jezak, Fall River Grange, Massachusetts

FRUCHTORTE (AUSTRIA) Fruit Tart

Yields: 10 to 12 servings | Pan Size: 9 inch | Preheat: 400°

½ c. butter
1½ c. flour
¼ c. sugar
1 tsp. cinnamon
1 egg, beaten
¼ c. sugar
⅓ c. cornstarch
¼ tsp. salt
1/16 tsp. nutmeg
2 c. milk
4 egg yolks, beaten
1 tsp. vanilla extract
2 c. strawberry halves
½ c. red currant jelly
⅛ tsp. nutmeg
¼ c. pistachio nuts

Cut butter into mixture of flour, ¼ cup sugar and cinnamon in bowl until crumbly. Add egg yolk; mix with fork until mixture forms ball. Chill for several minutes. Roll into 12-inch circle on lightly floured surface; fit into springform tart pan. Prick with fork. Chill for 1 hour. Bake for 12 minutes. Cool on wire rack. Mix ¼ cup sugar, cornstarch, salt and 1/16 teaspoon nutmeg in saucepan. Stir in milk gradually. Blend in egg yolks. Bring to a boil over medium-low heat, stirring constantly. Boil for 1 minute, stirring constantly. Stir in vanilla. Chill, covered, in refrigerator. Spread in tart shell. Arrange strawberries over top, leaving ½-inch border. Blend jelly and ⅛ teaspoon nutmeg in small saucepan. Heat until bubbly. Drizzle over strawberries. Sprinkle nuts around edge. Chill until serving time. Place on serving plate; remove side of pan.

Photograph for this recipe on page 237.

KATIE'S FRUIT PIZZA

Yields: 12 servings | Pan Size: 12 inch | Preheat: 400°

¾ c. butter
⅔ c. sugar
2 c. flour
¼ c. milk
¼ c. sugar
1 tbsp. cornstarch
¾ c. Gamay Beaujolais grape juice
2 to 3 whole canned or fresh pears
Kiwifruit slices
Blueberries
Seedless grape halves
Banana slices
Papaya slices
Cranberry sauce

Cream butter and ⅔ cup sugar in bowl until light and fluffy. Beat in flour and milk gradually. Press onto pizza pan to make crust. Bake for 13 to 18 minutes or until golden brown. Cool on wire rack. Combine ¼ cup sugar and cornstarch in small saucepan. Add grape juice. Bring to a boil over medium heat, stirring constantly. Boil for 1 minute or until thickened. Cool for 10 minutes. Arrange sliced pears on cooled crust. Top with kiwifruit, blueberries, grapes, banana, papaya or seasonal fruits. Dot with cranberry sauce. Drizzle with cooled glaze to coat fruit. Serve wedges for dessert, breakfast or brunch.

Katie Couch, San Jose Grange, California

Substitutions for Common Ingredients

If the recipe calls for:	Amount	Use instead:
Baking powder	1 teaspoon	¼ teaspoon baking soda plus ½ teaspoon cream of tartar
Bread crumbs, fine dry	1 cup	¾ cup finely crumbled crackers
Broth, chicken or beef	1 cup	1 bouillon cube or 1 envelope instant broth dissolved in 1 cup boiling water
Buttermilk	1 cup	1 cup plain yogurt or 1 cup whole milk plus 1 tablespoon lemon juice or vinegar (let stand 5 minutes)
Cake flour	1 cup	1 cup sifted all-purpose flour less 2 tablespoons
Catsup or chili sauce	½ cup	½ cup tomato sauce plus 2 tablespoons sugar, 1 tablespoon vinegar, and ⅛ teaspoon ground cloves
Chocolate, unsweetened	1 square (1 ounce)	3 tablespoons cocoa plus 1 tablespoon butter
Cornstarch (for thickening)	1 tablespoon	2 tablespoons all-purpose flour
Corn syrup, light (not for baking)	1 cup	1¼ cups granulated sugar plus ⅓ cup water
Cracker crumbs, fine	1 cup	1¼ cups dry bread crumbs
Cream, heavy	1 cup	¾ cup milk plus ⅓ cup melted butter
Cream, light	1 cup	¾ cup milk plus ¼ cup melted butter
Cream, sour	1 cup	⅞ cup plain yogurt or buttermilk plus 3 tablespoons melted butter
Garlic	1 small clove	⅛ teaspoon garlic powder
Half-and-half	1 cup	⅞ cup milk plus 1½ tablespoons melted butter
Herbs, fresh	1 tablespoon	1 teaspoon dried herbs
Honey	1 cup	1¼ cups granulated sugar plus ¼ cup water
Lemon juice	1 teaspoon	½ teaspoon vinegar
Liquid hot red pepper	3 to 4 drops	⅛ teaspoon cayenne pepper
Milk, whole	1 cup	½ cup evaporated milk plus ½ cup water, or 1 cup water plus ⅓ cup instant nonfat dry milk and 2 teaspoons melted butter, or 1 cup skim milk plus 2 teaspoons melted butter
Mushrooms, fresh	8 ounces	1 6-ounce can mushrooms, drained

Substitutions for Common Ingredients

If the recipe calls for:	Amount	Use instead:
Onion	1 small	1 tablespoon instant minced onion
Pork, ground	½ pound	½ pound mild sausage
Sugar, brown	1 cup, firmly packed	1 cup granulated sugar
Sugar, granulated	1 cup	1 cup firmly packed brown sugar
Tartar sauce	½ cup	6 tablespoons mayonnaise plus 2 tablespoons sweet pickle relish
Tomato paste	1 tablespoon	1 tablespoon catsup
Vinegar	1 teaspoon	2 teaspoons lemon juice
Yogurt, plain	1 cup	1 cup buttermilk

Equivalents for Common Ingredients

Food	Amount	Approximate Measure
Apples	1 pound	3 medium
Bananas	1 pound	3 medium
Berries	1 quart	3½ cups
Bread crumbs, dry	1 slice bread	¼ cup
Bread crumbs, soft	1 slice bread	½ cup
Butter or margarine	1 stick (¼ pound)	½ cup
Cheese, Cheddar	4 ounces	1 cup shredded
Cheese, cottage	1 pound	2 cups
Cheese, cream	3-ounce package 8-ounce package	6 tablespoons 1 cup (16 tablespoons)
Cream, heavy	½ pint	2 cups whipped
Flour, all-purpose	1 pound	3½ cups unsifted 4 cups sifted
Lemon	1 medium	3 tablespoons juice 1 tablespoon grated rind
Nuts in shell		
Pecans	1 pound	2¼ cups chopped
Walnuts	1 pound	1⅔ cups chopped
Orange	1 medium	⅓ cup juice 2 tablespoons grated rind
Potatoes	1 pound	3 medium
Sugar, brown	1 pound	2¼ cups (firmly packed)
Sugar, confectioners'	1 pound	4 cups unsifted
Sugar, granulated	1 pound	2 cups

Index

All microwave recipe page numbers are preceded by an M.

Photography Credits

National Dairy Council; American Spice Trade Association; Argo and Kingsford's cornstarch; The McIlhenney Company; National Peanut Council; The J. M. Smucker Company; United Fresh Fruit and Vegetable Association; National Live Stock and Meat Board; California Raisin Advisory Board; Idaho Potatoes; Alaska Seafood Marketing Institute; Quaker Oats; Florida Department of Citrus; Fleischmann's yeast; Hellmann's and Best Foods real mayonnaise; Mazola corn oil; California Kiwifruit Commission; North American Blueberry Council; Evaporated Milk Association; Diamond Walnut Kitchens; and National Kraut Packers Association.

★ ★

For Your Convenience . . .

Additional copies of National Grange *The Glory of Cooking* may be ordered, for $8.00 each copy, from:

National Grange Cookbook
1616 H Street N.W.
Washington, D.C.   20006

Library of Congress Cataloging-in-Publication Data
The Glory of Cooking.

Includes index.
1. Cookery, American. 2. Cookery, International.
I. Patrons of Husbandry. National Grange.
TX715.G5558   1986   641.5973   86-23872
ISBN-0-87197-217-4 (Favorite Recipes Press)